T0331751

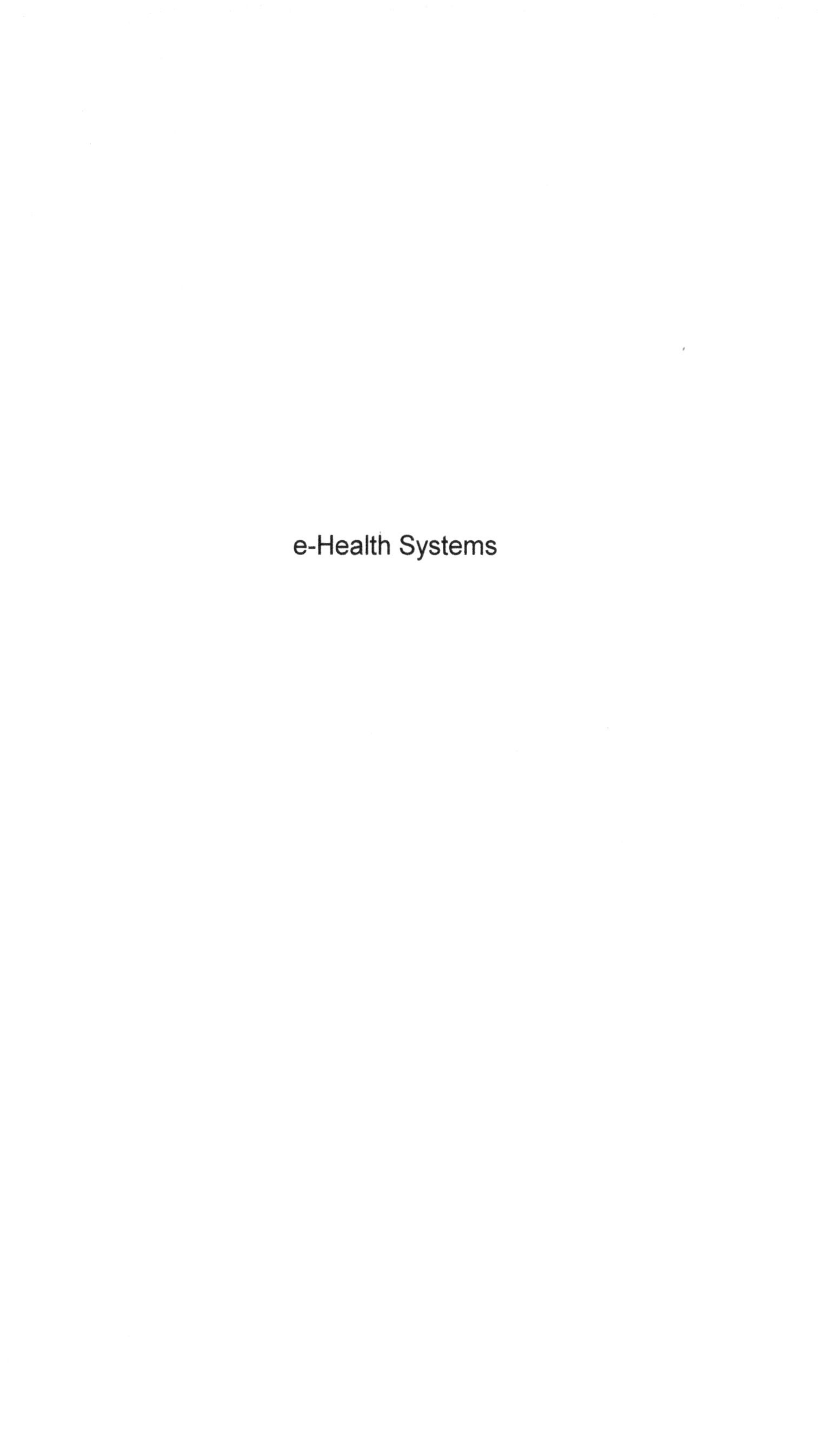

e-Health Systems

Sensor Networks Set

coordinated by
Abdelhamid Mellouk

e-Health Systems

Theory, Advances and Technical Applications

Joel José P.C. Rodrigues
Sandra Sendra Compte
Isabel de la Torra Diez

First published 2016 in Great Britain and the United States by ISTE Press Ltd and Elsevier Ltd

ISTE Press Ltd
27-37 St George's Road
London SW19 4EU
UK

www.iste.co.uk

Elsevier Ltd
The Boulevard, Langford Lane
Kidlington, Oxford, OX5 1GB
UK

www.elsevier.com

For information on all our publications visit our website at http://store.elsevier.com/

British Library Cataloguing-in-Publication Data
A CIP record for this book is available from the British Library
Library of Congress Cataloging in Publication Data
A catalog record for this book is available from the Library of Congress
ISBN 978-1-78548-091-1

Printed and bound in the UK and US

Contents

Preface

The present book intends to offer a global vision of all the parties involved in the deployment and operation processes of e-Health systems presenting the state-of-the-art on the issues addressed. It intends to be a useful guide in the context of research expertise in the development, deployment and evaluation of e-Health systems, which can help medical personnel to improve their work. It is aimed at researchers, professors and students of information and communications technology, computer science, healthcare and related areas. It will provide readers with an understanding of approaches to the critical nature and employment of different healthcare-based information systems and applications, such as web-based and mobile applications. Moreover, it introduces many interesting ideas on current issues including emerging technologies related to mobile and cloud computing, body area networks, social networks and security.

This book is divided into two main parts. The first part (consisting of the Introduction and five chapters) presents a comprehensive introduction to the concepts of e-Health and delves into the processes carried out to store information, as well as the standards that are used for this purpose:

– Chapter 1: This chapter discusses the main requirements that should be met by electronic health records, its benefits and the main standards used to deploy them.

– Chapter 2: This chapter explains Health Level 7 (HL7), including its background, goals and mission, architecture, standards, its transactional model and functional model.

– Chapter 3: This chapter addresses the aims and objectives of clinical document architecture (CDA), its levels, the structure of CDA document identifiers and its detailed design.

– Chapter 4: This chapter addresses the Digital Imaging and Communications in Medicine objectives, its relationship with other standards and the considered relevant parts of the standard.

– Chapter 5: This chapter elaborates on important standard contributions such as the ISO/TC 215, CEN/TC 251 standards and initiatives such as the Good European Health Record, OpenEHR, Integrating Healthcare Enterprise and Common Object Request Broker Architecture.

The second part of this book (Chapters 6–12) focuses on applications types and addresses the deployment of e-Health systems in-depth. In this part, we explain different types of wireless networks and security protocols employed to convert these systems into robust solutions avoiding any kind of data corruption and weaknesses:

– Chapter 6: This chapter elaborates on a review about body area networks covering all the aspects from device deployment up to communication architectures and protocols.

– Chapter 7: This chapter presents the most relevant mobile technologies and applications used in e-Health. It also analyzes different solutions for the most relevant platforms, different devices and operating systems.

– Chapter 8: This chapter combines the functionalities of the concept of mobile computing with medicine requirements in order to ensure that data acquisition runs smoothly. A case study on cardiology is presented and discussed in detail.

– Chapter 9: This chapter shows the different applications and services that can be developed from Chapters 6 and 7, and are used in the field of ambient assisted living to help elderly and disabled people to improve their quality of life.

– Chapter 10: This chapter analyzes the importance of social networks and social media in health. It also shows some examples of social networks used by medical professionals and platforms to assist people remotely.

– Chapter 11: This chapter shows the cloud-based solutions that solve some problems in traditional computing considering the risks in terms of safety and privacy. It also shows that cloud usage on e-Health can be useful for having lower integration costs, optimizing resources and performing a widely medical system.

– Chapter 12: In this chapter, privacy and security requirements in healthcare are analyzed, highlighting the importance of providing and enforcing privacy and security in healthcare. It also explains their importance and reviews both classical and novel security technologies that can fulfill these requirements.

This book tries to be considered as a source of inspiration for readers (students, professors, researchers, and professionals from related industry) who are interested in e-Health systems and applications and who are open to new research lines in this hot topic, which is being widely investigated.

We would like to thank Dr. Bruno M.C. Silva (Instituto de Telecomunicações, Portugal) for his cooperation as a co-author of the Chapters 7 and 12.

Joel J. P. C. RODRIGUES
Sandra SENDRA COMPTE
Isabel DE LA TORRE
April 2016

Introduction

The provision of health services at the local, regional, national, continental and even global level through the use of information and communication technologies (ICTs) has contributed to the emergence of an industry of electronic health (e-Health) with great economic importance. This is considered a wide concept that ranges from healthcare applications, such as teleconsultation, telemonitoring and remote diagnostics related to patient management, to patient training and healthcare professionals.

Nowadays, in most developed countries, e-Health systems offer many services such as individual health cards, the consultation of medical center guidelines, etc. In addition, e-Health systems are in charge of registering complaints and suggestions to the service. Some of the most recent topics or immediate actions are the electronic prescribing and electronic health records (EHRs), i.e. the registration of healthcare that people receive at the health institutions.

This book shows how technology is enabling the advancement on healthcare in terms of patient care and addresses the most recent contributions for the state-of-the-art on e-Health and key standards [ROD 12a]. Different applications and technologies such as Web 2.0/3.0, mobile devices, tablet computers or television with interactivity features allowing patients to be more informed and close to their physicians [BAI 98]. However, we are not talking about physical distance. Being close to these new technologies offers solutions to improve management and customer service through medicine at distance, otherwise known as telemedicine. After several assumptions performed in past decades on medical consultations and technologies evolution, including the Internet, the reality is that these dreams and utopias have become reality and have been imposed in our daily lives.

ICT on healthcare is an important tool that improves quality and patient safety, and also improving management and allowing for modern healthcare systems that can be adapted to suit the needs of patients and healthcare professionals. In order to obtain the best effectiveness, we need to assess the current organization and provide the appropriate technological support.

Technology can be defined as all devices that leverage resources to meet human needs. Applying this definition to the world of health, we should find amazing advances that make healthcare increasingly protected. A decade ago, it was difficult to associate the concept of health and the Internet. Because of technological advances and the development of next-generation electronic devices, currently and in a near future, it will be impossible to dissociate these terms in a common context that e-Health does not only provides comprehensive care that includes health promotion and preventive care but also facilitates access to information and offers privacy and quality assurance. More and more patients are seeking information through online platforms related to health issues in order to find out possible treatments and reach out to specialists. Frequently, the query does not require the physical presence of a physician and a patient in the same space. Consultations via the Internet to perform diagnosis and therapeutics significantly reduces the time and costs involved, which imply a shift in terms of saving time and money. The fact that a patient can access their medical records anytime and anywhere not only allows him/her to stay informed and but also to request a second evaluation outside usual consultations hours.

Internet and health form a link which aims to improve patient care either through appointments through the network, shipment of medical records, remote consultation or remote diagnosis, etc.

This chapter discusses the concept of e-Health, the essential requirements that e-Health systems should meet and the evolution from e-Health to t-Health (TV health) through m-Health (mobile health).

I.1. E-Health overview

The impact that the Internet and digital ICTs present over e-Health systems goes beyond the deployment of health portals. Speaking of e-Health is similar to talking about reinventing the information infrastructure of healthcare. In this way, the Internet has become the alternative low cost technology infrastructure to provide a common platform with global reach to perform multiple functions. In addition, it is also a good tool for the transactions relating to the management of patients and the general administration of a wide range of services. Of course privacy and related security issues should be considered. From this idea, we will able to provide a definition of e-Health [VAN 10].

Throughout recent years, several terms have been introduced that are often confused. There are terms like health telematics and telemedicine, as well as e-Health, online health, electronic health and network health that are defined as follows:

– *E-Health*: This term is the synonym of online health, electronic health and network health. It can be defined as "the infrastructure and applications of health which use the technologies of digital communications networks of multimedia data, primarily Internet. In simplified form, these terms are used to refer to the Internet in Healthcare". Currently, there is a tendency, especially in the European Union (EU), for using this term broadly and include all the health telematics applications under its usage.

– *Health telematics*: This is defined as the application of telematics technologies in the field of health. It is a term broadly accepted, including within administrative applications, information and in support to clinical practice. Telemedicine is also seen as a subset of health telematic applications, which can be also included under this term.

– *Telemedicine*: In the strict sense, it is understood as a provision of medical services remotely using electronic communications. There are telemedicine applications in e-Health (for example teleconsultation between groups of professionals). Nevertheless, some of the current telemedicine applications do not use the Internet.

Other definitions of e-Health performed by different organisms are shared below.

The World Health Organization (WHO) [WOR 15], in 1997, considers that e-Health *provides health care services, where distance is a critical factor, by professionals that appeal to ICT, with the aim of exchange data for making diagnoses in order to improve the health of people and communities in which they live*. Another definition is also used as follows: *The use, in the health sector, of digital information transmitted, stored or collected electronically to support the health care both locally and remotely*.

E-Health is based on the use of ICTs to improve patients' management, diagnosis and monitoring. Among the benefits provided to citizens, they offer information and the ability to promote an alternative diagnosis by doctors of other places because they have free access to the medical history at any time and place. Similarly, healthcare professionals can consult relevant information, new medical advances and have global access to data via computerized medical records.

Figure I.1 shows the pyramid of five levels describing the elements involved in telemedicine and e-Health [ROD 12b].

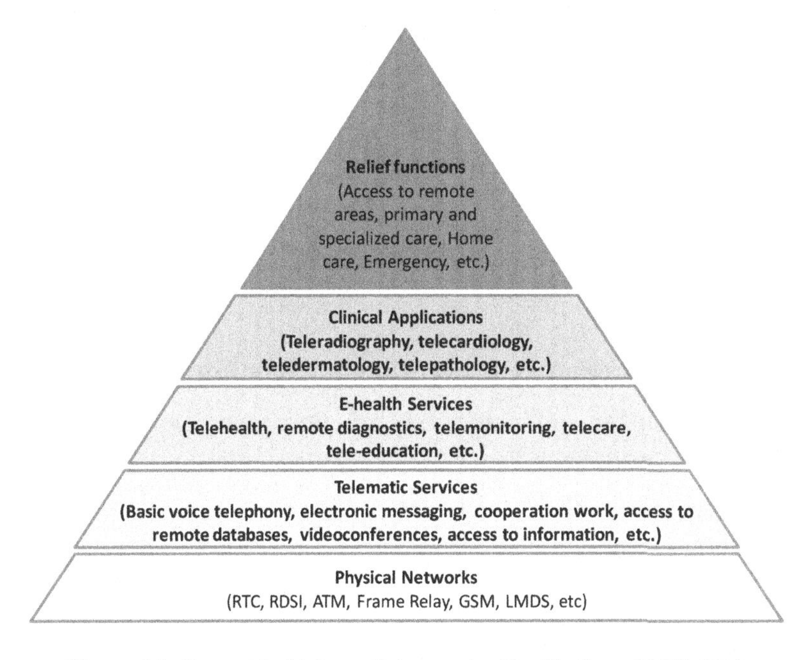

Figure I.1. *Pyramid of telemedicine and e-Health (from [ROD 12b])*

E-Health should not be described as an alternative or additional form of healthcare after the application of ICT. It is a new efficient and equitable way to improve accessibility, reducing response times and cost savings, with the possibility to deploy alerts and, ultimately, improve therapeutic and diagnostic efficacy, because of the potential for change provided by e-Health technologies.

Considering the movement of patients for working, studying, or simply pleasure, these tools offer access to information at any time when it could be vital to have a proper diagnosis. In most cases, these diagnoses allow to determine the most appropriate treatment and the use of ICT will facilitate the immediate therapeutics application. E-Health systems place the patients in the center of the health system improving the effectiveness and viability of the sector.

There are many advantages of e-Health beyond the simple medical consultation. Among them, the following should be highlighted:

– remote thermal digital imaging diagnosis;

– telesonography;

– teleradiology;

– surgery;

– diseases prognosis, prevention and monitoring;

– participation of citizens to improve policies and healthcare services;

– integration of the health system in the model of countries economic development;

– increase patient safety through reliable and effective systems;

– monitoring and methodical data storage on the patient's record;

– expediting medical outcomes.

In order to provide e-Health services with enough quality, they should meet several requirements, such as availability of information technologies and telecommunication systems to send and receive accurate information and remote healthcare. It is also necessary to ensure that all the procedures follow established medical ethics. Regarding security and privacy, the computer security plans established and approved by the corresponding instance should be considered. Hospitals should define a specific area to provide remote diagnosis services. This area must be sure and this safety should be certificated. Finally, it is also necessary to certify and register that medical staff is authorized to request and send information.

Regarding technical aspects, medical centers and hospitals should have terminal devices available to be used for efficient data exchange, biomedical signal reception and processing, and control of the patient environment where it is necessary. In addition, services, components and telematic applications that serve health management infrastructure are needed. Equipment and telecommunication systems, as well as generic telematics services and common equipment are also required.

I.2. E-Health evolution

To facilitate humanitarian work around the world, it is necessary to emphasize the importance of the use of ICT for health through the benefits that these technologies can bring to cope with disasters.

The development of ICT in the healthcare context is an ongoing concern which demands continuous improvement. Despite the growth that e-Health has experienced in recent years, research for its development and implementation has remained limited.

Since 2003, member states of the EU have been working together to improve the implementation of applications in health. These countries hold a rotating presidency of EU organized events. During these events, regular lectures about online health technologies, applications, tools and best practices are discussed. The events and meetings act as a platform to boost health services in Europe. Health area managers, physicians, researchers, policy makers and suppliers share experiences and discover new products.

In recent years, considering how much European society has aged, the "E-Health Ministerial Conference" recognized the need for urgent actions to improve patient services. Chronic diseases and increasing life expectancy are some of the problems that our healthcare system is facing, in terms of sustainability. The development of ICT applications in the health context has yielded results. For example, doctors have increased the available time to attend, in person, to their patients to 22%. In fact, the improvement of systems interoperability (both national and international) can solve this problem by reducing costs significantly.

In early 2005, the World Health Organization (WHO) launched an initiative dedicated to the study of e-Health, which aimed to strengthen the health systems of member countries. This initiative tried to encourage partnerships between public and private sectors to develop new proposals in I+D+I activities supporting capabilities creation for their use in the Member States to perform and apply rules and patterns.

The WHO intended to promote the adoption of quality criteria for e-Health material. It requested that Member States should adopt guidelines to improve the quality and reliability of published materials, the development of ICT infrastructures and applications to provide basic services. Indeed, some initial complications for the development were (1) the high cost of high-speed networks necessary for ICT applications, (2) lack of investment through traditional business models, and (3) lack of staff trained in ICT.

The Global Observatory for e-Health (GOe) [WOR 11] came into existence in early 2005. This organization is responsible for providing all Member States with the strategic information and guidance on practices, policies and effective standards in e-Health. The GOe is responsible for providing information on e-Health management to various international agencies and governments. It also analyzes and extracts information that significantly contributes to improving health through technology. The GOe seeks to find a compromise between business and governments to invest in ICT. It is in charge of elaborating and publishing the annual report and the development of special guidelines on fundamental research in e-Health in order to use them as references for legislators and government issues.

The aging of European society represents an enormous pressure for the healthcare systems. Currently, Europe has invested around 9% of its gross domestic product (GDP) in health. Because the healthcare industry is increasingly geared to information, the advancement of ICT can be more profitable allowing more money to become available for healthcare and not just for its administration. Figure I.2 shows the evolution of GDP for the main European countries and the difference between the value intended in 2002 and 2013 [SCH 13]. Figure I.2 also shows the average health expenditure in percentage (%) of GDP [IND 13].

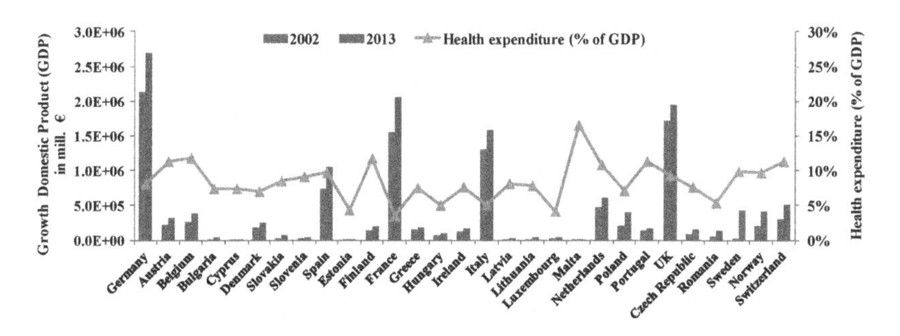

Figure I.2. *GDP for European countries in 2002 and 2013. For a color version of this figure, see www.iste.co.uk/rodrigues/ehealth.zip*

E-Health seeks not only to replace paper for electronic cards but it also aims for greater effectiveness and speed in diagnosis, to improve the quality of patients life and healthcare by allowing the patients to have medical examination in real time. It is important to ensure that this attention can be performed from home and on the move where processes such as medical images play a key role. Using supercomputers and next generation networks can also support the search for new cures.

At the European level, there is a lack of coordination regarding the e-Health industry. For this reason, governments are taking measurements and rules to ensure the leadership of the European industry in this field and benefit everyone in terms of better healthcare. Recently, on the occasion of the promotion ICT, Europe introduced a reform in the government's plans for e-Health through a new mechanism of cooperation: the European e-Health Governance initiative.

The project, called European Patient Smart Open Services, aims to generalize the digital medical records in Europe by unifying all health records on the EU. In this way, patients can have access to medicine abroad that have been forgotten, lost or consumed, and can communicate details about their health status to healthcare professionals who do not know their language.

I.2.1. *Mobile health (M-Health)*

Mobile devices offer a great potential for improving patient care because of its versatility and ubiquity (in tasks such as real time monitoring or reminders to take medication). The concept of mobile health (m-Health) is found within the terms of evolution of e-Health. M-Health can be defined simply as the use of wireless technology to deliver health services and information in mobile communication devices such as mobile phones, tablet computers, smart phones, monitoring devices, etc.: "mobile health (m-Health) delivers healthcare services, overcoming geographical, temporal, and even organizational barriers. M-Health solutions address emerging problems on health services, including, the increasing number of chronic diseases related to lifestyle, high costs of existing national health services, the need to empower patients and families to self-care and handle their own healthcare, and the need to provide direct access to health services, regardless of time and place" [SIL 15]. The latest versions of these devices present different options of wireless connectivity able to store health information accessible by healthcare professionals in local and remote ways. The GOe of WHO defines m-Health or mobile health as "medical and public health practice supported by mobile devices, such as mobile phones, patient monitoring devices, PDAs, and other wireless devices".

Within the field of medicine, m-Health [IST 04] has become a sub-class of e-Health where the first term is a part that configure the second one and which is differentiated by device independence. In order to explain the different types of m-Health applications, it is necessary to distinguish between developed and developing countries. The m-Health services that can put in place for both types of countries are very different. m-Health services in developing countries tend to optimize resources, facilitate the patient's life and the development of a population in the broadest sense of the word. Developed countries already have the technology, hospitals, medical resources, communications infrastructure and capacity. However, in developing countries the situation is very different considering less developed infrastructure and minor medical care. Bringing people closer to the health systems is becoming a major goal for most non-governmental organizations (NGOs).

When there is lack of infrastructure, mobile devices take the main stage. However, the fact that these are missing some key infrastructures, such as antennas, is a significant problem in these devices. Organizations such as *Télécoms Sans Frontière* and other NGOs try to improve these aspects to enhance healthcare. This is a key issue for recovering communications after, for example, a natural disaster.

Although it sounds paradoxical, in countries such as Mozambique and Zaire where poverty abounds, mobile phones play an important role in the daily lives of citizens. As said by Terry Kramer, from Vodafone Foundation, "When there are 2,200 million mobile phones in developing countries, 305 million PCs and only 11 million hospital beds, we can quickly see how mobile phones can provide solutions for healthcare" [NAI 12]. Moreover, Muhammad Yunus (the recipient of the 2006 Nobel Peace Prize for alleviating poverty in Bangladesh) said "The quickest way to get out of poverty right now is to have a mobile phone".

Regarding the current situation of m-Health, it is important to note that, recently, there has been a growing interest in the health sector to capitalize on the rapid uptake of mobile communication technologies. Indeed, the obvious technological jump has enabled developing countries, even those with relatively poor infrastructure, to move from landline phone to mobile phone technology. The number of mobile phone subscribers worldwide in 2001 was estimated at 1,000 million, while 11 years later, this value was over 6,000 million subscribers. In 2014, it was estimated that the number of mobile subscriptions exceeded the global population. In many countries, the number of mobile phone subscribers has surpassed the number of landline phones. Figure I.3 shows the growth in the number of mobile subscriptions worldwide from 2001 to 2012 [ITU 14].

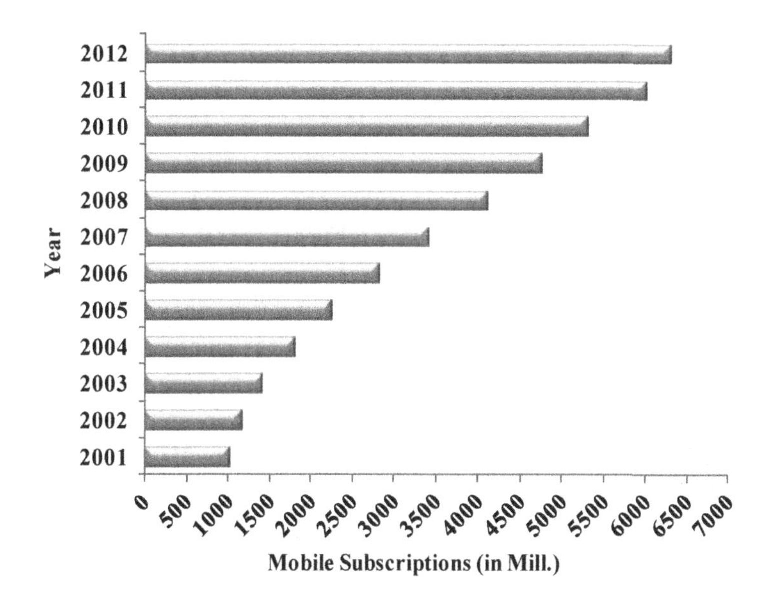

Figure I.3. *Worldwide growth from 2001 to 2012 in the number of mobile subscriptions*

I.2.2. *Television health (T-Health)*

The term t-Health indicates any type of health service offered via interactive digital television and, thereby, which provides or facilitates telehealth. This term implies remote healthcare through the interactive connection between home users and the person in charge of monitoring. Therefore, remote healthcare and services involve heterogeneous technologies including communications, databases, use of Internet and Intranet resources, image transmission and archiving, among others. All these utilities cover disciplines that exceed the traditional concept of medicine impacting on individuals and communities that receive such care.

Mobile devices offer advantages in the field of health because of the interactivity that digital television facilitates. Using these devices, citizens can make appointments with their general practitioners with the same tools that they use to watch their favorite TV series. Interactive TVs would have direct access via a channel to any medical information (information about diseases, diets, tips to quit smoking, etc.). The future will offer unlimited access to health resources through any device. This new medical and technological era is known as Health 2.0.

The t-Health mission contributes to the decentralization and integration of a country's health system and the universality of healthcare quality. This guarantees an improvement in terms of efficiency and equity for the benefit of excluded and scattered populations through the incorporation of ICTs.

The main principles that support t-Health are the following:

– *Equity*: It reduces, through t-Health, the gap to access health services for excluded populations. Healthcare should be available to everybody at the same quality and with similar options.

– *Efficiency*: The efficient use of health resources in the system through t-Health; the processes optimization and resource sharing among members of the system will allow an important saving in travel costs and support of diagnostic tests.

– *Quality*: It promotes comprehensive healthcare having user satisfaction as its main goal improving diagnostic accuracy and therapeutic decisions attitudes. As healthcare professionals can be trained remotely, the care for patients can be performed at different levels of care, without interrupting treatment.

– *Decentralization*: T-Health can be used as a strategic tool to facilitate change and thus moving toward decentralization of the health system.

– Promoting social development allows people greater access to health information and knowledge of their duties and rights in health, promoting the empowerment of people.

T-Health encompasses any remote health system. The latest evolution of this approach is based on the use of technological means such as TVs, camcorders, the Internet, among others. In fact, currently, there are many examples of applications which present similar services to the ones offered by t-Health. Some goals to achieve include controlling appointments of chronic patients, remembering and controlling the medication that patients are taking at each time, keeping tracking of pathological patients, studying the therapeutic benefits of digital terrestrial television (DTT) on patients, making use of DTT as a monitoring program integrated with other Hospital programs, among others.

It will probably take few years for the use of interactive DTT in Europe to be a given. However, there are already many projects that will work in this direction in less time than one may think.

I.3. Importance of new technologies for healthcare

Society and those responsible for its health should work towards creating a new image of aging that fits with the demographic and reflects the dignity of elderly people [HEI 11]. The aging of the population does not generate higher expenses, but aging is accompanied by poor health. This demographic evolution towards aging populations requires the improvement of health systems and social protection, healthcare and other related services from the point of view of an organization and its capabilities. Clearly, the demographic development depends on the type of country analyzed [EUR 12]. Figures I.4 and I.5 show the global population classified by age and sex [HAU 13].

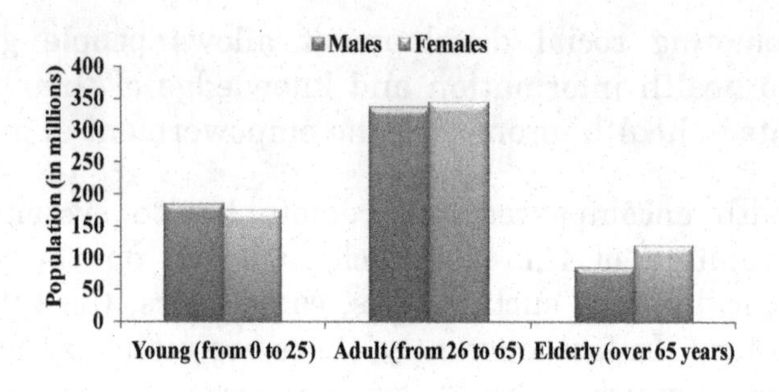

Figure I.4. *Population of developed countries by age and sex, 2012*

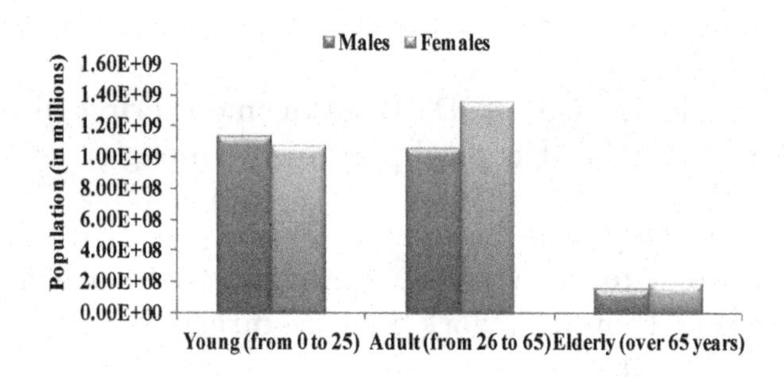

Figure I.5. *Population of developing countries by age and sex, 2012*

The aging population of the EU is due to an increased life expectancy. Life expectancy is an indicator with significant consequences for health, social and economic policies of a country. Longevity increased dramatically during the 20th Century. In 1900, the average life expectancy was 34.8 years, and now it is around 82.1 years. The factor that has had the greatest impact on increasing life expectancy is the declining mortality, especially in children. Figure I.6 shows the life expectancy for men and women at birth and after retirement [EUR 13].

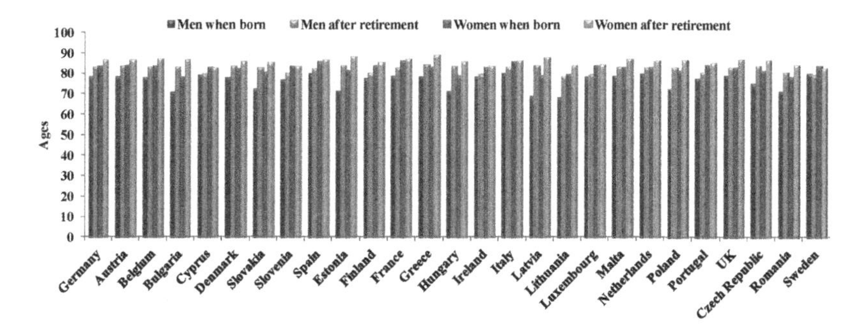

Figure I.6. *Life expectancy at birth and after retirement for men and women in Europe, 2013. For a color version of the figure, see www.iste.co.uk/rodrigues/ehealth.zip*

European forecasts indicate that for the percentage of people with 65 years of age and over, the total population will increase from 17.1% in 2008 to 30% in 2060. The average ratio of people at a working age (15–64 years old) and 65 years or more will change from 4:1 (currently) to 2:1 by 2050. Figure I.7 shows the percentage of the European population at or above 65 years. As may be seen, Germany, France, UK, Italy and Spain are the countries of the EU with the highest number of older individuals. They are also the most populous countries. Germany, Italy, Greece and Sweden are the oldest countries in relative terms [EUR 13].

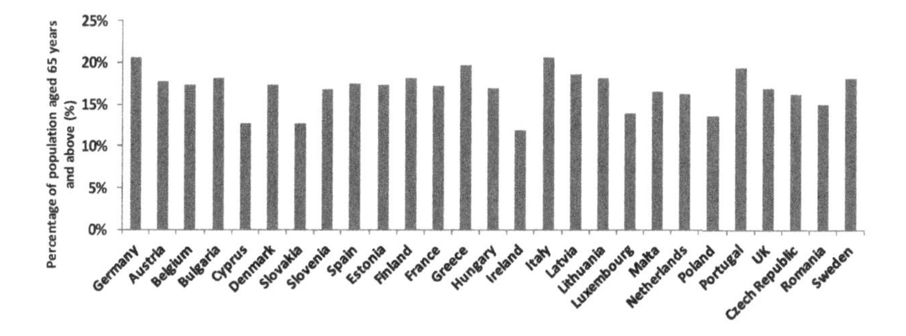

Figure I.7. *Percentage of the European population at or above 65 years (from [EUR 13])*

I.4. Structure of the book

This book intends to be a useful guide to support research expertise in the development, implementation and evaluation of telemedical and e-Health systems, which can help medical professionals to improve their work. It can be used by anyone interested in the use of ICTs in health, including people working in healthcare and related topics (physicians, nurses, etc.), ambient assisted living and wellbeing. The book will allow them to delve into various implementation issues, communication systems and data collection processes. It will provide possibilities for opening new research lines in different fields based on the issues addressed.

This book is recommended for researchers, professors and students of ICT, computer science, health, healthcare and related subjects. It will provide readers with an understanding of approaches to the critical nature and employment of different healthcare-based information systems and applications, such as Web-based and mobile systems and applications. Moreover, it introduces many interesting ideas on current issues including emerging technologies related to mobile and cloud computing, body area networks and security issues.

This book is divided into two main parts. The first part performs a comprehensive introduction to the concepts of e-Health and delves into the processes carried out to store information, as well as the related standards that are used on these technologies. The first part of this book consists of five chapters:

– Chapter 1: explains the reasons for the evolution away from medical records on paper and their requirements and benefits. It also discusses the importance of standards, as well as their needs and application rules for electronic medical records.

– Chapter 2: covers all the requirements needed to implement online consultations, to create integration systems without duplicating data and to provide information for systems that need to be updated. This chapter also presents a highly-technical report on HL7 clinical document architecture.

– Chapter 3: presents clinical document architecture as a tagging standard to define the structure and semantics of clinical documents that require the exchange of information in an environment of interoperability, formerly known as the patient record architecture.

– Chapter 4: presents the advantages of using digital imaging and communications in medicine for the exchange of medical images in digital formats.

– Chapter 5: elaborates on other initiatives and standards not addressed in the previous chapters regarding electronic medical records (EHRs).

The second part of the book is more technical. Different types of applications and implementations of e-Heath systems are discussed in detail. The chapters of this part explain, in depth, the types of wireless networks and security protocols employed to convert these systems into robust solutions, avoiding any kind of vulnerabilities associated with data corruption. The second part of this book consists of seven chapters:

– Chapter 6: elaborates on a deep review about body area networks covering all aspects from device deployment up to communication architectures and protocols.

– Chapter 7: presents the most relevant mobile technologies and applications used in e-Health. This chapter analyzes different solutions for several platforms, devices and operating systems.

– Chapter 8: shows the different applications and services which can be developed from Chapters 6 and 7, and how these are used in the field of ambient assisted living to help elderly and disabled people to improve their quality of life.

– Chapter 9: combines the functions of the concept of mobile computing with medicine requirements in order to ensure that data acquisition within the medical department runs smoothly.

– Chapter 10: analyzes the importance of social networks and social media in health. It also shows some examples of social networks used by medical professionals and platforms to assist people remotely.

– Chapter 11: shows the cloud-based solutions that solve some of the problems of traditional computing considering the risks in terms of safety and privacy. It also shows that cloud usage on e-Health can be useful for having lower integration costs, optimizing resources and making a widely medical system.

– Chapter 12: analyzes privacy and security requirements in healthcare, highlighting the importance of providing and enforcing privacy and security in healthcare. They also explain their importance and review both classical and novel security technologies that could fulfill these requirements. This chapter reviews their privacy and security requirements, such as data availability, data confidentiality, data integrity, accountability, anonymity and user awareness, and discusses the state-of-the-art technologies that address these requirements.

PART 1

Electronic Health Records: Standards and Other Initiatives

1

Electronic Medical Records and Their Standards

1.1. Introduction

Medical records are considered the quintessential clinical document. They are used as information support generated by the healthcare team, and are used as a transmission vehicle between the various team members who treat patients in another place or time. The traditional functions of medical records are care, teaching and research. From these, others have been developed which are closely related. These include:

– *assistance*: it is basically a document to assist care. Its main mission is to collect all pathologically relevant information on patients in order to derive the correct diagnosis or treatment in his/her case;

– *teaching*: each medical record should reflect the correct way of treating each clinical case, explaining exploratory and therapeutic decisions taken;

– *clinical research*: it establishes the precise mechanisms for locating medical records relating to a particular disease or a particular treatment, and it can be used as a source of knowledge of clinical activity itself;

– *epidemiological investigation*: it makes reference to research that relates to the causes of a disease and the influence of these over the emergence of disease;

– *clinical management and care resource planning*: it serves in clinical management, evaluation of local resource use and the planning of future investment;

– *documentary legal evidence*: this is a documentary account of the care and treatment provided;

– *care quality control*: medical records enable the assessment of scientific and technical objectives.

Medical records should be unique to each person, accumulate all their medical information and be integrated, so that they contain information on the all of the episodes of contact and disease.

The current holder of the medical record can present a number of problems relating to the information contained in it such as increased provider time, computer down time, lack of standards and threats to confidentiality [SEI 03].

The usual mass of documents leads to disorganization and fragmented information, with often poor success when trying to recover information in a rational and logical manner. The main problems with paper records are:

– the lack of uniformity in the documents causing uncertainty about their content;

– the illegibility of certain information contained in medical records primarily from handwritten documents;

– the changeability of information where existing support does not have access to mechanisms to ensure that their content is not altered by different users;

– questionable availability, and therefore accessibility, to information contained within the records. Technical support and level of access also vary. It is not possible for two or more people from different places to access the same record simultaneously;

– errors in partially stored documents (even in documents that are fully stored) that cause loss of value because of the lack of availability of the information contained therein;

– the problem of space and the personnel needed to handle it;

– technical difficulties in ensuring the anonymization of patient identifying data when using clinical data for analysis and research purposes to meet current data protection legislation [FAL 01];

– concerns over confidentiality because control to access to medical records cannot be ensured;

– the deterioration of supporting documentation and the risk of loss caused by water or fire caused by accidents or other events.

These problems are easier to solve with the use of electronic health records (EHRs), where its deployment implies no distortion in clinical activity. The computerization of the clinical history as well as offering a possible solution to the above-mentioned problems, EHRs provide the opportunity to integrate clinical information and to review the organization of services and professionals [MON 03].

Historically, one of the biggest challenges for healthcare professionals has been sharing information from different sources. With the growing trend toward EHR utilization, the need to achieve this goal has become urgent.

Computing and the emergence of new technologies are tools that help society to improve clinical applications [ROD 13a, FER 12]. The use of a simple, reliable and portable solution is essential to allow communication across different platforms. The structure and format of these electronic reports allow physicians the option to print them but also the ability to access the patient's medical record in a fast and simple way. It is assumed that a successful digital health information system must include information from the following systems [SEI 03]:

– health card database;

– current medical record, wherever it was generated;

– access to departmental clinical systems such as clinical analysis laboratory or diagnostic imaging services;

– health promotion and disease prevention programs;

– information on health facilities or other healthcare services;

– occupational health contingency;

– electronic prescription system;

– complementary health benefits;

– systems to aid clinical decision making.

An EHR includes all the health information relating to an individual, regardless where and when it has been generated. An objective of the EHR is interconnecting the different healthcare practitioners (patients, medical specialists, nurses, etc.) at a common point where all health information meets [KWA 05]. Figure 1.1 shows the health system in an information society.

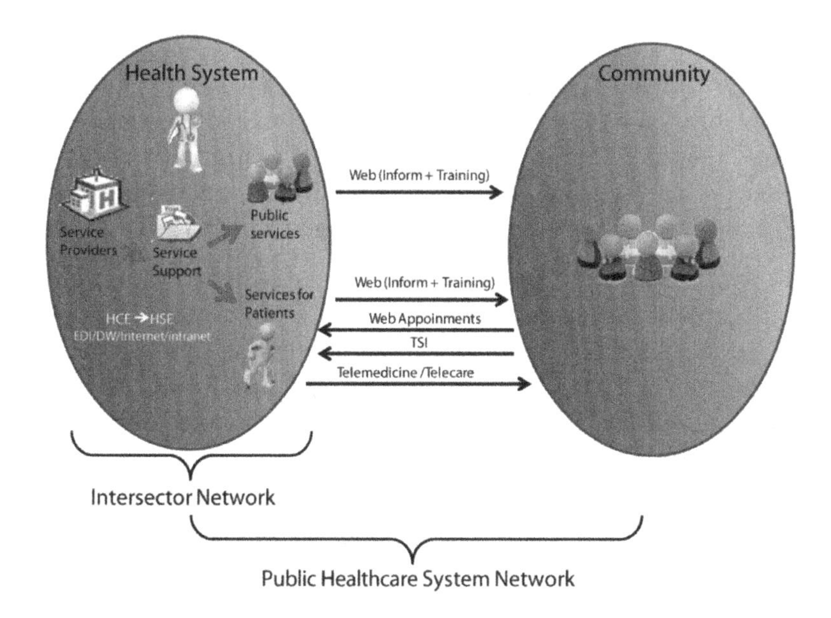

Figure 1.1. *Health system in an information society*

In all these systems, in order to interact with each other and exchange information related to individuals, it is essential that each person should be identified uniquely. This chapter discusses the main requirements of EHRs, their benefits and the main standards used to deploy them.

1.1.1. *Requirements of EHRs*

EHRs must include the following assumptions [KAL 12, FAR 10]:

– The relevant information of general interest should always be present, easy to access and extract from the general information. This is the case for both family and personal histories that are kept and increase/are added to over time so they can be used to inform clinical decisions, regardless of where they take place.

– The limited temporal information generated in isolated events may be well supported in closed electronic documents. These documents may contain the particularities of each specialty or service provided, in terms of design and functionality, as part of each care episode.

– The information is generated with temporal discontinuity but forms a unit in terms of content (clinical course, notes, etc.) that must be supported in electronic documents where previous entries cannot be altered. In turn, they also allow the addition of new comments or notes arising from clinical acts.

– The information generated by medical orders, both treatments and examinations, must be appended to electronic documents, allowing medical staff to send them to services where such orders should be completed without further input.

In this mobile society, the ability to access health records from different places is increasingly important. For this reason, in recent years, the computerization of medical records has become an important target for most of the work on telemedicine [SEI 03]. The replacement of traditional paper records with an EHR system and the ability to access it anytime and anywhere has the following benefits:

– it reduces/prevents the continuous growth of paperwork, which creates serious problems with physical storage;

– it allows the rapid transfer of patient health information to distant locations, unifying medical records above the limits of institutional care;

– it reduces includes the possible risk of loss and deterioration of conventional medical records;

– makes this information available to researchers and health planners in an easily accessible and treatable way.

The emerging demand for information structured properly in combination with the development of computer science has enabled the development of EHRs. The first steps in EHR development occurred in hospital environments and were focused toward those areas that are easy to structure: diagnoses, laboratory tests and drug treatments.

The clinical narrative (history, physical examination, etc.) has been extremely difficult to collect in a structured way. The efforts of groups currently working in this topic are focused on improving design and processing. In all healthcare institutions, medical records are the most important files because they contain vital information for clinical, administrative and legal management. It is the most important module of the system because all refer to it. Medical records may not be available in the main information system but their bases must be installed in order to guarantee that other modules can operate.

The basic medical record can integrate with different specialties such as laboratory tests medical histories and diagnostic exams with models of different and specific studies, depending on the needs of each user profile (healthcare professionals). It should be easy to use to store patient data in health environments (clinics and hospitals). It structures medical records in an ordered way, coding diseases according to world health organization (WHO) classifications, and compile statistics. It is also important to measure the quality of service offered to users considering the level of satisfaction that generates a global view of the service provided by an EHR application [DE 12].

Nowadays, a medical institution without a central information system, where information on each patient is distributed in several separate reports generated by each service and department, is unimaginable. The access to patient information by a locum medical doctor, for instance, may be extremely complicated. Overcoming this problem is a triumph of the EMR concept as a fundamental tool for medical care, regardless of other equally important aspects, such as its value as a legal document and instrument of medical practice audit.

The progressive accumulation of knowledge determines the income of a growing number of technicians and specialists. Sometimes they collaborate in a patients care but they are not in the same physical place. In these cases, medical records become the single means of communication between each member of this virtual working environment. While computerization of medical records does not solve the entire problem of hospital information management, in many cases it provides options that allow for reducing them or introduces benefits that make its implementation desirable.

1.1.2. *Benefits of EHRs*

Among many benefits offered by EHRs, it is important to highlight the following [ROM 10]:

– continuity of medical care;

– exchange of information and available online 24 h a day;

– control of the health profile for the population served;

– readability of prescriptions;

– loss of paper records is avoided;

– the ability to store large amounts of information, allowing advanced searches according to different parameters, such as forenames and pathologies;

– safer process of medical care;

– medical staff can schedule appointments.

Table 1.1 lists the main advantages of EHRs compared to traditional medical records.

As may be seen in many fields of information technology (IT), technical–theoretical vision has led to high expectations but meeting these expectations is taking longer than imagined.

Traditional medical records	**Electronic health records**
Clutter and disorganization	Order and organization
Lack of uniformity	Uniformity
Fragmented information	Unified information
Unreadable	Readable
Alterability	Fastness
Doubtful confidentiality	Access control
Questionable availability	Accessibility
Archiving errors	Error minimization
Deterioration of support	Guarantee of support
Storage	Other support
Problems in data separation	No problems in data separation

Table 1.1. *Features of traditional medical records and EHRs*

1.1.3. *An overview of EHRs*

Depending on their characteristics, a quick rating can be performed, considering three distinctions:

– *Computer-based patient record (CPR) systems*: They are the first telemedicine systems. Although the idea emerged in the 1980s, the CPR began to gain importance at the time the Institute of Medicine published: *the Computer Based Patient Record: An Essential Technology for Health Care* [INS 91]. The IOM proposed systems able to directly capture the paper records as an image for future reference.

– *Electronic medical record (EMR) system*: This is the current generation system. EMR systems encompass CPR systems and extend their definition. They have typically been thought as a proprietary system designed by an organization to provide specific services for creating and managing medical records electronically. Thus, EMR systems provide some interaction and access, in real time, to data in the organization where this system is located.

– *EHR systems*: These operate beyond the level of a proprietary information system. In this case, the data, their exchange and the modules of the architecture are standardized following general guidelines.

1.2. Standards for EHRs

In health, as in other fields of telematics applications, there is a general trend toward user demand for open systems that are distributed, interconnected and interoperable, with a high degree of reliability and increasingly demanding security requirements. The integrated management of health services and continuity in medical care requires the adoption of messages, formats, coding and structure of medical records to be widely accepted [DE 93, TOP 13, ROD 13b].

EHRs have become more attractive as costs have fallen and the market has developed. There are important arguments for considering similar effects in informatics and health telematics. This sector is characterized by market fragmentation, the proliferation of incompatible applications, the development costs of particular solutions, their short life cycle, maintenance problems and barriers to the operational integration of different and isolated systems [MON 03].

Standardization of the interface between telemedicine equipment and telecommunications systems is required. This section describes the objectives of EHR and some of the main issues of current healthcare systems [KOM 05].

1.2.1. *Goals of standards for EHR and the main issues of health information systems*

Currently, society tends to move to the heterogeneity of various devices in the healthcare sector. There are different user terminals, transportation systems, services and applications that could be adapted to the health field [MON 03]. The requirements of an information system are:

- extensibility;
- interoperability;
- portability;
- scalability;
- availability;
- reliability;

– security;

– low costs.

There are currently a number of issues that make it difficult to achieve these objectives [SEI 03]:

– market fragmentation;

– development of different applications;

– too short a life cycle of the systems;

– integration issues with other systems and applications;

– lack of compatibility;

– high cost of particular solutions.

Proprietary systems are usually closed systems where technical specifications are subject to secrecy or under patents held by the manufacturer. There are also open systems that make information public. These are usually based on public standards. This kind of system allows the design and implementation of pluggable and interoperable components, achieving most important objectives for the user.

1.2.2. *Standards and rules*

In telemedicine, manufacturers must adopt a set of rules such as [RIC 11]:

– interoperability and systems integration;

– independence of suppliers;

– reduced operating and maintenance costs;

– simplification of tasks;

– training and personnel qualification;

– increased security;

– this system should be considered an instrument for quality management;

– process re-engineering.

With these requirements, open standards are created. Following the sharing philosophy, the code is published and everyone has access to it. This method involves a process of open decision making which makes costs lower. The intellectual property rights of these standards are deposited in a non-profit organization that works with a policy of free access to repositories.

Following a layered architecture, it is easy to distinguish three levels: communication, services and application. These levels can be different for each user. The standards are considered as an interface that users can communicate with. The information system must include a set of rules for means of communication and generic services. A set of rules thus arise that are backed by a recognized authority and produced by a well-established public process designed to facilitate the consensus of stakeholders involved in the documents. There are rules at different levels: international (such as the International Organization for Standardization (ISO) or International Telecommunication Union), European (such as the European Committee for Standardization (CEN)) and national (such as, the Portuguese Institute of Quality and the Spanish Association for Standardization and Certification (AENOR)). However, in the case of an information system designed for telemedicine, it must meet another set of rules regarding the function of each term presented in each standard [MON 03]:

– distribution of components (CORBA, NET, etc.);

– internal communication bus (IP, FireWire, etc.);

– buses for devices (IrDA, USB, Bluetooth, etc.);

– internal communication media (Integrated Services Digital Network , Digital Subscriber Line (xDSL), etc.);

– user interfaces;

– medical devices (ISO/IEEE 11703, IEEE 1073, Point of Care Testing, DICOM, etc.);

– directory of the patient's history (ENV 13606, open EHR, etc.);

– communication of patient history (HL7, OMG, etc.);

– images (DICOM, CIAS, etc.);

– video (Session Initiation Protocol, H.323, etc.);

– safety and terminology (SNOMED, etc.).

Table 1.2 gives a summary of the main standards used in telemedicine.

Concept	ICD 9.0 and ICD 10.O				
Data	Medical images DICOM 3.0	Non-medical images JPEG/MPEG, M-JPEG	Text SGML, Hyper Text Markup Language (HTML), eXtensible Markup Language (XML), JavaScript Object Notation (JSON), Plain Text	Audio MPEG2	Video conferences (Commonly used standards that depend on the quality of the line)
Transmission	DICOM 3.0, HL7, File Transfer Protocol (FTP), Simple Mail Transfer Protocol (SMTP), Hyper Text Transfer Protocol (HTTP) and Transmission Control Protocol (TCP)				
Security	Authentication and encryption				
Infrastructure	Infrastructures commonly used in a network environment where they provide a network service				

Table 1.2. *Standards in telemedicine*

Figure 1.2 shows the typical evolution of the lifecycle of a standard. In the first stage (T0), there is early adoption of a standard that evolves; meanwhile, the older one remains in place. The second phase (T1) shows a massive migration to the new standard. During the third phase (T2), the current standard is used. In the fourth phase (T3), the old standard starts to be phased out and the new one begins to be used. The last phase (T4) registers a massive abandonment of the old standard and the new one begins to be used by users. The period between a standard that is adopted and a new standard is approximately 4 months.

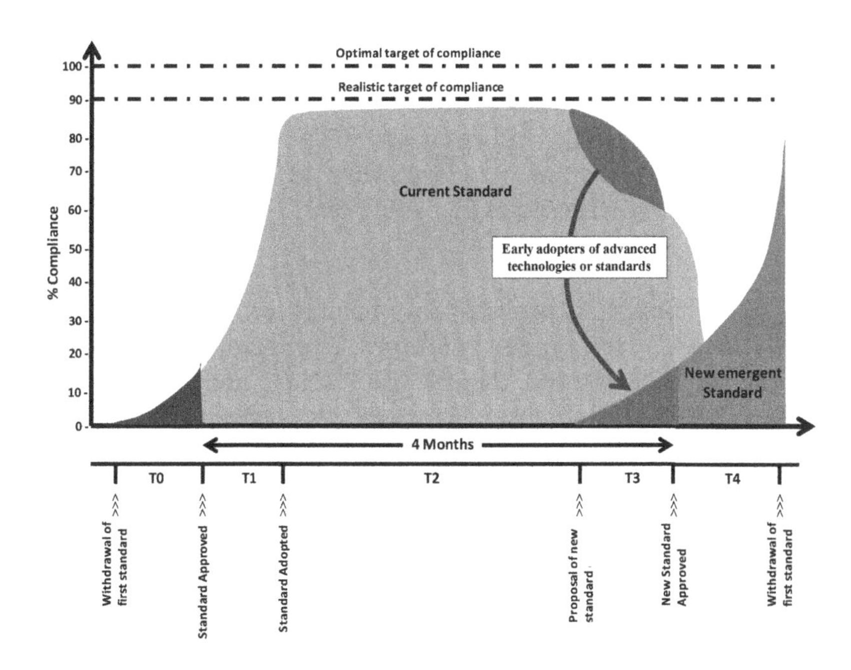

Figure 1.2. *Typical evolution of the life cycle of a standard*

The adoption of standards (formats agreements, messages, coding, data structures, files, etc.) is crucial for the successful coordination of activities (increase in safety, decrease in costs, promotion of the development of new services, etc.).

The standardization of EHRs is an essential factor for ensuring the interoperable sharing of health information. The European reference frame for the standardized exchange of EHRs is the recently approved ISO/EN 13606 standard. The general objective of the CEN/ISO 13606 standard is to define rigorous and stable information architecture for communicating part or all of the EHR. This standard follows an innovative dual-model architecture that separates information and knowledge [EN 16].

ISO 18308:2011 defines the set of requirements for the architecture of a system that processes, manages and communicates EHR information. There are different standards in the same category, such as ISO 10159:2011, ISO/IEEE 11073-10418:2013, ISO 11073-91064:2009, etc. [INT 16].

ISO 10159:2011 specifies the format of a manifest of Web access reference pointers, information object identifiers, information object filenames and associated information required by a target IT system [INT 16]. ISO/IEEE 11073-10418:2013 establishes a normative definition of communication between personal telehealth International Normalized Ratio devices and managers in a way that enables plug-and-play interoperability [INT 16]. ISO 11073-91064:2009 specifies the common conventions required for the cart-to-host as well as cart-to-cart interchange of specific patient data, ECG signal data, ECG measurements and ECG interpretation results [INT 16].

The other standard is Health Level 7 (HL7). This standard currently has six types of standards. HL7 v2 is the traditional standard for internal use in hospitals. HL7 v3 is a version for exchanges to ensure continuity of care across multiple care providers and different organizations. In the following chapter, HL7 will be looked at in depth.

2

Health Level 7

2.1. Introduction

Health level 7 (HL7) is a specification for a standard for electronic data interchange in the healthcare environment, which focuses on in-hospital communications. It is used for the exchange of clinical, financial and administrative information between computer systems [CHR 01]. HL7 is the result of work performed by a committee of providers' users, vendors and consultants in the area of health systems.

The average hospital has programs installed that deal with registration processes, admission and discharge of patients, mapping and reporting, clinical laboratory tests, radiology and pathology reports, billing and general administration, among others [HEA 08]. These applications are frequently developed by different vendors or groups, so each product can have very specific data formats.

As hospitals are expanding, the information processing operations are also expanding. The need to share data that contain this kind of information becomes critical [GAG 16]. The evolution and availability of global systems of hospital computerization that very few vendors have developed to date would mitigate the need for standards like HL7 for external data transmission. However, these programs are still scarce and their deployment requires heavy initial investment in both hardware and software, which makes the existence and development of specific low-cost applications very difficult. Figure 2.1 illustrates the interoperability of different clinical systems included in HL7.

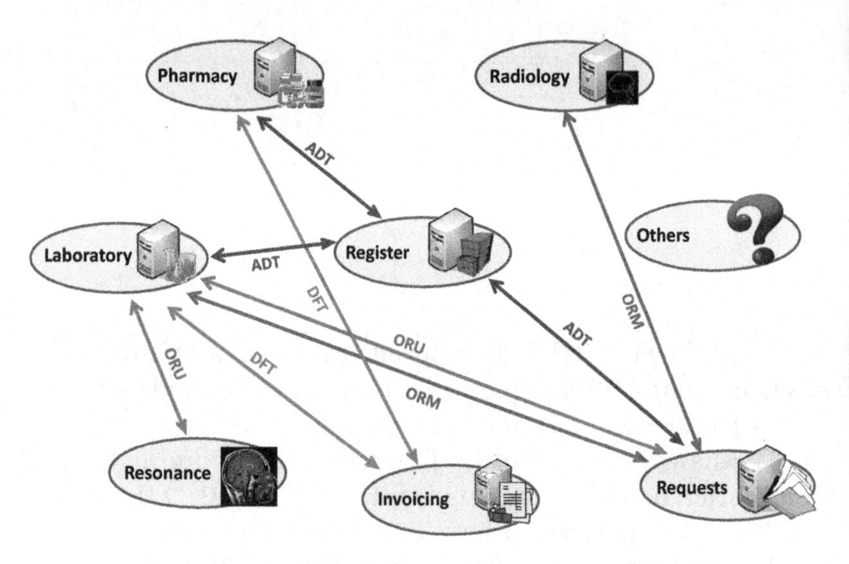

Figure 2.1. *Illustration of an interoperability scenario using HL7. For a color version of this figure, see www.iste.co.uk/rodrigues/ehealth.zip*

HL7 is a non-profit organization, open to anyone who wishes to participate, where its representatives are democratically elected. The main goal of this organization is to encourage the widespread use of standards between various stakeholders in the sector across international markets. This would benefit all projects because it would facilitate information systems involving data integration, application development, process development and encourage people to communicate in heterogeneous areas [HEA 08].

The necessity to develop standards that underpin interfaces between systems arises from the emergence of network technology for the integration of application programs in the topic of health stations, which are hosted in functional work stations and are technically different. Their integration often requires a huge amount of hours to be spent on a site-specific network environment and programming [MCN 12]. This occurs at the expense of the buyer and/or seller and prevents personnel involved from engaging in the more productive development of new modules or initiatives. The number of systems to be linked increases exponentially with the amount of time spent on the development of interfaces, while the attachment to a standard only requires the effort involved in its development. The main features provided by this standard are:

– it is an independent technology standard and platform;

– it provides the possibility to exchange information between applications developed by different vendors;

– there are reduced programming costs in developing and maintaining interfaces;

– it provides flexibility, because it is possible to develop applications in different technological environments and connect them together.

This chapter elaborates on HL7, including its background, goals and mission, architecture, standards, its transactional model and functional model.

2.2. The background to HL7

The HL7 Committee began operations in March 1987 following a conference organized by the University of Pennsylvania Hospital about health standards. Its purpose is to standardize the data exchange format and protocol between certain sets of application systems on health. The committee is organized in groups that are part of a healthcare system, which is voted for and approved by members of the working group.

In recent years, HL7 has experienced tremendous growth as an organization. There are currently over 170 organizations involved in the provision of health services that have deployed their system interfaces based on HL7 standards. In addition, there are many institutions that use it although they are not official members of the group.

The concept of "Level 7" refers to the highest levels of the Open Systems Interconnection (OSI) model of the ISO. This does not imply that HL7 is specifically under certain constituents of the seventh level of the OSI. In fact, HL7 does not specify a set of OSI specifications for levels 1–6. Instead, it specifically conforms to the conceptual definition of a link application strictly made to level 7 of the OSI model. The ISO-OSI architecture is illustrated in Figure 2.2.

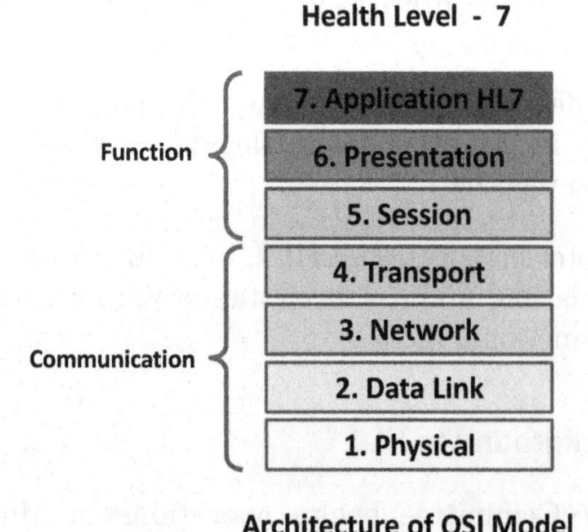

Figure 2.2. *Illustration of the ISO-OSI layered architecture*

In the OSI model, functions that communicate with various systems, both in terms of hardware and software, are divided into seven levels following an organization based on close activities. HL7 defines the data to be exchanged, the purpose of such exchanges and the communication of certain error messages for specific applications that are involved in the data exchange [MOR 11].

2.3. Goals and objectives of HL7

HL7 addresses the interfaces between systems that emit or receive log messages, admit transfer and discharge of patients, and information requests, orders, results, clinical observations, produce billing information and update master files. HL7 does not assume any particular architecture with respect to data location within the application, but it is designed to support both a central system of patient care and a more distributed environment where departmental applications are data repositories [SHA 09].

Considering the huge number of applications that are available for healthcare, as well as the variety of environments in which care processes and treatment are performed, it is clear that there are many additional interfaces that would benefit from the development of standards.

Other topics addressed by HL7 are:

- decision making support;

- nursing applications;

- ancillary services department applications;

– computerized EHRs;

– need for information outside the hospital setting.

The main goals and objectives of HL7 are:

– to develop and publish standards for approval by the American National Standards Institute (ANSI);

– to promote the use of HL7 in healthcare;

– to promote education and outreach standards;

– to promote service certification of conformity;

– to define methodological specifications to create extensions of the standard;

– acceptance and use of HL7 across the world through the creation of international affiliates.

In order to achieve the above goals, HL7 should perform a set of functions for each scenario. It defines the structure and coding messages to be exchanged. It profits from existing experiences in the development of protocols and standards that are continuously evolving products and technology and HL7 does not favor the interests of the owners of any company or organization [GRI 11].

2.4. HL7 format

HL7 specifies the format of messages created by computer applications aimed are supporting the healthcare process. The general format of the message data field presents items of variable length, separated by special characters, according to specific coding rules. The data fields are combined into logical groupings called segments, which are separated by specific characters. A message includes several lines and each line represents a segment. In its current version, HL7 encodes 27 message types, each one based on a specific set of processes in forming the overall process of healthcare.

2.5. Overview of the standards

– *Version 2.4*: This version was accredited by ANSI in October 2000. It includes new messages for laboratory automation, personnel management and application management.

– *Version 2.5*: This is the latest version to be released. It contains new posts over previous versions and offers lots of options for message content and the ability to define messages and *ad hoc* segments. This provides great flexibility but, on the other hand, it causes loss of interoperability.

– *Version 3*: This version adopts a rigorous methodology and message development called the coupled reference model (RIM) with messages.

– *Document Clinical Architecture or CDA* was recognized as an ANSI standard in November 2000 and it proposes a structure of XML documents. Thanks to the use of RIM and coded vocabularies, the CDA makes clinical documents, interpretable objects, a multitude of applications and is transferable through any electronic means.

– *The clinical context object workgroup* is managed by a working group that promotes the creation of standards for visual integration from the end-user's point of view with regards to healthcare applications.

2.6. Basic HL7 transactions model

The basic model of HL7 transactions can be observed in Figure 2.3 [ANS 07].

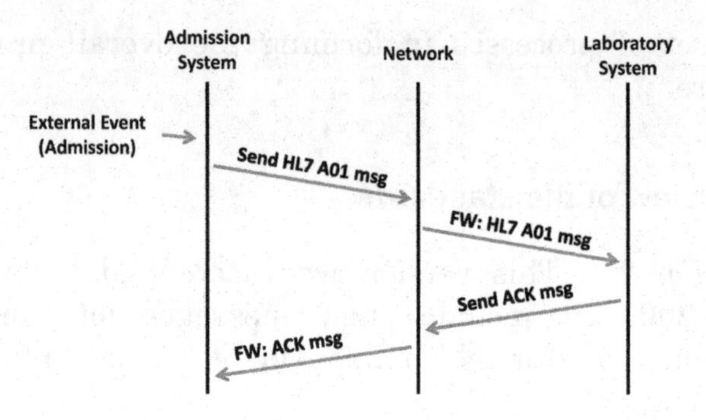

Figure 2.3. *HL7 basic transactions model*

Following the exchange of messages, the basic transaction model explains:

– *Step 1*: The sender system builds a HL7 message based on the application of data and sends it to the receiving system;

– *Step 2*: The receiving system receives the message and several options can be followed;

- syntactically validates the message. If it fails, it sends a rejection message to the sender. If not, it continues and passes to a second stage,

- sends the message to the application that can use one of the following options:

- create a reply message,

- create an error message,

- create a rejection message,

- send the message, error or rejection.

2.7. HL7 functional model

ANSI approved the first functional model for EHRs. This functional model developed by HL7 defined the most important ranges and functions that must be contained in an EHR system.

The functional model contains approximately 1,000 conformity criteria with 130 defined functions where features are included for assisted prescription, backgrounds, support systems, clinical decision making, order and security models. The model allows the creation of "profiles". These profiles are groupings of functions defined by administrations, associations, interest groups, etc. that gather a desirable set of characteristics to be met by a system. These sets are certifiable [GRI 11].

The functional model of HL7 (EHR-S) is based on a structure that has several parts:

1) the functional summary (which is divided into care, support and information infrastructure);

2) the functional profiles;

3) priorities assigned to the functions in each profile.

The functional summary should contain all the features of EHR and profiles must perform the above functions. Among the three main sections, there are 13 subdivisions [SLA 13]. The summary has more than 140 individual functions. Each one has a name, its statement and compliance criteria, and other information such as the description of the function. The functional model is designed to include features within each feature set, i.e. the user can create their own subset of functions [ANS 07] (see Figure 2.4).

The conformance clause explains the critical concepts for understanding and deploying the functional HL7 model such as the profile definition, compliance criteria and how to determine which is mandatory or optional. A conformance clause may also provide communication between businesses and consumers (buyers) as well as what is required. It serves as the basis for certification activities that can be performed by external HL7 organizations [ANS 07].

			Profiles
Direct Care	DC.1	Care Management	
	DC.2	Clinical Decision Support	
	DC.3	Operations Management and Communication	
Supportive	S.1	Clinical Suport	
	S.2	Measurement, Analysis, Research and Reports	
	S.3	Administrative and Financial	
Information Infrastructure	IN.1	Security	
	IN.2	Health Record Information and Management	
	IN.3	Registry and Directory Services	
	IN.4	Standard Terminologies and Terminology Services	
	IN.5	Standards-based Interoperability	
	IN.6	Bussiness Rules Management	
	IN.7	Workflow Management	

Figure 2.4. *Functional HL7 model including a functional summary and its subdivisions. For a color version of the figure, see www.iste.co.uk/rodrigues/ehealth.zip*

The functional summary provides a list of functions organized in different sections (as shown in Figure 2.5). The functions must be described as a system so the user can recognize the key elements of an EHR [ANS 07].

ID	Type	Name	Statement/description	See also	Conformance criteria	Row #
		Normative	Normative/reference	Reference	Normative	

Figure 2.5. *Elements of the functional HL7 model*

EHRs functions can be used for the following:

– to provide end-user outcomes such as patient safety, quality of service and cost in terms of EHR;

– to promote an overview of the EHR vendor's functions, users and other stakeholders to assess the functions of EHR;

– to provide the necessary framework to manage the requirements and standards for the next applications;

– to establish a method for each country to deploy these functions for their EHR scenarios, uses and priorities.

Every function of the functional HL7 model uses a set of elements or components as follows:

– *Element ID*: This identification element is an abstract function. Direct care functions are identified by "DC" followed by a number (e.g., DC.1.1.3.1 DC.1.1.3.2), support functions are identified by "S" followed by a number (e.g., S.2.1 or S.2.1.1) and the functions of information infrastructure are identified with "IN" followed by a number (e.g. IN.1.1, IN.1.2).

– *Element type*: Two possible values of H (to indicate header) or F (for indicating function) are in use.

– *Element name*: This element indicates the name of the function.

– *Element statement item / description*:

- a statement is a brief statement of the purpose of this function,

- the description is a detailed description of the function, including examples, if needed;

– *Element see also*: This element is designed to identify relationships between functions;

– *Element conformance criteria*: This is designed to check the conformity of the function in question.

3

Clinical Document Architecture

3.1. Introduction

Clinical document architecture (CDA), developed by the HL7, is a standard for defining the structure and semantics of clinical documents required in the exchange of an environment of interoperability, formerly known as the patient record architecture. A CDA document is a piece of information that may include text, images, sounds and any other type of media. It can be transported within an HL7 message [MAR 15]. CDA documents derive their meaning from the information model of HL7 RIM [SCH 00, SÁE 13].

A clinical document must have the following characteristics:

– *persistence*: a clinical document must be maintained over a period of time defined by local and regulatory requirements;

– *management*: a clinical document is maintained by a person or organization entrusted in its care;

– *authentication*: a clinical document is a collection of data created to be legal;

– *integrity*: authentication of a clinical document must be total;

– *readability*: a clinical document must be easily readable;

This chapter addresses the aims and objectives of CDA, its levels, the structure of CDA document identifiers and its detailed design.

3.2. Aims and objectives of CDA

The aims of CDA are summarized as follows [ALS 00]:

1) priority in the care of the sick;

2) using standards;

3) exchange of readable documents between users, including those with different levels of technical sophistication;

4) promote longevity of all encoded information;

5) allow a variety of applications for economic processing;

6) compatibility with a wide variety of applications;

7) allow the control of information requirements without extension to this specification.

The design objectives of CDA are as follows [KIM 06, TRE 06]:

1) this architecture must support eXtensible Markup Language (XML);

2) the technical barriers of architecture should be minimal;

3) the architecture should impose restrictions or minimum requirements in the structure and content of a document;

4) the architecture must be scalable;

5) documenting the specifications based on this architecture;

6) documenting the specifications for the creation and processing of documents;

7) CDA documents must be legible.

3.3. Levels of CDA

CDA is a hierarchy document type definition (DTD) of three levels where each one adds more sublevels and details. Currently, only the first level is fully defined. Level one is the basis of all and the most general is DTD. Although this is the most general, it is possible to differentiate between different types of documents such as clinical notes, completion of medical incomes, etc. [SPA 07]. Throughout the three levels of a document, the content does not change. It only varies by the granularity and semantic detail with which the document is described [ZHA 16]. This allows for great flexibility depending on the requirements of the application. Therefore, a document marked according to level three can be processed by an application that only needs a strong level one [DOL00]. Let us define the features of each of the levels:

– *Level 1* is the base of the hierarchy. It specifies the semantics of the document header [DOL 00], which is based on the information model of HL7 RIM. It is suitable for highly structured and narrative clinical documents where the body of the document does not contain semantics. Figure 3.1 shows level 1 of CDA.

– *Level 2* uses the same encoding for headers and sections as level one, but its results are more restrictive. It consists of a set of structures and semantics that depend on the type of clinical document which is specified [DOL 00]. Figure 3.2 shows level 2 of CDA.

– *Level 3* allows to define observations and services within the document body. It adds tags derived from a specific document within the RIM model [DOL 00]. Figure 3.3 shows the third level of CDA.

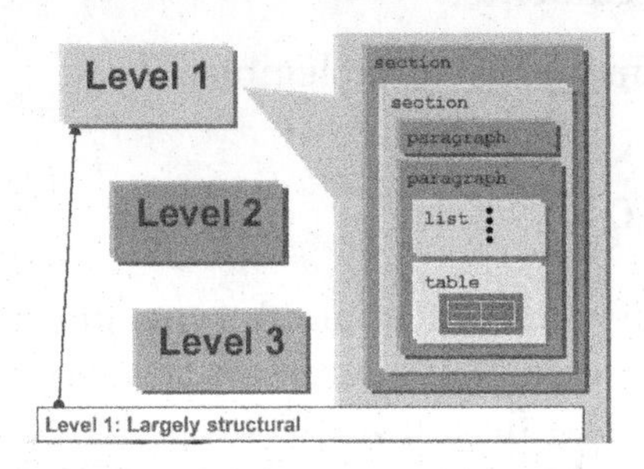

Figure 3.1. *Level 1 of CDA documents*

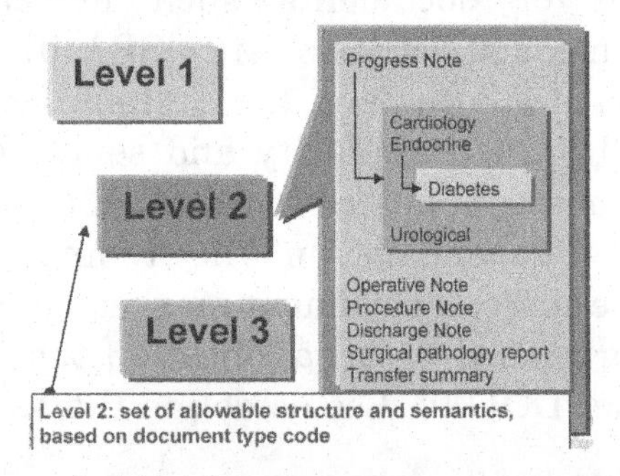

Figure 3.2. *Level 2 of CDA documents*

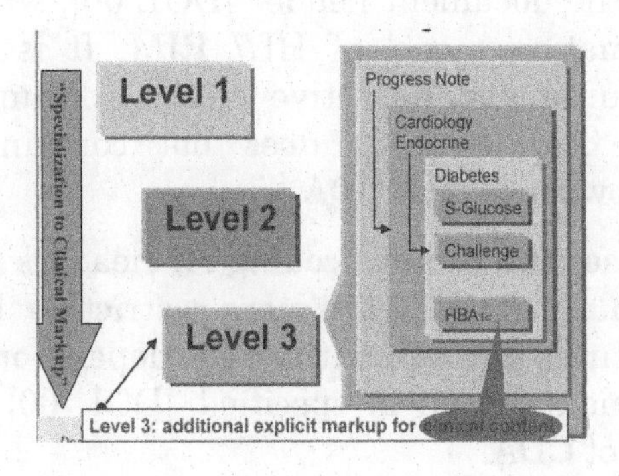

Figure 3.3. *Level 3 of CDA documents*

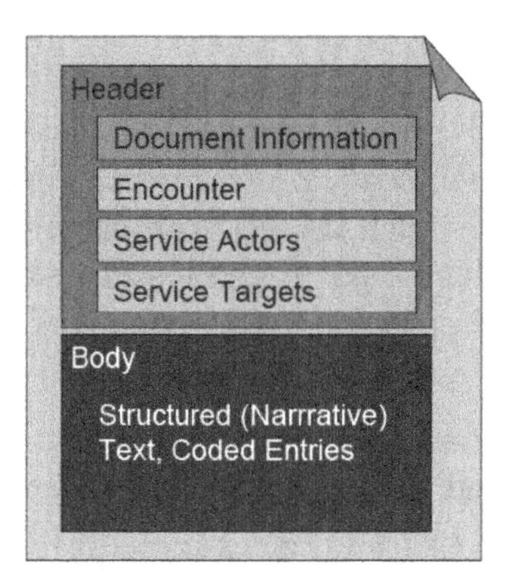

Figure 3.4. *CDA structure*

Currently, levels 2 and 3 are not fully defined. Level 1 is based on the following three technical specifications:

- CDA header;
- CDA level one body;
- HL7 v3.0 data types.

The CDA document structure can be seen in Figure 3.4. CDA extends the use of codes to identify the type of document, the sections in which it is divided, clinical procedures listed and clinical outcomes. It can use any code used in RIM, including internal and external vocabularies of RIM and codes such as Current Procedural Terminology, International Classification of Diseases (ICD), MEDCIN or Systematized Nomenclature of Medicine. The use of Logical Observations Identifiers, Names, and Codes (LOINC) is recommended for classifying document types, such as discharge reports and consultation reports. LOINC codes are available for commercial use under the terms of a license that ensures the integrity and ownership of the codes.

3.4. CDA identifiers

The global and unique identifiers necessary to build a CDA depend on each clinical document. There are some that will always appear (such as ID), and others that will appear less frequently (identifiers and roles of people who exercise, places, medical observations, etc.). Some of the identifiers to be defined in a CDA are the following:

– the unique identifier for each CDA instance (always required) is a fixed structure referred to in the regulatory scheme of the HL7 CDA;

– the identification of people: patients (*record Target* element), physicians (who take care of patients, etc.) and other possible agents as legal authenticators, patient accompanies, etc.;

– the identification of organizations: a physician's classification, which is responsible for the custody of the document, etc.;

– other identifications: confidentiality, clinical events, medical observations, diagnoses, procedures and treatments, medications and other observations, etc.

3.5. Design of a CDA document

A CDA document is made up of at least, a header that contains the essential information (author, *record Target*, etc.) and a structured body. The body does not require a mandatory class (text, component and section). In a structured body, clinical information is structured and defined by entry type (optional) classes, and although it is not mandatory, it is very interesting to use.

For the design of a CDA, it is important to know the refined message information model (R-MIM), the basic rules to build an XML file and the specific requirements of the clinical document. When the clinical document is very simple and we have some knowledge of HL7, CDA R-MIM and XML, we can directly address their development by following some general guidelines for developing a CDA, no matter how complex. The methodology used is as follows:

– basic study of the HL7 v.3 standard;

– checking that the domain for recording information is health and clinical management (and, in particular, CDA). To do this, we need to verify that the clinical document meets the standard features of a CDA document;

– analyze the reference model R-MIM HL7 CDA (R-MIM POCD_RM000040) and all of the classes therein;

– analyze the requirements and characteristics of the clinical document: the information provided, databases involved, etc.;

– identification of classes, attributes and necessary relationships of the CDA R-MIM. At this point, we need to verify that the document meets the features of the standard and of this domain;

– design of the CDA R-MIM restricted document.

3.5.1. *CDA header*

The purpose of the CDA header is to allow for the exchange of clinical documents across institutions, to facilitate clinical document management and the compilation of individual clinical documents in the electronic patient record.

The CDA header contains metadata that describes the document (illustrated in Figure 3.5). It can be divided into the following four logical components [ALS 00]:

– *document information*: includes the relationship between documents;

– *encounter data*: contains information about the service that is being given to a patient;

– *service actors*: information regarding the participants in the clinical service;

– *service targets*: information on service recipients, such as the patient.

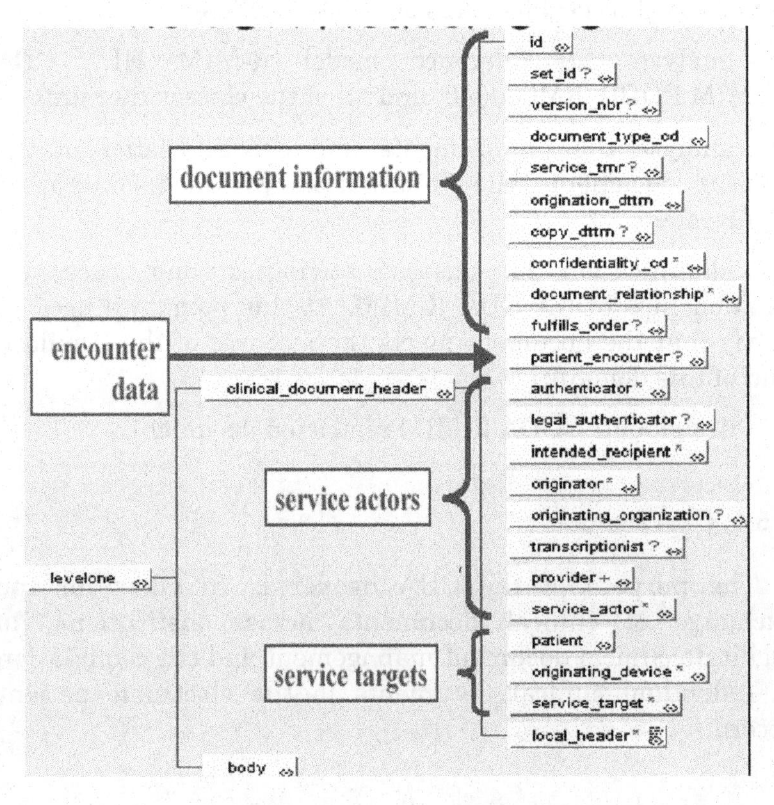

Figure 3.5. *Scheme of a CDA header*

The elements that frequently appear in a CDA header and which can be seen as an example of an obtained clinical header are:

– *Clinical_document_header*: this element is used to indicate the document header. Within it, the patient demographics are included;

– *Id*: Id represents the instance unique identifier of a clinical document. It is an element that defines a document uniquely and universally, and can be differentiated as follows:

- *Document_type_cd:* indicates the type of document you are creating. It contains the DN attributes (type of document), S (name of the coding system) and V (related document type code),

- *Origination_dttm:* represents the date on which an original document is created. Although a document is reviewed, its value remains the same. It contains the attribute V (date of document creation). Within the standard CDA, all dates are represented with the format *yyyy-mm-dd* (year-month-day),

- *Originator:* this element contains the data of origin (human) of the document. They are related to the item *originator.type_cd* who is the person who created the document and *participation_tmr* that indicates the creation date of the document,

- *Provider:* contains information about the person or organization that provides the medical service,

- *Patient:* this element includes personal data,

- *Patient_type*: always takes the value PATSBJ,

- *Id*: stores the patient identification such as passport or similar,

- *GIV*: name of the patient,

- *FAM*: surname of the patient,

- *STR*: address of the patient,

- *HNR:* house number of the patient,

- *ADL*: contains any additional information concerning the patient's address:

  - *CTY:* residence place of the patient (city);

  - *STA:* province/state of residence;

  - *ZIP:* zip code of the patient's home;

  - *CNT:* the country of the patient residence.

- *Phon*: telephone (mobile phone) number of the patient,

- *Local_header*: CDA standard defines special tags if set by the DTD do not conform to the information you want to store,

- *Birth_dttm*: date of birth of the patient,

- *Administrative_gender_cd*: gender of patient,

- *Local_header*: label with the descriptor "SS number" to store the numberofpatient social security,

- *Local_header shared:* this group of tags is used to define participants who have access to the history and type of each permission.

Other possible tags that do not appear in the clinical document that may be important are the following:

– *confidentiality code:* the code of confidentiality is a required contextual component of CDA, in which the value expressed in the header remains true for the entire document, unless overridden by a nested value. It is also used in privacy level coding (*coding with extensions*);

– *record target:* this represents the person to which that clinical document belongs. It usually coincides with the location where the tests/observations are performed, etc., but it also may not, such as with the case of a fetus. A clinical document normally has a single participant *record Target*. In the rare event that a clinical document (such as group meeting notes) is located in more than one patient table, it is possible to set more than one *record Target*. The *record Target* of a document is set in the header and transmitted to the nested content when it cannot be canceled;

– *author:* represents the people and/or machines that created the document. It may have one or more authors. In some cases, it represents the role or function inherent to the author of the document code. The *author* label requires these elements: *time* and *assigned Autho*r. The *assigned Person* and *represented Organization* elements are optional;

– *custodian:* this represents the organization in charge of maintaining the document. The *custodian* label indicates who is responsible for the care and security of the document. Every CDA document is assigned exactly one organization responsible for its maintenance. Figure 3.6 shows an example of a CDA header.

3.5.2. *Level 1 CDA body*

The body of the CDA document is comprised of a set of nested containers, including no-XML data, *sections*, *paragraphs*, *lists*, *tables*, etc. The *section* element can contain, at the same time, *paragraph*, *list* and *table* elements. The containers can include *caption* and *content* elements, which can be codified. Figure 3.7 illustrates the scheme of CDA documents.

```
<clinical_document_header>
<id EX="1e00a7c07dbd190e0000011270338695" RT="Aplication3.2"/>
<document_type_cd DN="Consultation note" S="LOINC" V="11488-4"/>
<origination_dttm V="2007-05-09"/>
<originator>
        <originator.type_cd V="AUT"/>
        <participation_tmr V="2007-05-09"/>
        <person>
                <id EX="123412344" RT="Aplication3.0"/>
        </person>
</originator>
<provider>
        <provider.type_cd V="CON"/>
        <person>
                <id EX="123412344" RT="Aplication3.0"/>
        </person>
</provider>
<patient>
        <patient.type_cd V="PATSBJ"/>
        <person>
                <id EX="12121212" RT="Aplication3.0"/>
                <person_name>
                        <nm>
                                <GIV V="James"/>
                                <FAM V="Smith"/>
                        </nm>
                </person_name>
                <addr>
                        <STR V="Burbon St."/>
                        <HNR V="14"/>
                        <ADL V="4d"/>
                        <CTY V="London"/>
                        <STA V="London "/>
                        <ZIP V="47007"/>
<CNT V="UnitedKingdon"/>
                </addr>
                <phon V="983123456"/>
                <local_header descriptor="email">jsmith@mail-
domain.com</local_header>
        </person>
        <birth_dttm V="1982-02-11"/>
        <administrative_gender_cd S="2.15.840.1.113883.5.1" V="M"/>
        <local_header descriptor="SSnumber">645363728273</local_header>

</patient>
<local_header descriptor="shared">
        <local_header descriptor="person">
                <local_attr name="V" value="123412344"/>
                <local_attr name="type" value="owner"/>
        </local_header>
</local_header>
</clinical_document_header>
```

Figure 3.6. *Example of CDA header*

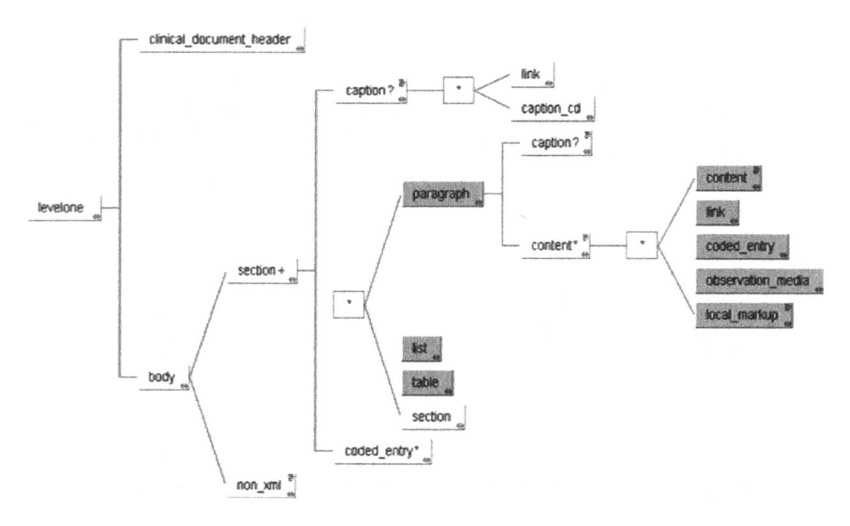

Figure 3.7. *Scheme of CDA documents*

Each CDA document has exactly one body associated with the *Clinical Document* class through the *component* connection. The body of a CDA can be represented through a structured body (*structured Body*) or through a structured body based on XML (*non XML Body*). Structured XML content is always inserted into a *structured Body* element, but never as an external archive. The data class non-XML (*non XML Body)* represents a document body that is performed with a different format of XML. It contains a required element, *text*, that is used as a reference and stored externally in the CDA document or to encode the data directly online. The *text* element has an optional attribute, *media Type*, that identifies the code, the encapsulated data and the method to interpret or present information. Presenting a non-XML body referenced requires a *software* tool that recognizes a particular type of MIME block.

The most used values of *media Type* are the following: "image/gif", "image/tiff", "text/rtf", "application/pdf", "image/g3fax", "text/html", "image/jpeg", "image/png", and "plan text". A *text* element may contain a reference that requires an attribute, *value,* which contains the uniform resource locator address of the external object pointed to it. An example is shown in Figure 3.8.

```
<component>
<nonXMLBody>
<text mediaType="plan text">
<reference value="pacient.txt"/>
</text>
</nonXMLBody>
</component>
```

Figure 3.8. *Reference that requires an attribute*

A structured body is composed of one or more component elements which can be composed, in turn, by zero or more sections (*section*), composed by entries (*entry*), which can be referenced as observations, meetings, etc. Each element is composed by optional elements, such as code, title and text. In Figure 3.9, the text content item may contain an element, which is used to add additional structure to the portion of the input text or add additional formal information.

```
<component>
<structuredBody>
<component>
<section>
<code code="10164-2" codeSystem="2.16.840.1.113883.6.1"
codeSystemName="LOINC"/>
<title>Anamnesis</title>
<text>
        <content>
Thispacientpresents...
</content>.
</text>
</section>
</component>
</structuredBody>
</component>
```

Figure 3.9. *Example of a code to add more structure to the entry text*

All these elements can be combined in the way that best suits the document being described:

– *section*: this tag is the basic node within the document body. In the defined records stored there are two sections within the corresponding *section* nodes. On the one hand, it contains all revisions of the patient and, on the other, it stores images associated with its history, as shown in Figure 3.10.

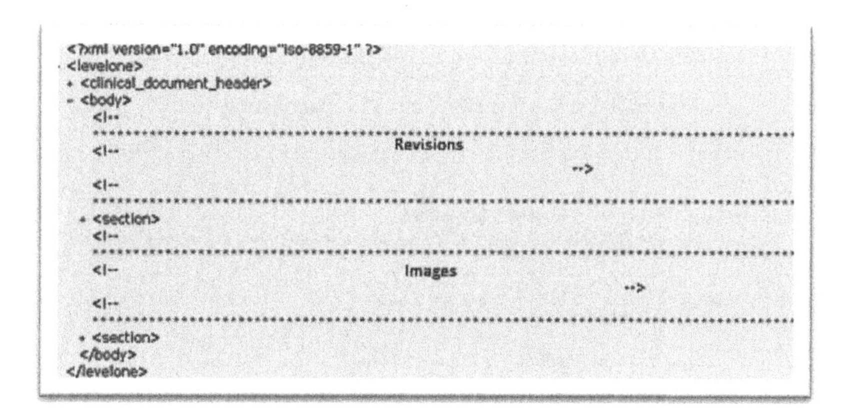

Figure 3.10. *Body of XML historical*

It can also be observed (in Figure 3.11) that each patient review is stored in a *section* node contained within the *revisions* node.

Each review is divided into sections corresponding to each piece of information from the records of the project: affiliation, motive, inquiry, ophthalmic medical history, general medical history, family history, examination, other tests/observations, diagnosis and, ultimately, treatment trial and recommendations. As in previous cases, each of these sections is a node section. Each review has an associated caption node where the date and time of its creation is stored;

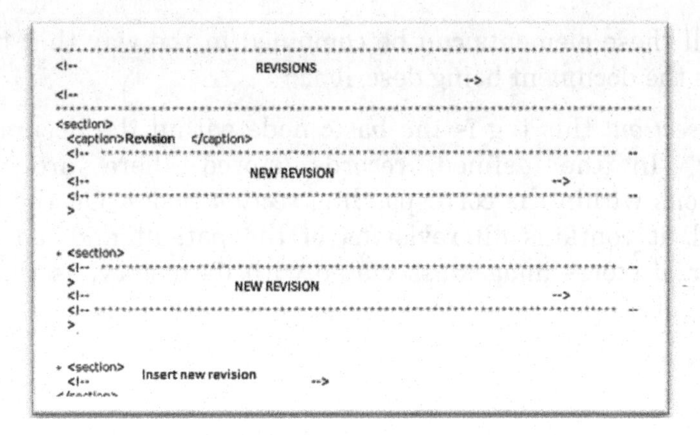

Figure 3.11. *Review within an XML historical record*

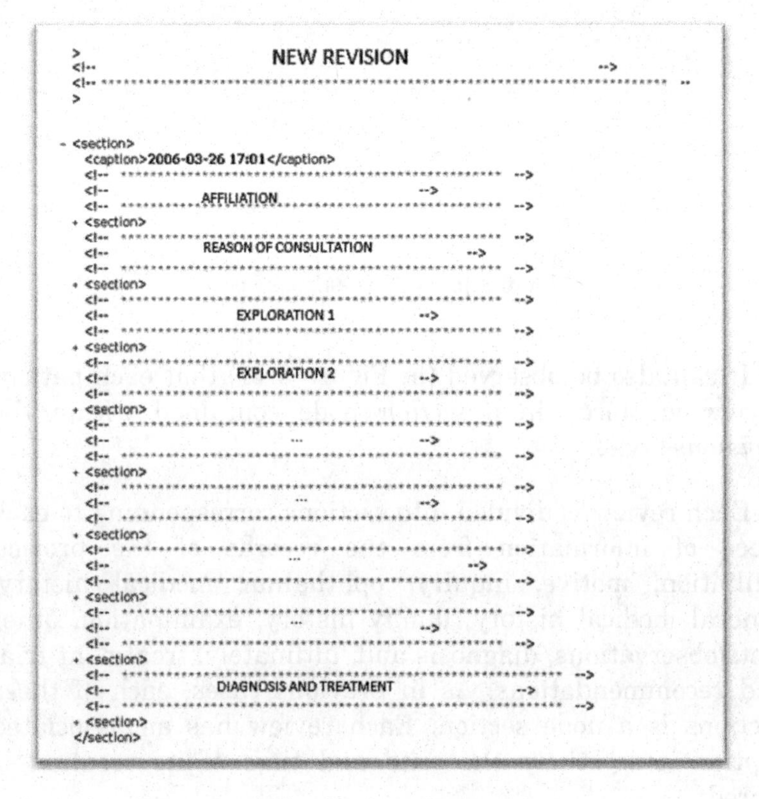

Figure 3.12. *Review of an XML historical record*

– *paragraph*: the *section* label can group the general sections, down to the specific data entered by users of the tool. The way in which these data are stored in the XML document may vary depending on the input format of the tool and may have lists, special tags, etc. The content of this tag is the data itself. This structure can be seen in Figure 3.13;

```
<section>
        <caption>Treatment </caption>
        <paragraph>
                <content>Complete rest </content>
        </paragraph>
</section>
```

Figure 3.13. *Part of a review of an XML historical record*

– *observation_media*: this label modifies images stored and encoded in base 64. These images are stored as items in a list in the corresponding section. Each image has a title where the ID of the image generated from a timestamp and the identifier of the user who entered it is stored. The images also have a child node containing the description and two for the original image (Figure 3.14) and the edited (Figure 3.15).

```
<paragraph>
        <caption>sagital</caption>
        <content>
        <observation_media>
                <observation_media.value ENC="B64" MT="image/jpeg"></observation_media.value>
        </observation_media>
        </content>
</paragraph>
```

Figure 3.14. *Code in which the digital image has not been modified*

```
<paragraph>
        <caption>frontal</caption>
        <content>
        <observation_media>
                <observation_media.value ENC="B64" MT="image/jpeg">/9j/4AAQSkZJRgABAgAAA
        </observation_media>
        </content>
</paragraph>
```

Figure 3.15. *Code in which the digital image has been modified*

3.6. HL7 v3.0 data types

As mentioned earlier, CDA documents derive their meaning from the HL7 RIM information model. The elements and attributes, and the relationships between these elements and attributes, are obtained from the reference model and embodied in XML.

Version 3 of the *HL7 Data Types* is a specification that attempts to define the data types for the exchange of clinical information [SCH 00]. Data types for strings, representing multimedia data, codes, identifiers for concepts and real-world devices, measurements, etc., are defined.

CDA specification allows to create components or coded elements whose names appear in the XML specification ending with a CD. These components have associated domains encoded with a vocabulary that represents sets of allowed values for them.

Each vocabulary has a unique identifier assigned by HL7 and every concept within a vocabulary has a unique code. The HL7 root identifier is 2.16.840.1.113883. As an example, the definition for the 2.16.840.1.113883.6.3 identifier is the coding scheme review International Classification of Diseases 10 (ICDR10). It is shown in Figure 3.16 where a piece of historical record using these codes is found.

```
<caption>MostResponsible Diagnosis</caption>
<section>
        <caption>Unstable Angina
                <caption_cd V=I20.0 S="2.16.840.1.113883.63"/>
        </caption>
        <paragraph>
<content>Y</content>
</paragraph>
</section>
```

Figure 3.16. *Fragment of the clinical historical record using this code*

It can be observed that the title of the paragraph is *Unstable Angina*. The code that represents the concept is I20.0 and it is taken from the source ICD10 vocabulary. This allows for the *caption* element to be read by a human or by an application processing *software*.

Although the HL7 standard emerged more than a decade ago, it has only recently begun to be used. We now need a mechanism to verify data integrity before the HL7 standard can be used [HUA 03].

4

Digital Imaging and Communications in Medicine

4.1. Introduction

The Digital Imaging and Communications in Medicine (DICOM) standard was established in 1992 to exchange medical images in digital format. It is somewhat complicated by its own specific "lingo". It is constantly changing to accommodate new imaging technologies and greater integration. Currently, it consists of 18 different sections, dealing with protocol, DICOM formats and specification compliance. DICOM is based on the standard *The American Collage of Radiology – The National Electrical Manufacturers Association* (ACR-NEMA) and it was released by the ACR to meet the needs of connectivity between imaging equipment. DICOM is affiliated with various American organizations and international standards working in related fields. The original DICOM standard was called ACR-NEMA, referring to these organizations. This standard was first published in 1985, and a second version (2.0) was published in 1998 [DIG 08]. In order to make clear their ancestral connection with the standard ACR-NEMA, the original version of DICOM has been called DICOM version 3.0. Normally, each year, updated versions of the DICOM standard are published. DICOM history dating back to the 1980s really was driven by users (i.e. ACR). Most manufacturers felt relatively comfortable supporting proprietary standards communication and data exchange, because it restricted their clients to purchasing equipment from the same company or developing custom software to connect to equipment acquisition. The development of a general purpose workstation, such as 3D workstations, was required for supporting a library of all the different types of tapes, floppy drives and other exchange formats. The availability of the ACR-NEMA standard in the 1980s proved to be a double-edged sword. Various manufacturers started to implement it over their own unstandardized network protocol, making the standard extensions as needed. Phillips and Siemens joined and even developed their own version, called Standard Product Interconnect. Early implementations of Picture Archiving and Communication Systems (PACS) and users dealing with systems of that era still have to deal with early ACR-NEMA 2.0 implementation and work with converters, interface boxes, etc., to reach the true level of DICOM.

DICOM is an ANSI standard, such as the HL7 standard, and is prevalent throughout hospitals, except in imaging departments [DIG 08]. The discussion on whether it should become an ANSI standard or not arises regularly within the DICOM standards committee, and has done for several years. It has now been decided that it would impose more restrictions than the additional benefits that it could bring. At this point, DICOM is widely respected and recognized as an authentic international standard. Furthermore, the standardization process is quite efficient. The DICOM standards committee meets several times a year mainly in the United States, but also occasionally in Europe and Asia.

This committee includes members from manufacturing and professional organizations. There are approximately 50 committee members who approve new work items, i.e. they determine new areas that can be standardized and approve the results. In fact, various working groups write standards and there are currently more than 20 with expertise in specific topics. There is a process, both internally and externally, involving a very thorough review, since each proposed change is subject to "public comment" by anyone who wishes to comment on it before being voted on by DICOM committee members. One of the working groups dedicated to the standard base (WG VI) ensures that new additions fit with the philosophy and the general integrity of the standard and acts to filter new additions.

DICOM uses a specific language and concepts that are common in object-oriented software engineering. Additionally, the standard itself contains several sections that are rarely used, due to the democratic process by which the standard was defined.

DICOM is based on concepts that are common in the domain of object-oriented programming, but are not yet in widespread usage. For example, ACR-NEMA defines images, while DICOM defines objects that include images and always refers to these objects in the context of applicable operations, such as store, move, look, create and print. The DICOM objects are called information objects, and operations or services are called classes of service (these are generalized definitions). Therefore, instead of discussing images, experts refer to DICOM service classes, objects and service–object pairs. Occurrence of a specific class is called, for example, a *CT_Store* of a particular patient. The use of new concepts and terminology requires a period of learning and familiarization before being able to truly understand and embrace the standard [NAT 08a].

One reason for the slow development of DICOM thus far is that, in general, the DICOM standard is used for medical imaging only, which is a very particular application compared with other standards and applications. This means that there are not many tutorials available to the general public. Moreover, as with any publication on a standard, documentation must be accurate and correct; this however means that, in the same way as when using legal terms, accuracy does not always facilitate simplicity and readability. Trying to understand and/or deploy DICOM using only a standard document is a real challenge, comparable to trying to learn a new language with just a dictionary. We can learn all the words beginning with A, B, etc., but that does not mean we can converse in that language. Unlike a dictionary, the DICOM standard also contains many sections and options that are rarely used. For example, we can have a pretty good conversation in any particular language using only a few thousand words. The same applies to DICOM. The standard does not identify which options are most frequently used, and which are used infrequently, or even not at all [NAT 08a].

The DICOM standard is continuously expanding. Not a week goes by without a DICOM working group meeting in some part of the world to discuss the definition of new objects and services. It is easy to extend the standard because of its modular nature. Regardless of whether someone is storing a Computed Tomography (CT) image or a dental, hemodynamic or endoscopy image, the same service object can be used. This approach can be compared with a furniture workshop, where information objects would be pieces of furniture, and tools, i.e. saws and hammers, are the

DICOM services. It does not really matter what types of furniture are being made, since in all cases the same tools are used. Furthermore, as illustrated in Figure 4.1, the images themselves are based on building blocks (modules) allowing specification of another object, reusing many predefined modules and studio equipment. As a result, many new applications outside of radiology (e.g. pathology, gross examination, endoscopy, radiation therapy, ophthalmology) are expanding the DICOM standard and using it as the basis for standardizing communications images.

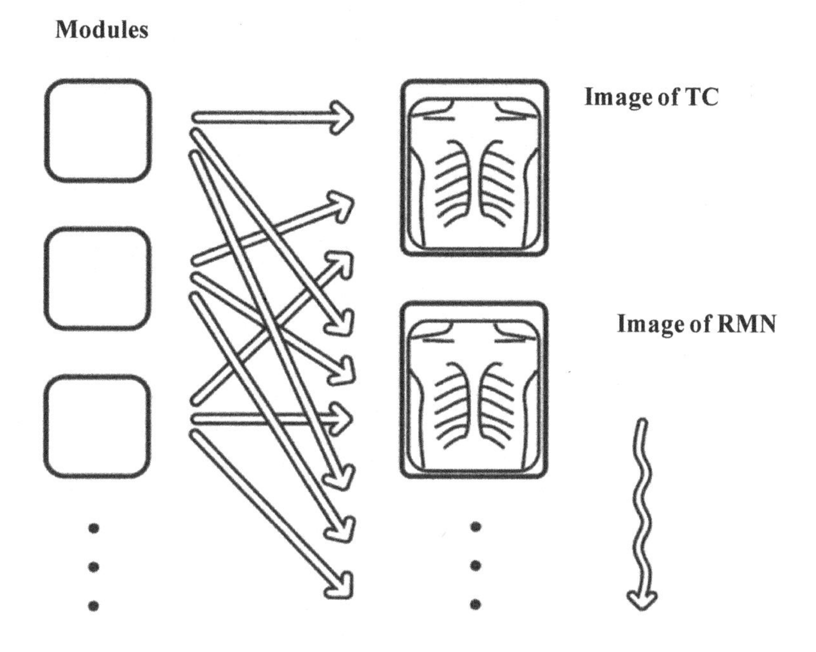

Figure 4.1. *Relationship module images*

The version of the standard also causes confusion. The DICOM standard is called DICOM 3.0. The number "3.0" indicates the evolution that began with the ACR-NEMA 1.0 and 2.0 standards. The title of ACR-NEMA DICOM was changed to highlight the fact that it is really a worldwide standard, with American institutions NEMA and ACR being committee members of DICOM, in the same way that other manufacturers and user organizations in Europe, Asia and other continents are also members. Both the DICOM standard as originally published in 1993 and the current version are referred to as DICOM 3.0. However, it is constantly growing and expanding. In fact, the community tried to remove "3.0" because it might cause confusion with a notion of versions. An updated review of the standard is printed and published periodically in an integrated document, usually every year. The completed standard not only consists of the last printed version, but also includes all additional services, changes and corrections, as approved by the DICOM committee members and published on the NEMA website, which is usually updated bimonthly (after the meeting of the Working Group VI). Therefore, the latest and most complete version of the DICOM standard is typically no more than 2 months old.

Regarding its implementation, DICOM inclusion is required for all purchases of new imaging equipment, except for those which are not connected to other device systems. Manufacturers have been offering DICOM services since the early 1990s. DICOM has several different services that includes image transfer to other storage devices, sending images to a printer, retrieval of a schedule including demographic information of a patient, updating the status of an exam in an information service, etc. However, the implementation of various services to storage is still somewhat limited in some types of equipment. Some devices limit their implementations to the core capabilities of image storage, query/retrieve and sometimes printing. To identify these different services, different "levels" of DICOM are mentioned. For purposes of inclusion in the DICOM documentation, a better term would be "usage profiles", a DICOM term explained below in the section addressing the definition of DICOM requirements.

Manufacturers have used DICOM to send, retrieve and print images. Recently, they have also started to use DICOM services to manage data. For example, a computed tomography (CT) team acquired a study of 120 axial slices, and sent them to a PACS system using the DICOM storage service.

The standard incorporates key improvements over its previous versions, as follows:

– it is applied to a network environment. Earlier versions were applicable only in environments from point to point; for operation in a network environment, an interface unit (network interface unit (NIU)) was required. Version 3.0 can support DICOM network communication standards used in industry, such as open systems interconnection (OSI) and protocols including transmission control protocol (TCP)/internet protocol (IP);

– it specifies how devices must meet the standard for the exchange of data and instructions. Previous versions have been limited to data transfer, but DICOM Version 3.0 includes the concept of service classes, the semantics of commands and associated data;

– it specifies the levels of compliance. Previous versions specified a minimum level of compliance; DICOM Version 3.0 explicitly describes how each implementation should structure a declaration of conformity to select specific options;

– it is structured as a document divided into several parts. This facilitates the rapid development of standards simplifying the addition of new features. The ISO guidelines that define how to structure multipart documents have been followed in the construction of the DICOM standard;

– it enters objects, not only images and graphics information but also used for studies, reports, etc.;

– it specifies an established technique for the unique identification of any information item, which facilitates unambiguous definitions of relationships between objects as they are interpreted by the network.

The DICOM standard does not specify the following:

– details of standard device features according to an implementation demand;

– the total set of features and functions, integrated for each device group following the standard rule system;

– a procedure test for evaluating and validating forms that meets the standard.

Throughout this chapter, the objectives and various parts of DICOM and its relationship with other standards are explained.

4.2. DICOM objectives

The DICOM standard facilitates device interoperability. It directs the semantics of commands and associated data. There must be rules about how interacting devices are expected to react to these orders and associated data, not only as information to be exchanged between devices DICOM's objectives include:

– directing the semantics of file services, file formats and information directories necessary for communication offline;

– explicitly defining compliance requirements for standard implementation. In particular, a declaration of conformity must specify enough information to determine the interoperable functions with another device claiming conformance;

– facilitating operation in a room connected to a network without requiring NIUs;

– accommodating the introduction of new services, thus facilitating support for future uses of medical imaging applications;

– making use of existing international standards, which themselves follow the documentation guidelines established for international standards.

While the DICOM standard offers the potential to facilitate implementations of PACS solutions, the use of this standard alone does not guarantee that all the goals of a PACS can be attained. The standard facilitates systems interoperability following compliance in a multivendor environment, but does not guarantee interoperability. It has been developed with an emphasis on medical diagnosis as practiced in radiology and related disciplines; however, it is now recognized as being applicable to a wide range of information-related images in clinical settings.

4.3. DICOM and other standards

As shown in Figure 4.2, there are strong connections between DICOM and other organizations to ensure that genuine international support exists in order to prevent duplication and increase credibility. In particular, two international standards bodies have committees for health informatics issues; namely, the CEN TC with the CEN/TC 251 and ISO with the Technical Committee ISO/TC 215. An alliance was established with the ISO Technical Committee 215 called Type A when it was created in 1999, and therefore, ISO/TC 215 has decided not to establish a working group for imaging, but to delegate to DICOM standards the treatment of bio-medical imaging.

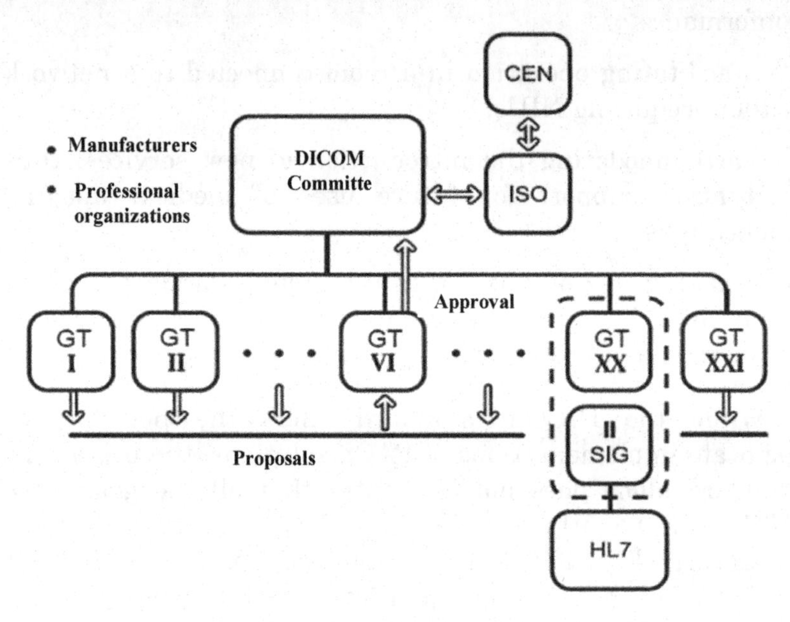

Figure 4.2. *Standard proposal*

Non-European standards do not normally participate in the work of CEN groups, except if there are DICOM members who participated in initial work. Worklist Services Team (Modalito Worklist) and Commitment Storage (Storage Commitment) were produced by the CEN project team. European standard working groups abandoned their participation a few years ago. However, DICOM and various working group committees, which include European members (as well as members from other non-American countries), meet regularly in Europe. CEN DICOM has been adopted by reference and has essentially become a European standard. The European Secretary is part of the European Coordinating Committee for Electrical Industry and Radiological (COCIR), the European equivalent of NEMA.

DICOM also meets with the HL7 standards organization for the coordination of both standards, and to facilitate the integration of image processing in healthcare organizations. Convergence with a Japanese DICOM exchange media format, called Image Sae and Carry (IS & C), took a lot of joint work with the Japan Medical Imaging and Radiological Systems Industries Association (JIRA) and the Medical Information System Development Center (médis-DC).

DICOM is also focusing on the development of Internet-related standards. It is important to ensure that the consistency of the DICOM standard is maintained with its large user base. DICOM uses standard intranets and health organizations, and can be exchanged as multipurpose e-mail extension objects.

4.4. Relation between DICOM standard parts

All parts of the DICOM standard are interrelated. As can be seen in Figure 4.3, Part 1 provides an overview, explains some basics and presents a good introduction to a new reader of the DICOM standard. It also explains the content and interrelationship of the various parts. Part 2 specifies the DICOM conformance. It requires that each device conforms to DICOM specifying services, so potential users, systems integrators and others can determine its connectivity. Part 2 specifies the DICOM conformance to be met by a product and also provides a template with several examples of typical DICOM conformance statements. This part is critical for anyone who needs to write a "DICOM Conformance Statement", and it is also useful for anyone who wants to be able to interpret it since all the aspects of DICOM are related to all other parts, as mentioned in Figure 4.3.

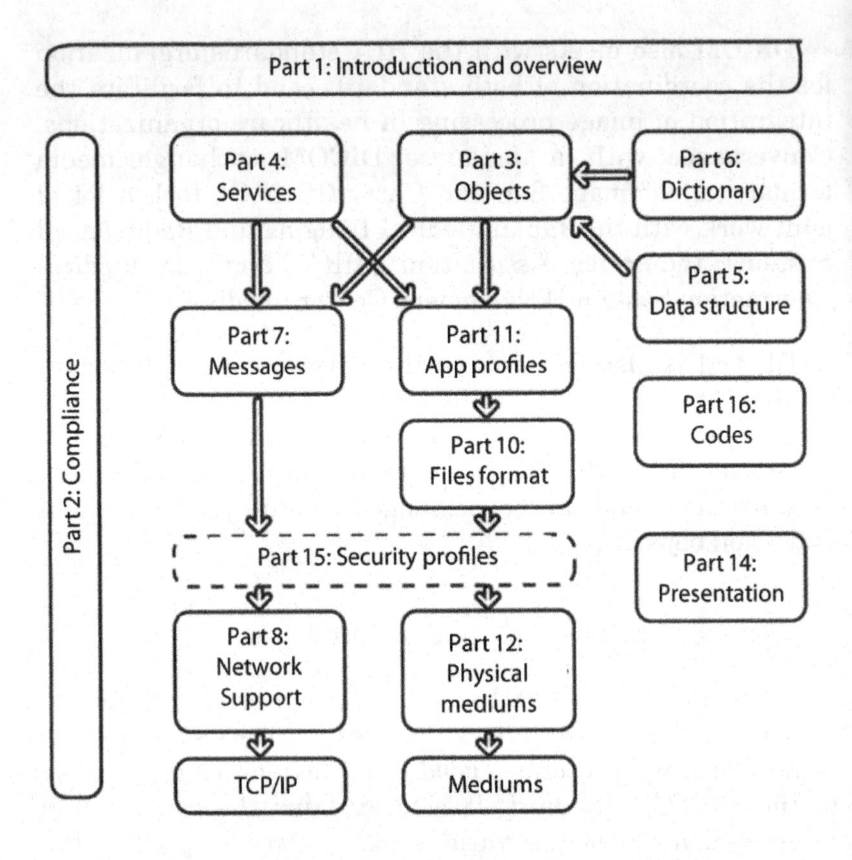

Figure 4.3. *Illustration of the relations between different DICOM standard parts*

Part 4 of the standard specifies the classes of service. It describes all the DICOM services from the storage and printing equipment work list. It specifies, in detail, the information exchanged with these services. In order to know precisely what information is exchanged when, for instance, an image is sent to a printer, it presents the details about how to change the print format. These services use specific commands to perform its functionalities. DICOM has several commands, depending on the required functionalities, and these commands are described in Part 7. Part 8 specifies the exact interface with the DICOM standard communication protocol, i.e. the TCP/IP. Application-level programmers probably need to use a set of DICOM tools that will handle all the details of the interface, and will likely not need to refer to parts 7 and 8. Nevertheless, it is important to keep in mind that these parts also contain all the errors that may occur during DICOM communication, including codes and descriptions. Therefore, for troubleshooting and support purposes, it might be necessary to use these parts as a resource.

The services described in Part 4 use the commands described in Part 7, exchanging information objects such as images and checklists. All these information objects are described in Part 3. The reason for continuously changing results from defining new image objects throughout time. For example, to know exactly how and when the mask information in an image is exchanged, it is necessary to refer Part 3. This part also specifies the definition of the Type for each individual data element, i.e. if a mandatory, optional or conditional element belonging to a particular part of the DICOM message. Part 3 is the "heart" of the standard. There are two parts that support Part 3, namely Part 6 (data dictionary) and Part 5 (data structures). Part 6 contains a list of all the individual attributes used to build these DICOM objects. Data structures specify the representation of its value, which can be compared to a definition of "type" in a software program. All DICOM elements have a specified value. For example, all names are of PN (Person Name) type, all dates of DA type, etc. To determine how these representations have a defined value, a specific format is used, for example the date format (YYYYMMDD), as may be seen in Part 5, which contains semantic data structures. Thus, both Part 6 (data dictionary) and Part 5 (data structures) support Part 3 (DICOM objects). Part 9 specifies a point-to-point using the 50-pin connector as defined by the DICOM predecessor, ACR-NEMA. There is no longer a need to consult this, except for historical reasons, or using an old device from the 1980s that still uses that kind of connection. The parts 10, 11 and 12 deal with format exchange on DICOM media. Part 10 specifies the format of files, including the directory structure. It is necessary to keep in mind that DICOM has a very specific directory structure, that can be read as DICOM CD exchange. It also displays key information for all images (which may be thousands in the case of a CD or DVD) and recover them. Since this directory is specific to DICOM, a DICOM application is needed to interpret the information. The file system itself is the standard for PCs, which means that when opened by, say, MS Windows Explorer, the available files can be easily seen. Part 11 contains the profiles which are defined for specific applications, such as hemodynamics and ultrasound, containing the definition of a specific subset of images and coding possibilities to store these images. Physical means are defined in Part 12. For example, information about the kind of DVD supporting the DICOM standard can be found here. Part 13 was defined early in the process of DICOM standardization in order to normalize the protocol for point-to-point printing and has been suppressed. Part 14 is about image quality. It contains function representation for DICOM standard grayscale mapping pixel values to a standard range of luminance values for a screen display and density values for printed representation, such as film. If information is needed to deploy this feature or there are questions about calibration, Part 14 can be referred to. Part 15 deals with security defined in DICOM. Specific profiles are identified, depending on the level of security desired. Part 16 (appeal for content mapper) contains all the code and templates. The latest DICOM object codes are increasingly used to uniquely identify items such as body parts and display codes. The templates are critical to facilitate interoperability when structured reports (SRs) are used.

The DICOM standard uses the figure as a guide to find the information needed by a reader requesting it. In particular, the electronic version of the DICOM standard is appropriate because it allows moving easily between the different parties, which, unfortunately, is necessary in most cases.

4.5. Parts of the DICOM standard

DICOM 3.0 considers the following 18 parts, although some of them have been withdrawn. All the parts are considered in order to offer a complete view of this important DICOM release.

PS 3.1. Introduction and overview [NAT 08a]:

– *PS 3.2. Compliance*: defines principles that implementations should follow [NAT 08b].

– *Requirements compliance*: specifies the general requirements that must be met by any DICOM implementation. It refers to sections under other parts of the standard.

– *Declaration of conformity*: defines the structure of a state of compliance. It specifies the information that must be present in a declaration of conformity. Moreover, it refers to sections of the compliance status of other parts of the standard.

– *PS 3.3. Defining objects*: specifies a class information object (IOD) that provides an abstract definition of real-world entities applicable to the communication of digital medical images [NAT 08c]. Every object class information consists of the description of its purpose and the attributes that define it. An IOD does not include the values for the attributes that comprise its definition. To facilitate the future growth of the standard and maintain compatibility with its previous versions, two types of IODs are defined: normalized and composite.

– *PS 3.4. Service class specifications*: defines a number of classes of service. A service class associates one or more items of information with one or more commands to be represented by these objects. Specifications indicate the class of service requirements for command elements and how the commands are applied to information objects. Specifications indicate the class of service requirements for providers and users of communications services. It defines the characteristics stored by all classes of service, and is structured as a judgment pursuant to a class individual service. This policy contains a number of annexes describing individual service classes in detail [NAT 08d).

– *PS 3.5. Data structure and coding*: specifies how DICOM applications construct and encode information in the data set resulting from the use of the information objects and service classes defined in Parts 3 and 4 of the DICOM standard. The support of a number of standard image compression techniques (e.g. JPEG) is specified. This part addresses the encoding rules necessary to construct a data stream to be converted into a message as specified in Part 7 of the DICOM standard. This data stream is produced by the collection of data elements created by the dataset. It also defines the semantics of a number of generic functions that are common to many of the information items. It defines the encoding rules for international character sets using DICOM [NAT 08e).

– *PS 3.6. Data dictionary*: registration is the centralized collection defining all the data elements available on DICOM to represent information [NAT 08f]. For each data element, this part includes the following information:

- the assignment of a unique label that includes the group and the item number;

- a name;

- specified value characteristics (character string, integer, etc.);

- specified value multiplicity (how many values per attribute);

- whether the user is retired.

– *PS 3.7. Exchanging messages*: specifies both the service and the protocol used by an application entity in a medical imaging environment to exchange messages regarding supported services defined in Part 8 or 9 communications. A message contains a flow of orders, defined in Part 7, followed by an optional data stream, as defined in Part 5 [NAT 08g]. It specifies the following data:

- operations and notifications (DICOM Message Service Element service) made available to the service classes defined in Part 4;

- rules to establish and terminate associations provided by the support specified in Part 7 communications, and the impact on pending transactions;

- rules governing the exchange of request and response commands;

- encoding rules necessary to construct command and message flows.

– *PS 3.8. Support communication network for messages exchange*: specifies the communication services and protocols required to support higher layers in a network, communication between DICOM application entities as specified in Parts 3–7. These communication services and protocols, that ensure communication between DICOM application entities, are carried out in an efficient and coordinated manner through the network [NAT 08h].

– *PS 3.9. Storage media and file format for data exchange*: specifies a general model for medical imaging information storage on removable media. The purpose of this section is to provide a structure enabling the exchange of various medical image types and related information on a wide range of physical storage media [NAT 08i]. It specifies the following information:

- a layered model for medical image storage and related information on storage media. This model introduces the concept of application profile storage media, which specifies application subsets of the DICOM standard to which a media storage implementation can claim compliance. Such conformity applies only to writing, reading and updating the contents of the storage medium;

- a DICOM file format supporting the encapsulation of any information object;

- a secure DICOM file format supporting the encapsulation of a DICOM file format in a crypto envelope;

- a DICOM file service providing independence from the underlying medium format and physical environment;

– *PS 3.10. Application profiles storage media*: specifies a subset of the DICOM standard for a given implementation that can claim conformance. This specific subset of application shall be referenced to an application outlining this section. Such a consent order applies to the interoperable exchange of medical images and related information on storage media for specific clinical uses. This follows the structure defined in Part 10 for information exchange on various types of media storage [NAT 08j].

– *PS 3.11. Functions and storage media format for data exchange*: facilitates information exchange between applications in medical environments [NAT 8k]. It specifies:

- a structure for describing the relation between the media storage pattern, a specific physical medium and the media format;

- the characteristics of the physical environment and associated media formats.

– *PS 3.12. Standard display function grayscale*: specifies a standardized function for consistent grayscale image display. This feature provides methods for calibrating a particular display system for the purpose of consistently presenting images on different media displays (e.g. monitors and printers) [NAT 08l].

The chosen display function is based on human visual perception. The contrast sensitivity of the human eye is clearly nonlinear to the range of luminance of the display devices;

– *PS 3.13. Security and system management profiles*: specifies the security and system management profiles for implementations that can demand conformity. The safety profiles and system management are defined by external referencing standard protocols, such as Dynamic Host Configuration Protocol, Lightweight Directory Access Protocol, Transport Layer Security and Integrated Secure Communication Layer. Security protocols may use security techniques such as public keys and "smart cards". Data encryption can use various standardized encryption schemes [NAT 08m].

This part does not address issues related to security policies. The standard only provides mechanisms that can be used to implement security policies regarding DICOM object exchange. This is the responsibility of the local administrator to set the appropriate security policy.

– *PS 3.14. Content mapped resources*: specifies the following [NAT 08n]:

- templates for structuring documents as DICOM information objects;

- sets of terms for use in coded information objects;

- a glossary of defined and maintained DICOM terminology;

- country-specific translations of coded terms;

– *PS 3.15. Clarifying information*: specifies the following [NAT 08o):

- informational and normative annexes containing explanatory information;

- this part of the DICOM standard contains explanatory information in the form of informational and normative appendices;

- thus, the following appendices are available:

– Appendix A: explanation of patient orientation (normative);

– Appendix B: integration modality work list and development mode of procedural steps in the original DICOM standard (informative);

– Appendix C: waves (informative);

– Appendix D: examples of SR encoding (informative);

– Appendix E: mammography CAD (informative);

– Appendix F: CAD pectoris (informative);

– Appendix G: explanation of cluster approach to IODs functional group multiframe (informative);

– Appendix H: examples of workflow identification of clinical trials (informative);

– Appendix I: template ultrasound (informative);

– Appendix J: management of identification parameters (informative);

– Appendix K: data management protocol for ultrasound;

– Appendix L: structure of hemodynamic report (informative);

– Appendix M: vascular ultrasound reports (informative);

– Appendix N: echocardiograms procedure reports (informative);

– Appendix O: logs (informative);

– Appendix P: transformations and maps (informative);

– Appendix Q: breast image reports (informative);

– Appendix R: use-cases configuration (informative);

– Appendix S: legacy transponder for configuration management (informative);

– Appendix G: quantitative analysis references (informative);

– Appendix U: ophthalmology use cases (informative);

– Appendix V: management protocols (informative);

– Appendix W: digital signatures in SRs use cases (informative);

– Appendix X: report based on dictation references images;

– Appendix Y: value-of-interest functions look-up-table (informative);

– Appendix Z: X-ray isocenter reference transformations (informative);

– Appendix AA: information on radiation dose use cases;

– Appendix BB: printing (informative);

– Appendix CC: storage commitment (informative);

– Appendix DD: work list (informative);

– Appendix EE: relevant questions related to patient information (informative);

– Appendix FF: template analysis report of cardiovascular CT/MR (informative);

– Appendix GG: JPIP (JPEG 2000 Interactive Protocol) referenced pixel data transfer syntax (informative);

– Appendix HH: coding segmentation example (informative).

– *PS 3.16. Web access to DICOM persistent objects (WADO)*: specifies the ways for expressing an accessing question to a DICOM persistent object as a hypertext transfer protocol uniform resource locator/uniform resource identifier request. It also includes a pointer to a specific DICOM persistent object in the format of a unique identifier [NAT 08p].

5

Other Standardization Initiatives

5.1. Introduction

In healthcare, as well as in other fields of telematics applications, there is a general trend of users demanding open, distributed, interconnected and interoperable systems with a high degree of reliability requirements and increasingly stringent safety. The integrated management of health services and continuity in medical care requires the adoption of messages, formats, coding and structure of electronic medical records to be widely accepted.

The role played by standards in increasing safety, reducing costs and encouraging market development in traditional industries is well known. The health sector is characterized by market fragmentation, the proliferation of incompatible applications, the development costs of particular solutions, their short life cycles, maintenance problems and barriers which hinder the operational integration of different and isolated systems [KHA 16]. A standardization of the interface between telemedicine equipment and telecommunications systems is necessary.

This chapter focuses on the International Organization for Standardization (ISO)/TC 215, CEN/TC 251 standards and initiatives such as GEHR, Open EHR, Integrating the Healthcare Enterprise (IHE) and Common Object Request Broker Architecture (CORBA).

5.2. International Organization for Standardization/TC 215

The ISO is a worldwide federation of national standards. The work of preparing International Standards is carried out through ISO technical committees (TCs). The draft international standards adopted by the TCs are circulated to member bodies such as the *Instituto Português da Qualidade* (IPQ) in Portugal or AENOR in Spain, for a vote. The publication of an international standard requires approval by at least 75% of the member bodies. The ISO is known for its wide range of standards used in many aspects of information systems, which take place within the Joint Technical Committee. One of the most popular contributions and broader impacts is the set of rules that support Open Systems Interconnection model communications.

In 1999, the American National Standards Institute (ANSI) took the initiative to promote the creation of a committee dedicated to ISO TC2 15 Health Informatics whose creation has received the support of the CEN (European Committee for Standardization), which includes IPQ and AENOR. The areas of interest of this committee are:

– messages and communication;

– representing medical concepts;

– security;

– coordination of modeling;

– medical records;

– biomedical images.

In August 1999, the ISO/TC 215 began to develop a set of standards on the requirements of the reference architecture of electronic health records (EHRs). The project has led to the Technical Specification ISO 18308, "Requirements for an Electronic Health Record Reference Architecture". It should be emphasized that the standard contains requirements for a functional EHR system, as the standard itself says: "a set of clinical and technical requirements for an architecture which supports medical record use, sharing and exchange of electronic records within and across different health sectors, different countries and different models of health care". Another ISO standard for EHR is the ISO DTR 20514, "EHR Definition and Scope", that is responsible for defining the EHR to specify their objectives.

The main users of this technical specification ISO requirement are standard developer architectures, e.g. CEN 13606, and other reference architectures such as the open EHR reference model. The development of the ISO 18308 has been performed in three stages. In the first phase, an exhaustive search for reference material was conducted in the literature, and direct contacts selected 35 primary sources including 20 sources originally collected by the EHCR-Supa project in Europe. In the second phase, working with over 700 requirements identified in the first phase, a hierarchical structure of "headings" under which requirements could be organized was developed. After eliminating redundancies, at the end of this phase requirements were reduced to 590 sources. In the final phase, a set of 123 requirements listed under a structure of 10 titles and 60 subtitles was consolidated.

5.3. European Committee for Standardization/Technical Committee (CEN/TC) 251

The European Committee for Standardization (CEN) is an organization founded in 1961 that contributes to the objectives of the European Union and European Economic Area with voluntary technical standards that promote free trade, safety of workers and consumers, networks interoperability, protection environment, exploitation of research and development programs, in addition to public achievement.

The Technical Committee (TC) 251– "Health informatics" – is one of the many sectors in which CEN is organized. It aims to achieve compatibility and interoperability between independent systems. This implies structure requirements for health information to support clinical and administrative procedures, quality requirements and safety, and technical methods to support interoperable systems.

CEN TC 251 differs from other standards organizations, as it is a standard development organization (SDO) between international or European SDO specific fields, aimed almost exclusively at technological content and not communication technology. The Business Plan of CEN/TC 251 is integrated in a process of change. The new direction of the TC, as the mandate of the European Commission (EC), will require joint efforts from the CEN, European Committee for Electrotechnical Standardization and European Telecommunications Standards Institute for balancing work with other international SDOs [CEN 16]. With respect to its structure, the CEN TC 251 includes several working groups (WGs). WG 1, models of information (WG1 information models), is responsible for developing standards relating to architecture and information models of EHRs. Magjarevic *et al.* [MAG 07] used different modules of CEN/TC 251 standard in a telemedicine network for cardiology (NEMESIS). In 1999, it published the prENV CEN 13606

"Communication with the electronic medical record", where a series of interoperability measures were proposed to facilitate communication between heterogeneous systems. So it was felt that the format of the clinical data should be maintained and presented at the receiving system but the underlying architectures are modified. This pre-norm considers four parts as follows [CEN 08]:

– *prENV 13606-1* (Extended Architecture): it is a part of the necessary components that define the architecture to allow for contents of medical history to be constructed, used, shared and maintained. With respect to the domain model, the result is a formal description of the context that surrounds the electronic health record (EHR);

– *prENV 13606-2* (Domain List of Terms): it provides a set of terms and definitions used by the medical staff, and enables all healthcare professionals to transmit and recognize the significance of clinical information based on the position of these terms within a medical record;

– *prENV 13606-3* (Distribution Rules): it defines a set of rules for medical record exchange in compliance with legal safety obligations. Medical records are made available to healthcare professionals through means of sharing and dissemination. It includes access to a physical patient record and creation of a virtual medical record that is built from the information stored in different sources and the communication of medical records, or portions of them, between systems;

– *prENV 13606-4* (Messages for the Exchange of Record Information): this pre-standard part specifies the different types of messages that allow information exchange between EHR centers or nurses. These messages allow information in an EHR to be sent from one professional to another. In this section, two properties of communication are considered: legibility and information processing.

In order to complete and adapt to new pre-standard requirements, the prENV 13606 underwent a period of public consultation. From multiple opinions, mostly based on experience with trading systems, and collaboration of representatives of HL 7 and open EHR, emerged the revised ENV 13606. This cooperation aimed to harmonize the already developed standard specifications and open EHR HL 7 to facilitate interoperability between them, i.e. to improve the ability of heterogeneous systems to communicate and exchange processes or data. The resulting document from the prEN 13606 review contains the following five parts [CEN 08]:

– *prEN 13606-1* (Reference Model): this part is a refinement of the prENV 13606-1. It proposes a generic information model defined to communicate with a patient's electronic medical record. Note that the preparation of this part involves receiving contributions from other organizations, such as HL7 and open EHR. They contribute to the interoperability among their standards;

– *prEN 13606-2* (Archetype Interchange Specification): this part was included at the occasion of the dual model adopted, establishing a generic data model and a language to represent and communicate the definition of individual instances of archetypes;

– *prEN 13606-3* (Reference Archetypes and Term Lists): it takes advantage of prENV 13606-2, defines a set of archetypes and is ready to support other parts of this standard;

– *prEN 13606-4* (Security Features): this part is based on prENV 13606-3. Sets of model concepts reflect accurate information within individual EHR instances. This is done in order to obtain a proper interaction with security components that may be required in any future EHR implementation;

– *prEN 13606-5* (Exchange Models): this part plays the same role as the prENV 13606-4 containing a set of models that are built on the earlier parts of the standard and may form the support or message-based communication services.

Specifically, the prEN 13606-1 dual model to design information architectures for communication with EHRs is adopted. Its goal is to design a scalable model to represent any possible input of health data records. The reasons for the adoption of this model are the following. First, due to the large number of different concepts available in the clinical domain. Second, due to the continuous variability of these concepts and, finally, due to the difficulty of representing this data digitally. This model includes a reference model and an archetype model.

This model is conceptually consistent with other models like GEHR–prENV 13601-1 or open EHR. It is used to represent the generic characteristics of the information in the history, how to add the background information required to comply with legal and ethical requirements of origin in order to define a set of classes that form the generic building blocks of EHR and reflect the characteristics that do not change from EHR. This information model needs to be supplemented in the domain of knowledge by a formal method of communicating and sharing hierarchical structures within the EHR, data types and ranges of values that can take the registrations and other constraints. This is to ensure the interoperability, consistency and quality of data. Their representation is performed through diagrams using a unified modeling language.

This reference model assumes that information in HC is inherently hierarchical. Therefore, it must reflect this structure and a hierarchical organization which meets the requirements to be faithful to the original clinical context, and ensure that meaning is preserved when the records are communicated between heterogeneous clinical systems. The contextual requirements of EHR are key to such fidelity and are related to a set of classes of logic block construction proposing appropriate attributes for each level in the hierarchy of EHR extraction.

According to an archetype model, archetypes are used to represent the specific characteristics of the different types of clinical data, which potentially represent the need to meet the requirements of different professions, specialties and metadata services. Each archetype case must be adjusted to an archetype model, which is formally related to the reference model. Thus, an archetype provides the following:

– a framework for information-based EHR reference model elements;

– a high-level semantic description of clinical concepts that can be processed automatically by health information systems. Archetypes are used by systems for the creation and validation of data to create user interfaces for knowledge sharing and retrieval. The version control archetype reviews ensure that new revisions do not invalidate data created with previous releases. The diversity of health information stored on paper, which exists in every healthcare organization, can lead to a wide range of possible archetypes that might be needed in a community with shared EHR. Also archetypes should be created by medical specialists.

After passing the phases of analysis and corresponding approval periods, four of the five parts of EN 13606 have been adopted as a standard EN 13606-*x* (where *x* is the number for each part). Parts 1, 2 and 4 were adopted as a standard in 2007, while Part 3 was approved in 2008.ISO 13606-5 was prepared by Technical Committee ISO/TC 215, Health informatics and by Technical Committee CEN/TC 251, Health informatics in collaboration.

Notably, the EN 13606 standard is especially designed for communication of EHRs. It allows for great flexibility in the representation of information structures that are transmitted through the use of archetypes, which also serve to semantically describe such information. This allows the same semantic processing and a reduction in errors of information insights. The EN 13606 standard is robust and does not need to deploy the underlying systems.

5.4. Common object request broker architecture

The Object Management Group (OMG) is the largest consortium of software in the world and aggregates more than 800 companies. It is a non-profit organization. One of the major achievements of this organization has been the development of the CORBA standard, a standard that has been developed for the integration of systems using object-oriented technology [MON 03].

CORBA defines an infrastructure architecture (Object Management Architecture) of OMG, and specifies the required standards to invoke methods on objects in distributed and heterogeneous environments. Intuitively, an object can be seen as a "piece of software" that provides one or more services and a method as one of the services offered by the object. Grimson *et al.* [GRI 98] performed an integration of a telemedicine system based on CORBA EHR. However, the most interesting aspect is the CORBAmed, which is an adaptation of the CORBA standard to the field of healthcare. Gritzalis and Lambrinoudakis [GRI 04] describe the possibilities of CORBA and CORBAmed activities. CORBAmed CORBA is a division responsible for defining a set of core middleware services as well as the domain of healthcare. The mission of this WG is summarized as follows:

– to improve quality of care and cost reduction through the use of CORBA technologies;

– to provide a definition of standardized object-oriented interfaces between services and health functions.

In the health sector, where CORBAmed usually coexists with countless other heterogeneous systems, the standard tries to provide a services specification in order to create some technological interoperability among them. Seven of the most important services are listed below:

– *Patient identification service*: allows for the unambiguous association of different clinical information added to a single patient. This service is in charge of establishing different correlations regarding patient identification in various systems to maintain the index information. This is a very important and critical task considered as the main barrier to the development of a reliable environment for achieving EHRs.

– *Service medical terminology lexicon*. It is used for:

- *information acquisition*: assistance in the process of entering coded information;

- *mediation*: processing messages or data elements from one representation form to another;

- *indexing and inference*: whether some associations may exist between various pieces of information;

- *manipulation or composite concepts*: it helps in the entry, validation, translation and simplification of composite concepts.

– *Service access to multimedia information*: used to extract and manage multimedia resources, including medical images for instance. It allows for information retrieval and knowledge extraction from heterogeneous systems to interoperate with each other.

– *Service decision to access resources*: used to obtain approvals, permits management and access to medical information.

– *Clinical observations access service*: implements standardized interfaces for public access to clinical information from a federation of heterogeneous systems. It requires the creation of gateways for each standardized clinical information system connected to import, export, propagate and index patient clinical records.

– *Service management abbreviated information*: used to compile and manage medical summaries to transmit information among dispersed systems. This service is optional.

– *Service to facilitate data interpretation*: used to aid the decision-making process of health information extraction from different sources.

5.5. Good European Health Record

The Good European Health Record (GEHR) is a Telematics project which provides a multimedia architecture of patient data in electronic format. This advanced computing project in medicine has created a multimedia architecture to use and share electronic healthcare records and clinical, technical, educational, ethical and legal information. The project involved 21 GEHR organizations from seven European countries along with their clinical departments in which various professions and disciplines related to medicine participated. Furthermore, this standard has developed two formal definitions to support its architecture: the GEHR object model and GEHR exchange format. To support the development of electronic record systems, the project has produced a set of 2,000 health record items available in nine European languages and a comprehensive set of 47 anatomical drawings.

5.5.1. *Patient requirements*

The GEHR architecture has been developed through extensive research of patients' needs. Physicians, nurses and other medical-related professionals were involved in deriving a set of requirements in different key areas. The GEHR that summarizes the electronic file must be readable and portable, serving as a support for clinical care. Experts rate this opportunity to create electronic files. Classifications and standard languages cannot be assumed by other individuals.

5.5.2. *GEHR architecture description*

All the information in EHRs is implicitly related to the patient. GEHR architecture has an original data structure and appears as grouped entries in the file. It has made a great effort to propose, as much as possible, a generic, flexible and reliable architecture. The main characteristics of the GEHR architecture are the following:

– EHR provides a particular container for each particular patient;

– the transaction provides most of the features needed for the legal medicine aspects. Because of these data, it can be transferred safely between different EHR systems;

– it is possible to aggregate other formats EHR and other EHR collections.

5.6. Integrating the Healthcare Enterprise

IHE is an initiative lead by healthcare professionals (including professional associations of physicians) and suppliers, which aims to improve communication between information systems used in patient care. IHE integration profiles define the use of available standards for system integration in order to provide effective interoperability and an efficient workflow. IHE enables the required level of integration in the era of the HER to be achieved.

Each IHE integration profile describes a clinical need for systems integration and solution to carry it out. It also defines the functional components, which are called IHE actors, and specifies the possible transactions that each actor shall perform in detail, which is always based on standards such as DICOM and HL7 [IHE 08].

The main benefits of IHE are presented as follows:

– it makes use of advanced information technologies that greatly assist health workers to improve the quality and efficiency of health care;

– it increases patient safety by ensuring the integrity of medical information;

– it reduces the time spent in problems solving, such as data loss and the appearance of no relevant studies, thus optimizing the use of staff time;

– it provides well-structured patient information, so medical staff can perform medical decisions based on the best information as possible;

– it defines the most pressing integration issues;

– it defines technical solutions;

– it tests product solutions from vendors;

– it promotes demonstrations of multivendor integration;

– it channels the translation of these solutions products;

– it offers support for training providers of the healthcare sector.

In its first year, the IHE initiative has focused on the Hospital Information System, Radiology Information

System, Picture Modes and PACS using both HL7 and DICOM as summarized in Table 5.1.

	HIS	*RIS*	*PACS*	*Modalities*
HIS	HL7	HL7	–	–
RIS	HL7	HL7	HL7/DICOM	DICOM
PACS	–	HL7/DICOM	DICOM	DICOM
Modalities	–	DICOM	DICOM	DICOM

Table 5.1. *Imaging modalities and PACS HIS, hospital information system; RIS, radiology information system*

In the following years, the IHE initiative considered other standards. Siemens has always played an active role developing technologies and standards, with representation in more than 20 WGs and committees in many organizations and standards initiatives (DICOM, HL7, CORBAmed IHE) and lead WGs in key areas.

5.7. Open EHR

Open EHR is a foundation that makes open research, development and implementation of EHRs. Their results are based on a combination of more than 15 years of research in EHR, which include templates, information and service models, population size and clinical work.

The open EHR foundation was created to enable the development of specifications, software and open source systems for health information, particularly EHR. Post all its specifications and implementations as open source. It also develops "archetypes" and terminology for usage with EHR [OPE 08].

The main objectives of this foundation are the following:

– promotion and publishing the requirements for representing and communicating electronic health information based on the experience of implementing and evolving over time as health care and medical knowledge;

– promotion and publishing EHR information architectures, models and data dictionaries, and tests in applications;

– evaluation and validation of EHR architectures;

– keep applications running under license;

– collaboration with other groups and health information systems, achieving interoperability systems in the computer-related healthcare fields.

Health information systems can be constructed by defining information models, executing them and uses databases, as well as adding clinical terminologies. However, the implementation of an environment containing the abovementioned information is still required. Firstly, the requirements must be defined, without which a suitable model cannot be prepared. The open EHR conditions should include the following:

– the GEHR project requirements;

– EHRs technical requirements written for the Australian GEHR project;

– the requirements for GEHR in Europe, as documented in the doctoral thesis of Dr. Dipak Kalra [KAL 02];

– the requirements of ISO 18308 for an EHR architecture.

The improvements offered by the open EHR foundation are the following:

– software maintenance is reduced, since the software should not change every time the model changes some clinical data – it only changes archetypes;

– increase the validity of the data because the archetypes are used to validate all the input data to the EHR. From a clinical point of view, data are more trustworthy;

– increase interoperability: because of this information sharing between clinicians within a hospital, a network of community care and greater distances are improved;

– standard: the reference model of open EHR is based on standards of ISO and CEN EHR and is interoperable with HL7 message standards and EDIFACT. This can be integrated with other software and open EHR software systems;

– integration with systems: this standard can be integrated with many systems using well-known standards for data interoperability.

5.8. Security standards in EHRs

Security in an information system should include all the possible threats that are identified in all elements of the information system: machines, software, data, networks and network electronics. Threats can be both voluntary and involuntary, similary to disasters, such as fires and floods [GAR 03].

Table 5.2 shows the security objectives and security measures or mechanisms available to ensure compliance.

The two basic security mechanisms use public and private keys, and algorithms summary of an address. These are the foundations for the construction of other security mechanisms.

Objective	Description	Measures
ID	Process of identifying the client application or service	Digital certificates
Notice	To ensure that access to information is performed only by authorized entities	Encryption
Integrity	Set of actions to ensure the information has not been transformed during processing, transport or storage	Digital signature
Non-repudiation	Procedure to ensure that none of the parties involved and identified can deny their participation in a transaction	Digital signature, audit
Authorization	Determines what information can be accessed and what tasks can be undertaken by an authenticated client. This process determines the privileges associated with a user profile	Organizational issues that every organization must design and carry out their particular systems
Audit	It is possible to track the accesses made to information and transactions made on it for each user and the circumstances performed by them	Raw access and data operations
Availability	Part of the security to have and access information when needed. It should protect the systems and, then, they remain operational and can access information at any time	Operation and level of systems services

Table 5.2. *Objectives and security measures*

Combining all the abovementioned security objectives, it is possible to protect information systems through encryption, digital signatures and certificates. The basic and technical mechanisms are complemented by organizational authorizations and auditing, as well as the operation and service level.

5.9. CEN ENV 13608-1:2000: security for healthcare communication

The CEN ENV 13608-1:2000 standard is a comprehensive security framework, with security policies and procedures, and which defines access of issues and tools. The rules on security and data protection systems include deployment of certificates, public keys and digital signatures. Therefore, safety standards for health standards where data integrity, back-up and safety messages exchange are defined. Therefore, the CEN TC251 standard has been approved and presents the following characteristics:

– secure identification of user passwords for healthcare management and security authentication (ENV 12251);

– strong authentication is also defined using microprocessor cards for secure user identification (ENV 12251);

– an algorithm for digital signature services in healthcare defined at ENV 12388.

There is another group of organisms that have defined important standards for health security. In this case, ISO has defined the use of public key infrastructure (ISO/CD 17090). There are also WGs on security, such as the standard defined by the American College of Radiology (ACR) and the National Electrical Manufacturers Association (NEMA) for DICOM (ACR NEMA/DICOM). It has been proposed as a standard method for communicating images (transfer files and corresponding information) between devices manufactured by different vendors. The American Society for Testing and

Materials Standards includes several subcommittees and defining standards for:

- privacy, confidentiality and access;
- data safety and health information systems;
- medical transcription and documentation.

PART 2

Emerging e-Health Technologies and Applications

6

Body Area Networks

6.1. Introduction

A wireless sensor network (WSN) can be defined as a network of small embedded devices, called sensors, which communicate wirelessly following an ad hoc configuration. They are located strategically inside a physical medium and are able to interact with it in order to measure physical parameters from the environment and record the sensed information [YIC 08, NYC 04].

The nodes should be small devices in order to avoid causing any visual impact to the ecosystem, and they should not consume too much energy. It is important to keep in mind that nodes have limited data process and storage capacity. WSNs should implement a security system in order to avoid intrusions, as with any other network. The typical structure of a WSN usually includes sensor nodes. They are radio processors that take the sensor data (physical magnitude values of the medium) and send the information to the base station. The base station gathers data, which is usually a common computer or embedded system with higher process capacity. The gateway is the interconnection between the sensor network and the data network [CAM 11].

It is important to define the number of sensors and their best position for sensing the environment or taking measurements from the surrounding areas [OLI 11]. Sensor nodes need to communicate between themselves. For this reason, it is also essential to know the signal behavior in each medium, their scalability [LLO 08] and their connection strategy for communication [GAR 08].

WSNs are considered spontaneous networks because they are formed dynamically depending on the connectivity between nodes, their position and nodes drop due to failures. These kinds of networks are characterized as being easy to deploy and self-configuring [ROD 10]. We can highlight the following features in WSNs [SEN 13b]:

– *Dynamic topologies*: in a WSN, the topology is always changing because nodes can fail or new nodes can join the network. These changes affect the communication between sensors.

– *Variability channel*: the radio channel is highly variable. There are several situations, such as attenuation, fast fainting, slow fainting and interference that can cause data errors.

– *Ad hoc networks*: generally, sensor networks do not have a wired network infrastructure. All motes or nodes are transceivers and routers simultaneously. However, the concept of a sink node is important; this node collects the information and sends it to a central computer capable of processing the data.

– *Failure tolerance*: a sensor node should be able to continue operating despite the existence of errors in the system.

– *Multi hop or broadcast communications*: these types of networks use any routing protocol to enable multi hop communications, although it is also common for the use of messages sent in broadcast.

– *Power saving*: one of the most important features in these networks. Currently, the motes have limited energy. A sensor node should have an ultra-low consumption processor and transceiver radio. This is one of its most restrictive features.

– *Limited hardware*: in order to get an adjusted consumption, the hardware should be simple; this brings a limited process capacity.

– *Production costs*: sensor networks are formed by a high number of nodes. Motes must be economic to create a reliable network.

Despite the evolution of these networks, it is always possible to improve their efficiency, their operation and interaction with the environment.

Sensor nodes are able to gather data from the environment. It is necessary to choose the adequate transducer. Sensor networks can be useful in many areas of application, such as habitat monitoring, fire detection, personal tracking, animal monitoring, reservoir water controlling, or intruder sensing, among others [DIA 12].

This chapter focuses on deployment in four main areas. Each application presents particular characteristics:

– *Rural and natural monitoring* [LLO 09, GAR 11, LLO 11, OLI 11];

- where a scientist wants to collect measurements of an inaccessible and hostile environment over a period of time to detect changes, trends, etc.;

- energy constraints;

- a large number of synchronized nodes are required to measure and transmit periodically;

- it is necessary to have high life time of the WSN;

- the coordination of information needs synchronization in WSN;

- it usually presents a relatively stable physical topology;

- no strict latency requirements;

- this type of network does not need frequent reconfiguration.

– *Building monitoring [SEN 14a, SEN 14b]*:

- these kinds of applications need a continuous sensing;

- but nodes do not send continuous data;

- low energy consumption;

- high importance of the “status” of a node;

- real-time requirements: the importance of communication latency.

– *Terrestrial animal monitoring and tracking systems [SEN 13a]*:

- application to control animals that are labeled with sensor nodes in a given region;

- the topology of these networks is very dynamic, due to the continuous movement of the sensor nodes;

- energy constraints;

- the WSN should be able to discover new nodes and form new topologies.

– *WSN for underwater environments [SEN 13, HAN 15, HAN 16, JIA 16]*:

- underwater communications can be based on the use of optical signals, electromagnetic signals and the propagation of acoustic and ultrasonic signals;

- great reliance for water parameters;

- energy constraints;

- high attenuation due to the conductivity of water;

- the performance of these networks depends on the technology used.

– WSN for people monitoring and e-Health systems [SEN 14c, DIA 14, CAL 12]:

These kinds of networks present very similar requirements to the previous cases. In this case, the benefits are directly related to users. A WSN mainly conducts people monitoring and e-Health systems may be used as follows:

– improve patients' health monitoring by exporting professional expert knowledge to the patient for everyday life. Risk detection and professional recommendations will be available, in real time, and not only during physical interaction with doctors. This will increase effectiveness of therapies and minimize risk detection times [COS 15];

– increase the efficiency of the health system by saving time and resources along the entire health chain (patient-care with nurses and physicians) because of the supervised automation of repetitive monitoring tasks. This will reduce the number of patient visits to the hospital/clinic and increase the number of patients that can be managed by each professional;

– introduce the benefits of artificial intelligence, machine learning and data analysis over existing records in medical diagnosis to facilitate professionals' tasks;

– facilitate self-management of disease by patients and caregivers, allowing them to build their own disease management models with the graphical system tools.

Depending on the specific disease, this will result in a series of measurable improvements that will be evaluated in real world trials, such as the following:

– a reduction in the number of physical visits of a patient to the clinic/hospital;

– a reduction in the average time devoted to each patient by physicians;

– an increase in the maximum number of patients that can be monitored/treated by a health service at once;

– a reduction in detection times of health status degradation;

– a reduction in procedure (therapies, drug dosage optimization, etc.) execution times.

6.2. Wireless technology used for sensor communication

It is possible to use several wireless technologies to support communication among nodes. The main wireless technologies used in WSN are the following.

Bluetooth is an open specification for wireless networks based on the radio frequency that operates in the industrial medical frequency band (2.4 GHz) forming wireless personal area networks (WPAN) [IEE 05]. It has low energy consumption and a fairly low cost. Bluetooth controls its interference and susceptibility to interference by using spread spectrum modulation. It uses a frequency hopping spread spectrum signaling method. Bluetooth was formalized in the IEEE 802.15.1 standard, version 1.2. Bluetooth technology uses a small area network without infrastructure (piconets). Nodes share a physical channel with a clock and a unique sequence of jumps in the same piconet. In Bluetooth, different channels can coexist. While a master can belong only to one piconet, any other device can belong at the same time to several piconets. This overlap is called a scatter net (dispersed network), although defined routing capacities do not exist among them. This technology is developed to be used for the interconnection of devices such as computers, MP3, and portable digital assistants at a distance of about 10 m, although the latest products in the market achieve 100 m of coverage radius. Nevertheless, this coverage range can be greater; higher antenna gain and bigger distances can be achieved using signal repeaters.

Zig Bee is an alliance of more than 100 companies, most of them manufactures of semiconductors. Zig Bee and the standard IEEE 802.15.4 are standards-based protocols that provide the network infrastructure required for WSN applications [IEE 06]. The IEEE 802.15.4 defines the physical and MAC layers, and Zig Bee defines the network and application layers. This technology is focused on creating low rate personal area networks. Their objectives are to develop and to implant a wireless technology of low energy consumption and low cost. It is presented as a very economic solution for WSNs, and is also positioned toward energy management, automation and remote control applications. Zig Bee products work in a band of frequencies that includes 2.4 GHz, using the modulation OR-quadrature phase shift keyed (QPSK) with expansion direct sequence spread spectrum signaling (DSSS), and 868 MHz in Europe or 915 MHz in North America with the modulation BPSK with expansion DSSS. Its energy consumption is very low; it consumes 20 times less energy than IEEE 802.11 standard and their implementation is relatively simple. Their typical coverage range is around 50m, although this value could increase depending on the environment.

Inside the IEEE 802.11 standard [IEE 07], standard variants such as IEEE 802.11a, IEEE 802.11b, IEEE 802.11g and IEEE 802.11n are included among others. The original standard also defines the CSMA/CA as “Carrier sense multiple access" with collision avoidance among the data frames. The 2.4000–2.4835 GHz band is divided into 13 channels, each of width 22 MHz but spaced only 5 MHz apart, with channel 1 centered on 2.412 GHz and 13 on 2.472 GHz, to which Japan adds a 14th channel 12 MHz above channel 13. The availability of channels is regulated by country, constrained in part by the radio spectrum allocated to various services. IEEE 802.11b data are encoded using DSSS technology. It uses Complementary Code Keying modulated with the QPSK technology to achieve a maximum raw data rate of 11 Mbit/s. IEEE 802.11a/g use orthogonal frequency division multiplexing methods with a maximum of 52 subcarriers, achieving a maximum raw data rate of 54 Mbps. IEEE 802.11n is a new standard for wireless communications that presents a significant increase in the maximum raw to a maximum theoretical value of 600 Mbit/s. The current state of the art supports a Physical (PHY) rate of 450 Mbit/s, with the use of three spatial streams at a channel width of 40 MHz. Furthermore, IEEE 802.11n uses multiple-input multiple-output (MIMO); this is the utilization of multiple transmitter and receiver antennas to improve system performance. MIMO technology provides spatial division multiplexing, where multiple independent data streams are transferred simultaneously. It increases data rate and coverage area, in contrast with the other variants. IEEE 802.11 can work in two ways: (1) ad hoc mode, when the stations communicate to each other directly, and (2) infrastructure mode, in which the stations access the network through one or more access points. Its coverage can reach more than 300 m. The effective overall range of IEEE 802.11a is less than that of IEEE 802.11b/g. In theory, IEEE 802.11a signals are absorbed more readily by walls and other solid objects in their path due to their smaller wavelength and, as a result, cannot penetrate as far as those of 802.11b.

The main obstacle to Bluetooth and IEEE 802.11 technology becoming a wearable technology at the level of a sensor network is the complexity of the protocol and the topology rigidity of the networks, as well as the high power consumption of the devices. Depending on the case, in our implementation we may require a higher coverage range than the one offered by Bluetooth; although many WSN developers have adopted Bluetooth and Zig Bee technologies for sensor communication, we usually prefer to use the IEEE 802.11 standard. We can see their differences in Table 6.1.

	WLAN (IEEE 802.11)	Bluetooth (IEEE 802.15.1)	Zigbee (IEEE 802.15.4)
Frequency bands	5 GHz (a/n) 2.4GHz (b/g/n)	2.4 GHz	2.4 GHz 868/915 MHz
Raw data rate	11 Mbps (2.4 GHz in b) 54 Mbps (2.4 GHz in g or 5 GHz in a) 500 Mbps (2.4 GHz and 5 GHz in n)	1 Mbps	250 kbps (2.4 GHz) 40 kbps (915 MHz) 20 kbps (868 MHz)
Number of channels	11–14 (depends on the country in b/g/n), working at 2.4 GHz 24 non-overlapping 20 MHz channels and up to 12 non-overlapping 40 MHz channels, working at 5 GHz in n. 52 channels in a	79	16 (2.4 GHz) 10 (915 MHz) 1 (868 MHz)
Coverage range	100–300–900 m	10–100 m	30–50 m

Table 6.1. *Comparison of the most popular wireless technologies*

6.3. What is a sensor?

A sensor is a device, composed by sensitive cells, that transforms physical or chemical magnitudes (instrumentation variables) as useful signals to measure or control systems (electrical magnitude). The instrumentation variables depend on the type of sensor, and can be temperature, distance, acceleration, inclination, displacement, pressure, humidity, pH, etc. The electric magnitude can be a value of electric resistance, or an electric capacity, or a voltage, or an electric current, etc.

A transducer and a sensor are different devices and they should be differentiated. A transducer is a device that transforms one physical magnitude into another (such as mechanical energy into electric energy). A transducer can be a microphone that converts an audio wave into an electric signal. On the other hand, a sensor is a device that provides an output signal given a specific physical quantity. The input value is called a measure and it causes a response in the sensor. An example is a linear variable differential transformer, which converts a position into electric signal [NYC 04]. Therefore, a sensor can be considered a transducer and vice versa. All sensors can be classified and included within one of the groups shown in Table 6.2 [TOM 10].

Criterion	Type	Description
Energy contribution	Modulator	The output energy comes from an external source
	Generator	The output energy is given by the input
Output signal	Analogical	The output varies in a continuous mode
	Digital	The exit varies discontinuously
Operation mode	Defection	The measured magnitude causes a physical effect in some parts of the device
	Comparison	It tries to stay the defection to zero, applying opposed effects to the one generated by the magnitude

Table 6.2. *Sensor classification*

Commonly, the signals obtained from the sensors are not useful for processing and additional circuits are necessary, such as a Wheatstone bridge, or signal conditioner circuits based on amplifiers, in order to adapt the voltage levels from the rest of circuit.

Most of these sensors offer analog output signals and, in many cases, these signals are required to work with digital control devices such as a PC. In these cases, it will be necessary to use an analog to digital converter. Figure 6.1 shows an example with all necessary circuit blocks.

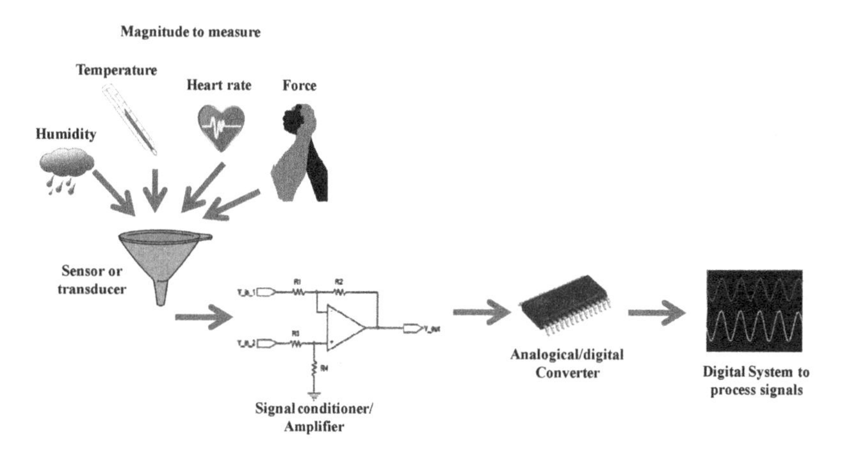

Figure 6.1. *Block diagram of a monitoring system*

6.3.1. *Type of sensors*

A sensor converts a magnitude without any electric characteristic into electric signals due to its physical effect [TOM 11]. The physical effect can be resistance, capacity, inductance, magnetism, charges and electric field, piezoelectric effect and Hall effect [FRA 03]. The sensors can be classified according to the sensed or controlled magnitude [TOM 11]. In this section, we are going to see the most used sensors used for environmental monitoring. Table 6.3 shows a complete description and properties of the main sensors and transducers.

Measurable physical value	Type of sensor	Description
Light (visible, infrared, ultraviolet)	Light dependent resistor (LDRs) or photo resistors	Its operation is based on the photoelectric effect. If the light incident on the device is of high frequency, resistance decreases.
	Photocell or photovoltaic cells	Solar panels are silicon compounds. They are made of silicon mixed with other materials such as phosphorus and boron that create positive and negative charges to generate electricity.
	Photodiodes	A photodiode is a pn junction structure or P-I-N. When a light beam of sufficient energy impinges on the diode, it excites an electron and a hole creates positively charged. The movement of carriers produces a photocurrent.
	Phototransistors	Sensitive to light, usually infrared. The light incident on the base region generates carriers therein. The movement of carriers produces a current flow.
	Charge-coupled device (CCD)	Integrated circuit that contains a number of linked or coupled capacitors. Each capacitor can transfer its electric charge to one or more adjacent capacitors on the printed circuit
	Video cameras	The image sensor is the main element of an electronic camera. It captures the light that makes up the image and becomes a signal in analog or digital format. This is a chip made up of millions of light-sensitive components (diodes or transistors) which capture the projected subject when exposed to the image light.
Sound and ultrasound	Microphone	The microphone is an electrical transducer. Its function is to translate the vibrations due to acoustic pressure by the sound waves on the capsule into electrical energy, which allows recording of sounds from any place or element.
	Piezoelectric sensors	A piezoelectric sensor is a device that uses the piezoelectric effect to measure pressure, acceleration, strain or force; transforming the readings into electrical signals.
	Ultrasonic rangers	In the measurement module, a transmitter launches a train of ultrasonic pulses, with a frequency in the order of 38–50 kHz, and the receiver expects the rebound. The time between emission and return is measured, which results in the distance between transmitter and object where the rebound occurred.

Gravity (tilt position)	Accelerometers, vibration sensors	The accelerometer is one of the most versatile transducers, the most common piezoelectric compression. It is based on the response when a piezo electric crystal lattice is compressed: a force proportional to the applied electric charge occurs.
	Pendulares sensors (inclinometers)	Inclinometers or tilt sensors are designed to convert a physical quantity into an electrical one. In this case, the physical quantity is the inclination that can range from a few degrees to the full 360°. The output signal may be proportional to the angle or proportional to the sine wave of the angle, and may be incurrent, voltage or digital output.
	Mercury contact	A mercury switch is a device whose purpose is to allow or interrupt the flow of electrical current in an electrical circuit, depending on its alignment relative to a horizontal position.
	Gyroscope	Detection is based on the vibration of ceramic pieces subject to a distortion produced by the Coriolis effect (changes in angular velocity).
Temperature	Thermistors	A thermistor is a resistive temperature sensor. Its operation is based on the variation of resistivity with temperature.
	Resistance temperature detector (RTDs)	A resistance temperature detector is based on the variation of conductor resistance with the temperature sensor temperature.
	Thermo couple or thermo couples	Transducer formed by the union of two different metals that produces a very small potential difference, which is a function of the temperature difference between metals, called "hot spot" and the point "reference" (See Beck Effect).
	Diodes	The terminal voltage V_d of a diode depends on the current I_d flowing through it and the temperature T_d of the diode.
	Pyro sensors	A sensor that detects distance calls with high sensitivity. It offers a driving circuit that measures the photons of the ultraviolet spectrum associated with flames and fire in general.
Humidity	Capacitive sensors	The sensor is based on when a liquid or fluid enters the electric field between the sensor plates; it varies the dielectric and consequently the capacitance value. In this case, the sensor changes its permittivity with respect to humidity.
	Resistive sensors	Resistive humidity sensors are constructed on a thin polymer tablet capable of absorbing water, on which two interwoven metal materials or conductive carbon contacts are printed. The parameter measured is the electrical resistance through the polymer, which changes with the water content.

	Integrates modes	Integrated humidity sensor calibrated at the factory with digital output. Communication is via a synchronous serial bus using a protocol. The device further has in its interior a temperature sensor to compensate the moisture measurement with respect to temperature.
Pressure and/or force	Micro switches and touch sensors	Electrical devices, pneumatic or mechanical, located at the end of a moving element such as a conveyor belt, in order to send signals that can change the status of a circuit.
	Pressure sensors	Pressure sensors or pressure transducers are elements which transform a physical quantity of pressure or force per unit area into another electrical quantity to be employed in automation equipment or standard acquisition. Measurement ranges widely from a few thousandths of a bar to thousands of bars.
	Force sensors	Force transducers and HBM force sensors measure tensile loads and static and dynamic compression with virtually no displacement
	Robotic skin	The sensor consists of several organic or plastic transistors plastic placed on a flexible base material. Thus, dense sensor arrays can be constructed which may extend over wide areas.
Velocity	Tachograph	A tachograph is an electronic device that records various events originating in a land transport vehicle during transport, whether cargo or passenger and road or rail.
	Encoders	Electromechanical device used to convert the angular position of a shaft to a digital code.
Magnetism	Hall effect	The Hall effect sensor uses the Hall effect to measure magnetic fields or currents, or for position determination. If current flows and a magnetic field flows in the vertical direction to the sensor, then the sensor creates an outgoing voltage proportional to the product of magnetic field strength and current. If the current value is known, then you can calculate the magnetic field strength.
Location	GPS	The global navigation satellite system (GNSS) is used to determine the position of an object, a person or a vehicle with an accuracy up to centimeters (if used differential GPS) worldwide, but typically of a few meters. The system was developed, installed and used by the United States Department of Defense. The GPS system consists of 24 satellites and uses triangulation to determine position around the globe, to an accuracy of several meters.

Proximity	Capacitive sensors	Capacitive proximity sensors are used to detect metal and non-metallic objects (liquid, plastic, wood etc.) contactlessly. Capacitive proximity sensors use the variation of capacitance between the sensor and the object to be detected. When the object is at a predefined distance from the sensitive part of the sensor, an electronic circuit within the sensor begins to oscillate. The rise or fall of oscillation is identified by a certain threshold circuit leading to an amplifier to operate an external load.
	Inductive sensors	Inductive proximity sensors are used to detect metal objects contactlessly. Its principle of operation is based on a coil and an oscillator that create an electromagnetic field in the immediate environment of the target area. The presence of a metal object (actuator) in the operating area causes a damping of the oscillation amplitude. The rise or fall of oscillation is identified by a circuit that changes the threshold sensor output
Distance	Ultrasonic distance meters	Ultrasonic sensors are mainly based on object detection through the emission and reflection of acoustic waves. They work by emitting an ultrasonic pulse against the object to be sensed, and to detect the reflected pulse, a timer to start its count by issuing the pulse tops. This time is referred to below.
	Distance measuring infrared beam	Distance can be measured with light by a laser. Like sound, light takes time to travel, so if you measure the time between pulse and emit back, you can calculate the distance directly.
Acidity	Ion sensitive field effect transistor (ISFET)	An ISFET is an electronic–chemical sensor that reacts to changes in the pH. When the ion concentration (e.g. the basic pH or acidic pH properties changes), the quantity of ions that passes through the membrane and is deposited on the transistor gate varies. This occurs when the sensor is in contact with the substance to be tested and varies the current flowing through the transistor.

Table 6.3. *Sensor description*

6.4. Wireless body area networks

The technology of WSNs for medical monitoring is an attractive alternative to traditional medical systems. Today, biomedical sensors are used in a few applications, such as health monitoring, which are not yet integrated into communication networks [DIA 14, CAL 14].

It is important to communicate the data measured by a detection device (sensor) to other devices that will concentrate and process information. Therefore, it is important to have a communication network biomedical sensor. This would have a radical impact on the quality of life of patients and their treatment success rates. One can also have a wide range of future applications, such as monitoring of cardiovascular disease, diabetes and asthma consultation through telemedicine and health systems, etc.

Body area networks (BAN) have recently emerged as a solution to solve this problem. BANs are a new generation of WSNs suitable for human body monitoring. A BAN consists of a small set of nodes equipped with biomedical sensors, motion detectors and wireless communication devices. These nodes collect vital signs of the body which are then transmitted wirelessly to a united central database where all information collected is processed. Because of its wireless nature, BAN nodes have many advantages, such as ubiquitous connectivity, mobility and interoperability. Some nodes can also be equipped with actuators, such as pacemakers or instruments for storing and injecting drugs. Smart phones can be used to convey all information collected with the outside world (health, emergency services, etc.) [SIL 15a].

BAN networks have their own characteristics, as discussed below, that distinguish them from WSNs, and technical challenges also create new architecture. A wireless body area network (WBAN) has two categories of nodes: sensors and actuators in or on the human body, and coordinators users WBAN nodes around or second-level devices equipped radio users, which function as an infrastructure to transmit data. However, in a WSN, each network node acts as a sensor node as well as a coordinator node:

– *Density*: the number of sensors and actuators deployed in the user depends on the use cases. Usually, it does not present high redundancy for fault tolerance in wireless network nodes as conventional sensors, and therefore do not require a high density of nodes.

– *Transmission rate*: most WSNs are applied to control or monitor events, where events may occur irregularly. In contrast, BAN networks are used for monitoring of human physiological activities, ranging from a more regular basis. As a result, application data streams exhibit relatively stable rates.

– *Mobility*: WBAN users can move. The WBAN nodes are associated with the same user and they move together in the same direction. In contrast, the WSN nodes are generally considered static and any node which moves can do so individually and not in groups.

6.5. WSNs, BANs, wearable sensors and deployment for e-Health, disabled and elderly people

This section presents a summary of some of the most important research projects and proposals where systems for e-health applications are developed. This kind of WBAN can be developed using small devices specially designed for this proposal [MIS 14]. However, in many cases, researchers prefer to use smartphones as a central processing unit because of their processing capacities [SIL 15a].

6.5.1. *Systems, wearable sensors and deployment for e-Health applications*

In the last 15 years, research in the field of m-Health have proposed new solutions and designed new clinical decision support systems (CDSSs) for physician and caregivers. These systems and prototypes help health professionals with management and decision-making tasks. Advances have been made in research and the market for improving healthcare and patients' quality of lye [LOP 13]. In fact, there are some organizations, public and private, that focus their efforts on improving the health field, e-learning systems for medical tasks and medical applications (useful for physicians, caregivers and patients). They aim to develop responsive innovations and provide rigorous evidence-based support for mobile ICTs to improve global health [JHU 15]. In general, these companies try to address different aspects and parts of health from the basic development of devices to programs and use policies. For example, the American Health Information Management Association [THE 15] is working on advancing the implementation of electronic health records (EHRs) by leading key industry initiatives and advocating high and consistent standards, while the Healthcare Information and Management Systems Society [HEA 15], which is a not-for-profit organization, is dedicated to promoting better healthcare and information management systems and leads efforts to optimize health engagements and care outcomes using information technology.

These medical management solutions combine software and clinical services to reduce administration costs and improve medical outcomes. An example of CDSS is Care SERV [CAR 15]. This solution provides support to the care management and utilization management. This kind of software provides transcription tools support for interpreting and formatting medical documents. These applications should allow clinicians to record, review and edit dictations by medical record, account or job number. In fact, the utilization of CDSS should be very easy without any requirement for training of clinicians, and permitting the use of voice macros to automatically insert their pre-defined content [THE 15]. Su and Wu [SU 11] presented a highly distributed information infrastructure called MADIP. This system uses the Intelligent Agent paradigm, which is able to automatically notify the responsible care provider of abnormality, offer medical advice from a distance and perform continuous health monitoring for those who need it. To develop this architecture the authors considered aspects such as interoperability, scalability and openness in heterogeneous e-health environments. The system allows the user to access his/her medical record, to find out the medical information of the city and to make a booking to be visited by a particular kind of doctor. Doctors may request the performance of clinical tests on the patient and update the medical record of the patient during a visit.

The platforms must be built to meet needs such as generating more transparency between doctors and patient outcomes and to reduce fragmentation in cost and management solutions for the care of patients. Along these lines, inFinite [INF 15] is a health management technology platform that enables connectivity, utility and interaction between each element (physicians, patients and caregivers) of the entire medical management interventional relationship. InFinite also uses active forensic claims surveillance, building a complete historical record for use in real time. It helps to enhance the relationship between clinical and cost solutions and delivers cohesive results before, during and after care, and integrates document and medical record management. This solution provides real-time record viewing, retrieval and outcome reporting capabilities throughout the interventional process. The truth is that the common primary objective of any of these applications must provide to clinicians access to up-to-date patient data from connected biometric devices, so they can more efficiently monitor and manage patients at their home or when they are on the go [VER 15]. Furthermore, all these systems should guarantee the protection of patients' private medical information. They should also place the patients as an important piece within the whole process allowing their own health management, which encourages their compliance with physician-directed care plans and helps them to manage chronic illnesses more effectively. Finally, these improvements should lead to an improvement in economical and management costs [ALC 15].

In some cases, access to these platforms can be provided by a proprietary solution or by other kinds of software developed for smart and mobile devices [MAC 13]. These applications usually permit users and physicians manage medical information such as pictures, EHR, and appointment reminders. They can be developed for iOS to be used in Apple devices or for Android devices. The main advantages of the latter type are that they are open code solutions and in most cases their acquisition is free. Some examples of applications for Apple devices include Gazelle or ISCRUB. The first one allows users to chart their lab results and manage various medications with medical reminders. The application can be used as a schedule for the next lab appointment and to find the nearest Quest Diagnostics Patient Service Center location [QUE 15]. It provides an easy and safe place to store, see, share and access important medical and health information in case of emergency. ISCRUB is a little different. This software is an infection-control application and shows to doctors, nurses and other staff where they should be most scrupulous about washing their hands or to take more specific hygiene measures. The app gives medical staff a way to send and share their observations about special hygiene measures, in a hospital or medical center, via a wireless device to a central database, where the results can be calculated and shared with all staff the same day.

Regarding infectious diseases, Freifeld *et al.* [FRE 08] presented the design principles, software architecture and implementation of Health Map, a web application and an automated system for querying, filtering, integrating and visualizing unstructured reports on disease outbreaks. SmartHEALTH also developed an open integrated architecture for new biodiagnostic systems to support European companies exploiting bioassays or new application concepts. One of the main goals of this project is to miniaturize the technology and cost engineered into a portable and consumer product. This system takes into account the healthcare user identity and ambient environment, respecting confidentiality and information access rights. smartHEALTH performs multianalyate sensing and interpretation for nucleic acids, proteins and others and handles multiple biological sample types. Results are interpreted and presented using bioinformatics [SMA 09].

For making a diagnosis, doctors and nurses usually use images and pictures that are kept as medical health records. Regarding these images, it is of the utmost importance to protect patient privacy. Following these premises, CLINICAM [LAN 15] is an application for Apple mobile devices (iPhone or iPad) that allows clinicians to capture clinical images and transfer them directly to the patient's electronic medical record (EMR). This application is used at Brigham and Women's Hospital that sends such photos directly to the patient's EMR without storing them on the phone.

6.5.2. *General purpose wireless nodes used on e-Health applications*

In the market, there are many mixed applications that allow patient monitoring of him/herself by medical devices connected to mobile or electronic devices. These systems also allow a wireless connection for uploading the data to the cloud or to request them at any time. Using this kind of application, solutions developed from commercial hardware can be proposed, such as the case of Platforms of Arduino and Raspberry Pi Hacks (the open hardware division of Libelium) that implement an e-Health Sensor Platform to help researchers and developers to measure biometric sensor data for experimentation and test purposes [COO 15]. These platforms allow users to perform biometric and medical applications where body monitoring is needed by using nine different sensors: pulse, oxygen in blood (SPO_2), airflow (breathing), body temperature, electrocardiogram, gluco meter, galvanic skin response (sweating), blood pressure (sphygmomanometer) and patient position (accelerometer). Blumrosen *et al.* [BLU 11] also described the design of an m-Health platform for continuous real-time remote patient monitoring called C-SMART. The platform is based on a set of sensors for assessment of patient's physiological condition, a mobile phone, and a centralized healthcare utility. C-SMART is implemented in the form of an application and is compatible with different existing telemedicine and medical database standards such as IEEE 11073. The proposal tries to reduce the platform overhead with minimal user intervention and minimal cost.

There are more professional platforms which allow medical device connectivity and data management. These have special platforms designed to be interoperable with different medical devices and applications, providing end-to-end wireless connectivity, as the case of Qualcomm Life, Inc. and its 2net Platform [QUA 15]. Other systems, such as Preventice Care Platform [PRE 15], capture patient data and make it available to healthcare professionals via mobile devices and personalized Web portals. It can also be integrated with the EMR systems and other patient systems that house information about patients and their care plans. Remote and real-time monitoring helps healthcare professionals to exercise greater control over patients with problems that need a rapid response to counteract harmful effects [COS 15]. This biometric information, such as blood sugar and blood pressure, gathered for each system can be wirelessly sent using available connectivity options such as IEEE 802.11, 3G, GPRS, Bluetooth, IEEE 802.15.4 or ZigBee, depending on the application. The data is transmitted instantly and securely to a database, where it can be interpreted by the healthcare professional.

6.6. The alternative: using smartphones to deploy WBANs

This section reviews the related literature that takes advantage of smartphones' embedded sensors and shows some real life applications [SIL 15a, GAR 14]. Other works that describe useful implementations to improve the quality of life of disabled and elderly people were considered.

Nowadays, there are millions of people carrying mobile phones. Many developers have unconsciously deployed a strong infrastructure, which can help users to implement new proposals based on the sensing capabilities of these devices [SIL 15a]. Following this idea, Lane *et al.* [LAN 10] discuss the state of the art of mobile phone sensing. This work analyzes some aspects in many different disciplines such as business, healthcare, social networks, environmental monitoring and transportation. In addition, they review the main sensors embedded in mobile phones, and discusses possibilities for opening this technology up to society.

Taking into account that processing capabilities of mobile devices are ever increasing, the incorporation of several sensors and an increase in the complexity of the applications needed to control all these sensors is possible. In this line, Muldoon *et al.* [MUL 06] propose the use of a multi agent system called "collaborative agent tuning" to optimize system operation in devices with limited computing capacities. This solution permits developers to manage and control all available sensors in mobile devices and smartphones.

When WSNs are mentioned, people think about networks composed of geographically dispersed sensors that work together to monitor the environment. The increased use of smartphones suggests the development of large sensor networks using these mobile devices as sensor nodes [TUR 09]. In [KAN 07], the authors present a first attempt toward the understanding and implementation of a programmable sensor network using the infrastructure created by mobile devices. The proposed system uses the collected samples of the phone sensors and shares the data with other users, publishing it in a data repository.

The advances of wireless network technology and the development of body sensors are helping to improve the care of patients with reduced mobility in hospitals and health centers [CHE 11, CAL 13, CAL 15]. Accidental falls by elderly and disabled people are considered a major health problem, in terms of primary care costs, of the public and private health systems [LOP 13]. If a fall is detected, the system generates a message with the GPS position coordinates that are sent via SMS and at the same time the device can make emergency calls. This proposal has low computational cost, which implies less battery power consumption. In addition, the traffic generated into the network is acceptable. It has a fast mechanism to reduce the impact of falls for elderly people, while permits an automatic and quick response to potential incidents.

The care of elderly people living alone and the extension of their independence are the goals of the activity tracking system described by Fahim *et al.* [FAH 12]. Moreover, Kaluža *et al.* presented a system with the same goals by using a multi agent approach, which is able to send an alert when there is an emergency or unusual behavior.

There are some other mobile applications that give support about drugs and treatments, first aid information and local health listings. WebMD is an Android application that helps medical staff and patients with their decision making by providing mobile access 24/7 to mobile-optimized health information and decision support tools [KAL 10]. WebMD [WEB 15] also has a proprietary platform that improves this service. The application acts as a handy guide for medical emergencies, from insect stings to broken bones, and helpful treatment tips are always available, even without an Internet connection.

7

Mobile Health Technologies and Applications

7.1. Introduction

With the proliferation of mobile communications using smart devices that support 3G and 4G networks, mobile computing has attracted both research and business communities including the health sector. Mobile communications offer enormous opportunities to create efficient and innovative mobile health (m-Health) solutions. M-Health proposes to deliver healthcare anytime and anywhere, surpassing geographical, temporal and even organizational barriers [AKT 10, TAC 03]. M-Health applications and their inherent mobility functionalities have a strong impact on typical healthcare monitoring and alerting systems, record maintenance, clinical and administrative data collection, healthcare delivery programs, medical information awareness, detection and prevention systems, drug counterfeiting and theft [ZUE 09]. In this context, physicians can easily download or gain access to lab results, medical records, medical images and drug information. In the same way, patients can check their diagnostics (if allowed by the medical staff) remotely, using mobile devices anywhere.

The success of m-Health was led by the emergence of a market for mobile applications. According to a report by the IMS Institute for healthcare informatics, there are more than 165,000 mobile applications related to health in several catalogs [IMS 15]. Most of these offer support tools that help individuals to follow certain health parameters, in addition to providing other health-related information. This report shows that these apps may be clustered in several general wellness areas, such as fitness, lifestyle and stress, diet and nutrition, as well as medication reminders and management.

In order to compare the abovementioned apps related to wellness with those that may have impact on diseases (in the society), the WHO study for the period from 2000 to 2012 was analyzed [WOR 12]. In a total of 30 million deaths around the world, the top 10 causes are the following: ischemic heart disease (12.8% of deaths), cerebrovascular disease (10.8%), infections of the lower respiratory tract (6.1%), chronic obstructive pulmonary disease (COPD) (5.8%), diarrheal diseases (4.3%), human immunodeficiency virus (HIV) (3.1%), cancer of the trachea, bronchus and lung (2.4%), tuberculosis (2.4%), diabetes (2.2%) and traffic accidents (2.1%). In 2011, preterm birth and low birth weight was just below the 10th position in the ranking (1.91%). The WHO study also discusses the global burden of disease, which shows the conditions that generate the greatest number of new cases of sick people in the world and the most prevalent diseases for 2014 [QUE 13]. The diseases that generate the greatest number of cases are also the illnesses that are new to the study, such as malaria (241.3 million new cases), measles (27.1 million) or pertussis (18.4 million).

The most prevalent diseases are those whose symptoms do not occur continuously. The top 10 of these, given the millions of people affected by them, are the following: anemia (1,159 million), hearing loss (636.5 million), migraines (324.1 million), loss of vision (272.4 million), malnutrition (238.9 million), asthma (234.9 million), diabetes (220.5 million), osteoarthritis (151.4 million), unipolar depressive disorders (151.2 million), strong intestinal infections (150.9 million) and related disorders by alcohol usage (125 million).

This chapter focuses on addressing the most significant of m-Health research work and novel services and applications available in mobile markets and in the healthcare industry. Moreover, it presents a conducted study showing the number of mobile apps available for each disease, identifying the strong and weak points of each topic, generating a starting point for the development of new solutions, mitigating the identified gaps and improving available functionalities.

7.2. Mobile health: an overview

Mobile health was defined in the early 2000s as "emerging mobile communications and network technologies for healthcare systems" [LAX 00, IST 03]. Since then, research and development of novel m-Health services and applications have been given priority by the research community [SIL 15b]. Several health and wellness areas have gathered important findings and contributions from m-Health, such as cardiology [MAR 13, BIS 14, FAY 10, LIN 10], diabetes [SIE 13, KIR 13, CAF 12], obesity [SIL 13, MAA 12, LOP 11a, ZHU 10], quitting smoking [FIN 13, WHI 11] and elderly care and chronic diseases [SIL 15b, COS 15, FON 13, CHI 13]. These different specialties make use of m-Health applications for monitoring, prevention and detection of diseases. Research and market interests in this topic are growing every day, as is the diversification of the areas of influence. A comprehensive study performed by

Fiordelli *et al.* [FIO 13] demonstrates and analyzes the impact of mobile phones on healthcare contexts in the last decade. The authors conducted a literature review of 117 articles published between 2002 and 2012 in 77 different journals. The results shown that, in 2007–2008, the number of research articles almost doubled, exponentially growing every year.

The fast evolution of smartphones and applications also trigged the appearance of new mobile solutions and markets. Figure 7.1 presents the worldwide smartphone sales to end users by operating systems in the third quarter of 2015.

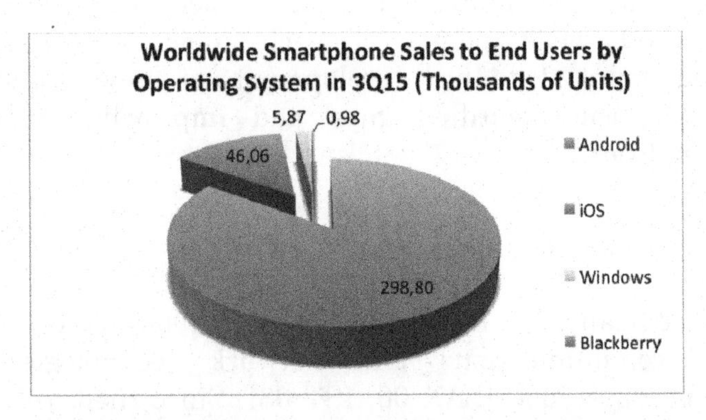

Figure 7.1. *Worldwide smartphone sales to end users by operating systems in 3Q 2015 (from [GAR15]). For a color version of this figure, see www.iste.co.uk/rodrigues/ehealth.zip*

Google's operating system (OS) – Android – and Apple's iOS dominate the market. The quality of both OSs is unquestionable and their online application stores both sustain financial successes in the mobile market. These online markets allow developers to sell or offer all kind of mobile applications opening up new potential areas of research and development, such as m-Health applications. At the end of 2010, more than 200 million m-Health applications were downloaded and about 70% of worldwide citizens were interested in accessing at least one m-Health application. It is forecast that, in 2017, more than 1.7 billion people will have downloaded health apps with an m-Health market income of about 26 billion dollars [RES 13]. The market of mobile health applications is directed toward patients, clinicians and healthcare professionals. These applications are mainly suited for management of diseases, self-monitoring and drug control as well as other clinical and educational applications.

7.3. Study and analysis of current m-Health applications

This section focuses on a study considering commercial applications available for the general public in the various app stores considering the most important platforms [RIV 13, MAS 13]. In descending order of market share, the sequence is the following: Google Play by Android [GOO 16], iTunes App Store by Apple [APP 16], Windows phone Apps+games by Microsoft [MIC 16], BlackBerry World by BlackBerry [BLA 16] and Ovi Store by Nokia [NOK 16]. Only apps in "medicine" and "health and welfare" ("health and fitness") were considered. Exceptions include locators for Alzheimer's patients or depressive disorders-related apps that allow users to interact with other mode considering as "social network".

7.3.1. *Overview of available m-Health applications*

The search for commercial applications conducted for a total of 26 diseases shows that 2,837 applications have been found in different mobile platforms, as presented in Table 7.1. Google Play presents the higher results (1,254 applications), closely followed by iTunes (with 1,251 results). The mobile applications market is very dynamic and is constantly growing and evolving so, regarding the volume of medical applications, the first position can change periodically. However, the other platforms do not present significant positive data. BlackBerry is placed as the third platform with 158 discrete applications, a step above of Apps+games with 136 apps. Ovi Store remains almost forgotten with just 40 related applications.

	Play	iTunes	BB World	Apps + games	Ovi	Total
Cardiology	240	252	14	13	1	520
Cerebrovascular disease	46	48	5	2	0	101
Lung cancer	57	53	4	2	0	116
Alzheimer	59	63	4	9	0	135
Lower resp. infections	28	18	1	6	0	53
COPD	15	18	0	2	1	36
Cancer of the colon and rectum	6	9	1	0	0	16
Diabetes	423	451	61	28	16	979
Breast cancer	30	37	6	5	5	83
Diarrheal diseases	29	25	6	5	1	66
HIV/AIDS	48	53	10	7	5	123
Tuberculosis	8	3	0	2	0	12
Traffic accidents	0	0	0	0	0	0
Prematurity	1	0	0	2	0	3
Malaria	7	5	0	4	1	17
Measles	5	3	0	0	0	8
Pertussis	0	0	0	0	0	0
Anemia	11	6	0	3	0	20
Hearing loss	22	20	2	3	0	47
Migraines	61	55	8	4	0	128
Loss of vision	23	25	5	8	0	61
Malnutrition	0	0	0	0	0	0
Asthma	53	60	12	4	1	120
Osteoarthritis	27	31	4	5	1	68
Depressive disorders	55	26	15	22	6	124
Intestinal infections	0	0	0	0	0	0
Alcohol disorders	0	0	0	0	0	0
Total	1254	1251	158	136	38	2837

Table 7.1. *Volume of apps per platform by wellness topic*

In percentage terms, as presented in Figure 7.2, Google Android and iOS have a share of about 44.20% and 44.09%, respectively, showing a similar level of importance. The remaining 11% is divided almost equally between

BlackBerry OS and Windows Phone. Symbian has a token presence with only 1%. This similarity between iOS and Android is evident when we observe that, in 12 of the 22 groups, Android platform holds a larger number of the results for a specific application, while iOS is more popular in nine of the remaining 10.

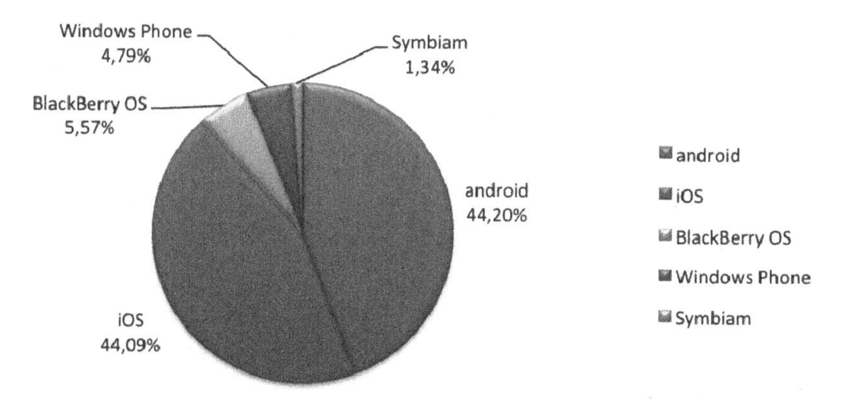

Figure 7.2. *Market percentage per platform. For a color version of the figure, see www.iste.co.uk/rodrigues/ehealth.zip*

Figure 7.3 presents the number of available applications per disease. As may be seen in this figure, diabetes-related apps have the highest number of applications (almost 1,000), representing almost 35% of the total (34.50%). In second place are cardiology-related apps, with 520 applications, representing 18.33% of the total. At considerably lower rates we find the rest of the available applications that may be divided into three main blocks. A first group includes Alzheimer (135 apps and 4.75% of total), HIV (123 apps and 4.33%), asthma (120 apps and 4.23%), trachea, bronchus and lung cancers (116 apps representing a percentage of 4.08%), and cerebrovascular disease (with 101 apps, 3.56%).

A second group includes breast cancer (with 83 apps representing about 2.92% of the total), osteoarthritis (68 apps, 2.4%), diarrheal diseases (66 apps, 2.32%), loss of vision (61 apps, 2.32%), infections of the lower respiratory tract (53 apps, 1.86%), hearing loss (47 apps, 1.65%) and COPD (36 apps, 1.27%).

The latter group involves wellness areas with few or no available apps, such as anemia (20 apps, 0.7%), malaria (17 apps, 0.59%), colon cancer and RCTO (16 apps, 0.56%), tuberculosis (13 apps, 0.46%), measles (8 apps, 0.28%), preterm delivery (3 apps, 0.1%), traffic accidents, intestinal infections, malnutrition, whooping cough and alcohol-derived disorders that do not have any application.

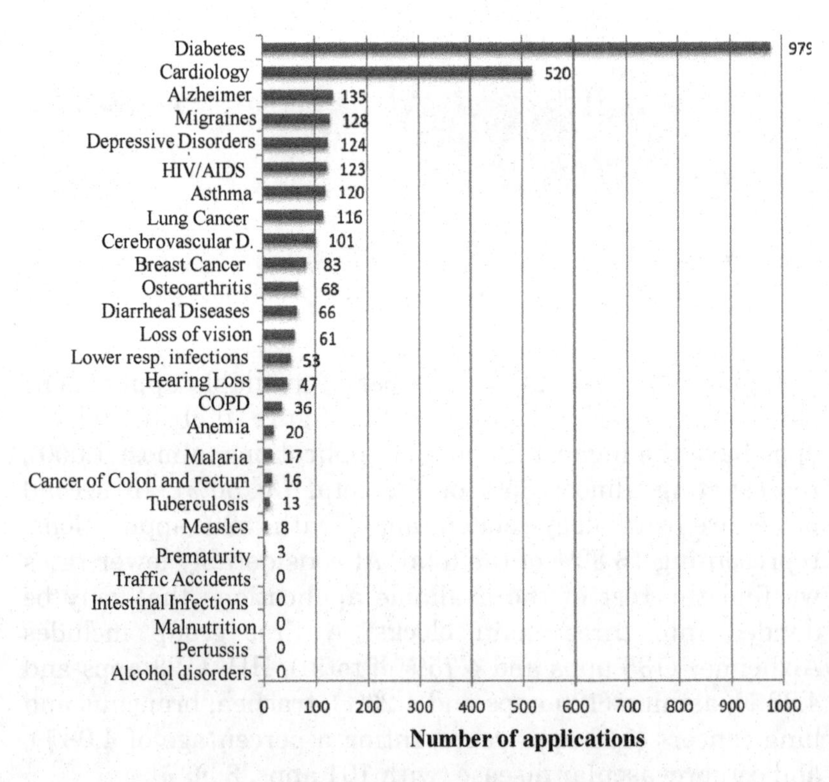

Figure 7.3. *Number of applications as a function of the above-identified diseases*

Measles (with 62.5% of total), tuberculosis (61.5%) and anemia (55%) are examples of diseases with higher percentages in Android applications. Colon and rectum cancers (56.25%), chronic obstructive pulmonary disease (50%) and cardiology (48.5%) are the preponderant for iOS.

7.3.2. *Analysis of the available m-Health applications*

Table 7.2 presents a list of m-Health applications and their most relevant features, those which directly influence their number of downloads. The name, note/mark given by other users and price are some of the properties that users use when searching app stores. Moreover, other characteristics are important to distinguish between different apps of a medical nature, such as type of application (whether it is clinical or not), if there is contact with the medical practitioner or other users, or the type of target audience. The apps usage is also considered, namely, presentation of data to users or whether an Internet connection is needed.

There is great heterogeneity among apps even within a same illness. The best-known and downloaded app has hundreds or even thousands of votes, while others only have a few scores, if any. The average score of all ailments apps is about 1.91 points out of 5. If we only consider the apps that have been rated by users, the valuation rises to 3.8 out of 5. In this case, all the categories obtained scores between 3 and 5 points, with anemia (4.33 points), tuberculosis (4.21 points), breast cancer (4.19 points) and diabetes (3.99 points) being the most valued.

Diabetes-related applications perform best among all the mentioned applications, consistently scoring above 3 points.

Google Play									
Name	Mark	Type	Internet connectivity	Clinical	Data visualization	Contact with MD/other users	Use	Public	Price
Prognosis: Cardiology	4.8	Education	Yes	No	Text, image, graphics	No/No	Occasional	Students general	Free
Hear Runastic Heart Ratet	4.6	Monitoring	Yes	No	Text, Graphic	Yes/Yes	Occasional	General	Free
Beat Rate	4.4	Monitoring	No	No	Text, Graphic	No/No	Occasional	General	Free
Cardiac Mobile ECG	4.6	Monitoring	No	Yes	Text, image, graphics, audio	Yes/No	Continuou s	Specialists patients	Free
Epi m Health Lite	4.7	Monitoring	No	No	Text, Graphic	No/No	Continuou s	Patients	Free
Sense View Sensor	4.9	Monitoring	No	No	Text, image, videos	Yes/No	Continuou s	Specialists patients	Free
Cardiograp h	4	Monitoring	No	No	Text, Graphic	No/No	Occasional	General	Free
Cardio 3 Echo	4.2	Diagnosis	Yes	Yes	Text, image, graphics	No/No	Frequent	Specialists students	29.99€
ECG Pocketcards	4	Diagnosis/ Education	No	Yes	Text, image, graphics, tables	No/No	Frequent	Specialists students	3.81€
ACCC Pocket GUudes	4.1	Diagnosis/ Education	No	Yes	Text, image, schemes	No/No	Frequent	Specialists students	Free
Heard Sounds	4	Education	No	Yes	Text, audio	No/No	Occasional	Specialists students	2.26€

Table 7.2. *M-Health applications as a function of their most downloadable features*

Figure 7.4 illustrates the percentage of each type of application. As expected, the most abundant applications are prominently informative and account for nearly 4 in 10 apps (about 37.76%), because they do not need to deploy special features. The second group of apps is of an educational nature (17.47%).

In essence, these two groups are the same, but are different in their approach and way in which they teach the user. Considering these two groups as only one, they comprise about 55.23% of apps. Therefore, it can be considered that one in each two applications provides informative content to users.

Monitoring tools and diagnosis are the following two groups in terms of importance, both hovering around 14%. The other classes are related to treatment (7.62%), calculators (5.48%), healthcare (2.74%), pagers/beepers (1.71%) and alarms (0.17%). The latter two kinds of apps are types that specialize in Alzheimer's disease and strokes, respectively.

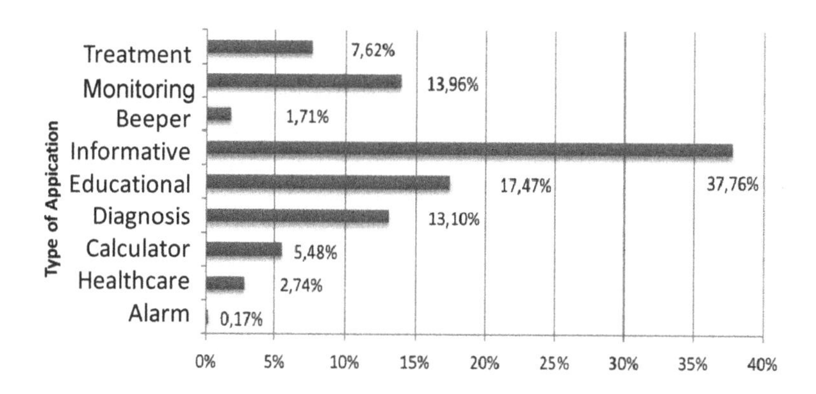

Figure 7.4. *Percentage of applications types*

Many of the apps need an Internet connection to work properly or to make all their functions available. Several of the features that need Internet connectivity include reviews of other users, explanatory videos, etc. There are also apps that need to regularly update the displayed information, such as news servers, downloading packages, encyclopedias, medical information or guides. However, this study showed that the vast majority of applications only need Internet connectivity to send information about results obtained by the user, either by email, social networks or through specific functionalities deployed in each particular application and where both physicians and users may be recipients of this information.

One important issue considered by users when deciding which applications to use, aside from the aforementioned characteristics, is the support from specialists for their clinical application, the results of which are shown in Figure 7.5 for different diseases. The ailments with a higher percentage of apps of this type are, in descending order, tuberculosis (53.85%), cardiology (50.7%) and chronic obstructive pulmonary disease (50%). These supported apps have many monitoring and diagnosis tools and, above all, different medical calculators.

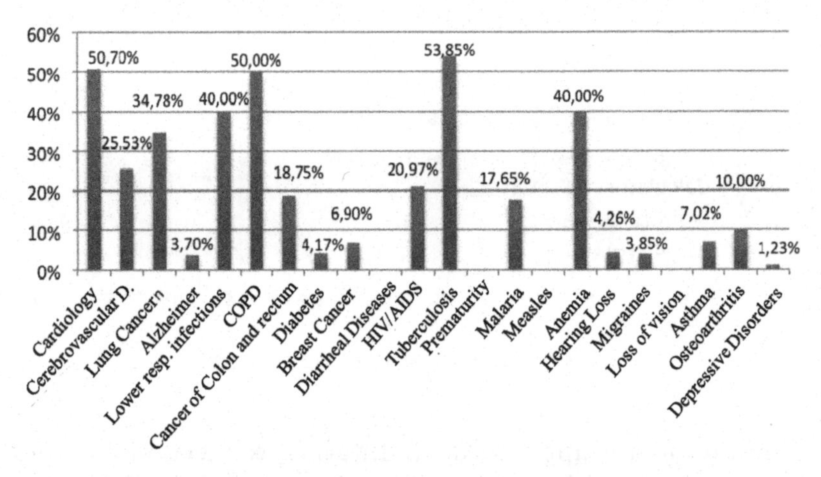

Figure 7.5. *Percentage of clinical applications per disease*

Figure 7.6 presents the overall low percentage of apps that allow for users to contact specialists. None of the groups studied provides more than 20% of tools with this feature. Considering contact with other users, the situation improves. Alzheimer's apps allow users to contact other people (about 51%) because these apps usually include tools for communication with patients. Diabetes-related applications are used foremost as monitoring tools, representing 13.54% of all the available applications. In terms of use for retrieving information (informative use), colon and rectum cancer applications have their share of 12.5%. Finally, applications related to unipolar depressive disorders represent 12.35%. Given the value of direct patient communication for these types diseases, these applications all support tools for contact/interaction between users.

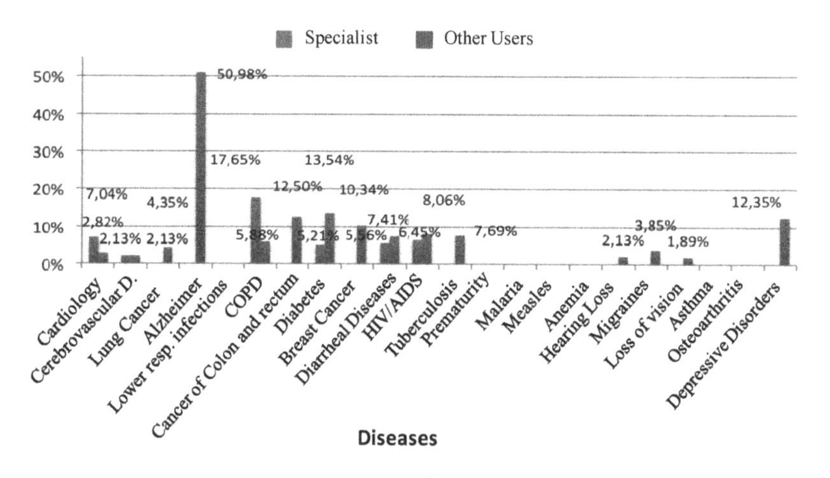

Figure 7.6. *Percentage of applications that allow/promote interaction with other users. For a color version of the figure, see www.iste.co.uk/rodrigues/ehealth.zip*

Given the characteristics of the abovementioned apps, the next step focuses on evaluating the frequency that each medical app is used and the corresponding reason. Figure 7.7 shows that nearly 6 out of 10 applications can be used randomly, basically when a user sees it. 3 out of 10 apps (33.5%) are used often as educational tools or for consultation by scholars, students and the general public. About 6.40% of this corresponds to frequent use directly linked to the different existing monitoring tools. Another 1.12% refers to special situations that may occur in cardiology (how to exercise cardiopulmonary resuscitation) and cerebrovascular disease (rapid diagnosis of possible cerebrovascular problems by health emergency personnel).

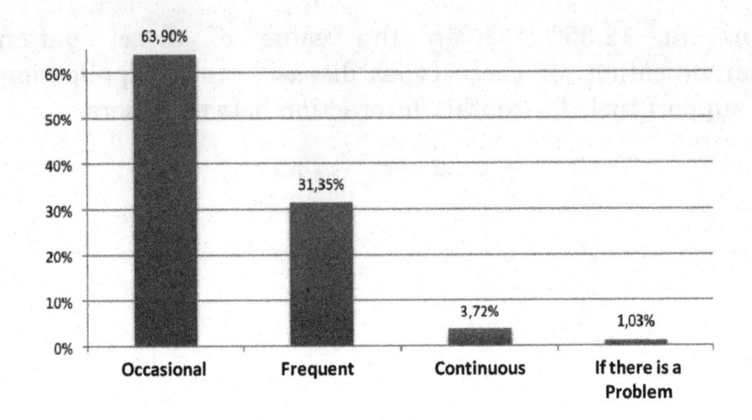

Figure 7.7. *Frequency that each medical app is used and the respective reason*

Given that an application may have several target users, Figure 7.8 shows that almost half of the applications (about 44.87%) are intended to be used by anyone and are general in nature. Apps which focus on monitoring patients make up about 27%, and 15% were created for specialists. Students, family and/or parents and children focus only on 8, 3 and 1%, respectively.

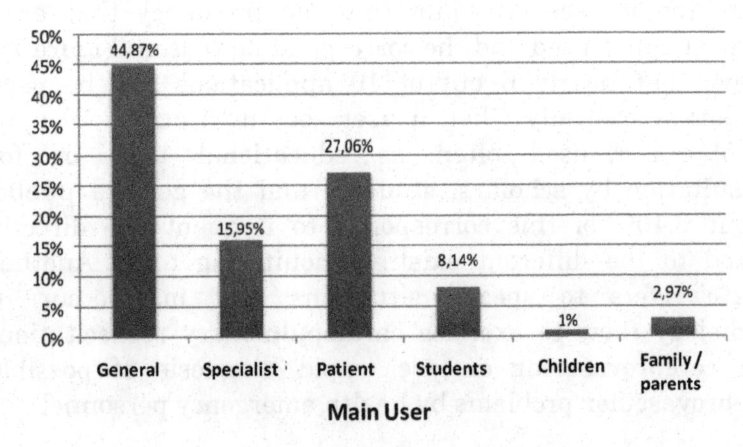

Figure 7.8. *Percentage of users as function of their intended use for medical apps*

Finally, the feature that makes the biggest difference in terms of the success of an application is the price. Users interested by a particular app will not hesitate to pay for it, but more general users looking for an app with certain features and functionalities, will compare among the available options, and unless paid versions offer additional features, they will choose a free version or one at a low price. Figure 7.9 presents the percentage of free apps from the list of the studied applications. On average, about 56.9% of the applications are free.

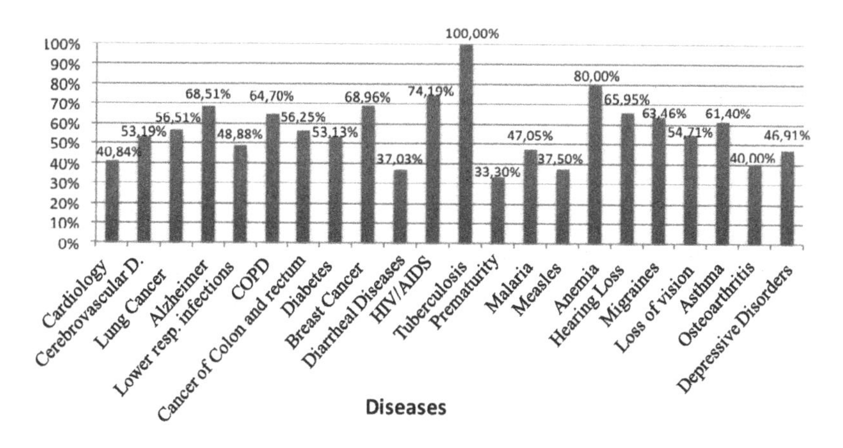

Figure 7.9. *Percentage of free available medical apps per disease*

The average cost of all the applications, both free and paid, is shown in Figure 7.10. In most cases, the price ranges from 0.01 to 2€. This means the cost associated with purchase and application is not high. Other applications, such as those for loss of vision, osteoarthritis, HIV and lung cancer, have prices ranging from 2 to 4€. The most expensive apps are those for malaria (with a price around 7.67€, on average) and cardiology (with an average price of 11.02€). For malaria, a shortage of apps may justify the price. However, in cardiology there are two main reasons for the price, one being that the app is dealing with a clinical specialty (this generally means that apps will have higher prices) and, secondly, that although there are many diagnostic, educational and informational tools available for free, others are very expensive (with prices ranging from 25 to 130€).

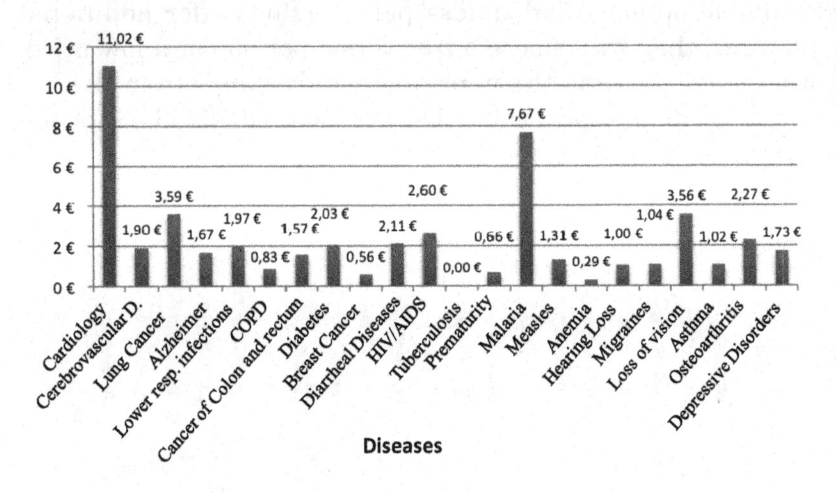

Figure 7.10. *Average price of available medical app per disease*

7.4. Conclusions

M-Health proposes to deliver healthcare services anytime and anywhere, thereby overcoming geographical, temporal and even organizational barriers with low and affordable costs. The proliferation of m-Health applications through online stores is a profitable business model that is widely used by both patients and physicians. The main reason for the increase in the m-Health market is the affordable costs and inherent mobility offered by these applications. They aim to be a major asset in patients' lives, especially in elderly, disabled and chronically ill individuals. By association, they have a strong impact on all healthcare services such as hospitals, care centers and emergency attendance.

From this study on the popularity of m-Health applications, a clear imbalance between different groups or diseases is observable. This imbalance is due to the fact that some m-Health applications are only for educational or informational purposes and are not for treatment or diagnosis.

The future of m-Health relies on creating applications that involve communities and social networks. m-Health solutions may use social networking to promote healthy behaviors and awareness among patients involved in networked groups and communities. A future study could address the technologic interoperability between m-Health applications and cloud services. Finally, a study addressing the impact of reducing financial costs to end-users/patients and how public and private healthcare systems are affected by this is needed.

8

Mobile Computing in Medicine: Case Studies

8.1. Introduction

Mobile health (m-Health) involves the clearest sense of e-Health evolution. The term mobile health was coined early in the 2000s and can easily be defined as "using wireless technology to deliver health services and information through mobile communication devices, such as mobile phones, personal digital assistants (PDAs), smartphones, monitoring devices, e-book readers and iPODs (i.e. any device with wireless connectivity that is capable of storing health information accessible by health professionals, if necessary, or having the ability to access the information remotely) [LAX 00, IST 03].

M-Health applications include the use of mobile devices in the collection of community health and clinical data, scheduling of health information professionals, researchers and patients, real-time monitoring of body signals and direct care provision (via mobile telemedicine) [BRO 14, SIL 13].

Non-communicable diseases (NCDs) are the leading cause of death in the world. According to a World Health

Organization (WHO) study, within an average of 56.8 million deaths in 2009, 36 million were caused by NCDs. Concretely, chronic diseases are a significant part of this group, cardiovascular diseases (CVDs) being the deadliest diseases responsible for 17.3 million deaths in 2008, representing about 30% of all deaths worldwide [WOR 10]. Additionally, despite the advances in healthcare, these numbers are estimated to increase to more than 23 million individuals by 2030 [WOR 11, BER 14, TSA 11, MAR 14, MAR 13].

Among CVDs, heart conditions and heart diseases are a significant factor in the number of deaths [THE 14]. Coronary heart disease (or ischemic heart disease) is especially fatal and was responsible for 7.25 million deaths in 2008. With other cardiac conditions, such as hypertensive heart disease and inflammatory heart disease, coronary heart disease contributes a significantly high percentage to the global number of deaths [MAR 13]. However, not only are the deaths caused by a disease important, they also create disabilities. Coronary heart disease alone caused a total of 62,587 million disability-adjusted life years (DALYs) in 2008, which gives an idea of the huge number of DALYs that heart diseases incur. These disabilities mean more hospitalizations and more medical interventions, which directly contribute to the costs of the healthcare systems, not considering the economic costs of that lost productivity by the affected people that can be felt by enterprises and the economical sector. In the United States, for instance, the costs derived from heart diseases were estimated to be about $448 billion in 2008 [WOR 11].

The advent of information technology in healthcare and the incredible expansion of the market of smartphones and tablets have created a new mobile health applications software industry [MCM 13, JAR 11, SIL 15a]. These new health apps continue to increase in number. Focusing only on the most important app stores, there are more than

11,000 apps in the category of health and fitness and almost 5,000 in the category of medicine in Android's Google Play, and around 20,000 apps in the health and fitness section and more than 14,000 in the medicine section in Apple's app store. Focusing only on cardiology, 439 apps for iOS and 271 for Android were found in 2013 [MAR 13]. In 2015, there were more than 165,000 mobile applications related to health in several catalogs [IMS 15].

Since heart diseases make up a significant percentage of deaths and disabilities caused by non-communicable diseases, it is obvious that there are many health apps focusing on these diseases [WOR 14]. Many of them are designed for patients' use, such as those for heart rate monitoring in order to detect abnormal rhythms and warn the user, others for cardiac rehabilitation, some for resuscitation in case of heart infarction, and even those for self diagnosis, among others [JAR 11, YU 13, MÜL 13]. There are also apps for healthcare professionals, such as those that continuously monitor patients, those that use mobile phones in order to assist the professional in their decisions, or even some that use smartphones for phonocardiography applications to evaluate the cardiovascular function, amongst others. Summing up, there are many apps in cardiology developed for different objectives and, in general, they have been proved to positively influence chronic diseases, in general, and heart diseases, in particular. However, the authors have identified a lack of apps for self-management of heart diseases and conditions [MAR 14], and so decided to create an app for this purpose. This chapter also presents this app, called Heart keeper, showing the outcomes of its design, its development and its validation. Before this, different m-Health apps will be addressed in the next sections.

8.2. M-Health applications

In order to present and give an overview of the current m-Health applications context, it is necessary to distinguish between developed and underdeveloped countries. m-Health services that can be used in countries are completely different from those that can be used in developing countries. The first group tends to optimize resources and make life easier for patients while the second group is basically for assisting the people's development, i.e. for improving life conditions and extending life expectancy [BIL 12].

Developed countries have the technology, hospitals, medical staff, communication infrastructure and capacity that favor certain types of applications. In these countries, the following medical applications are usually available:

– *Remote data collection*: many patients perform their own checks. The data resulting from this self-monitoring can be introduced into a simple Java application that is submitted to a central monitoring information and, if an abnormality is detected, a pre-determined protocol is activated.

– *Remote monitoring*: monitoring is very important in chronically ill patients. Such monitoring can be returned to an automated control. When there is a collapse, alarms are set off, the application detects it automatically and, in addition, the person can be located using a global positioning system (GPS) and/or an automatic request may be sent through the global system for mobile communications to mobilize careers or relatives.

– *Reminder services*: using either short message service (SMS) or voice messages, reminders for taking medication, physician appointments and even tips related by the precautions that should be followed, for instance, in a heat wave or a flu epidemic.

– *Appointment management*: focusing not only on a simple appointment request, but taking it a step further, showing symptoms to the physician to get an idea about what is happening to the patient when he/she goes to a consultation.

– *Monitoring*: automated systems and voice messaging can provide proactive monitoring by the health system and, based on the results, take corrective action.

On the other hand, in developing countries the perspective changes radically. Poverty and a lack of infrastructure presents challenges and mobile devices play a key role in addressing them [SAN 12]. Obviously they cannot solve some issues, such as antennas, but organizations such as Telecom Sans Frontiers complement other non-governmental organizations focusing more on medical care. This is a key issue when communications must be used to recover from a natural disaster. In these countries, the main actions are the following:

– *Awareness action*: in places where diseases such as AIDS affect large proportions of the population, information is extremely important in preventing diseases and it is a scenario where SMS is revealed as a key media.

– *Monitoring of epidemics*: based on field data that medical staff have sent from their mobile devices, a progress map of an epidemic can be followed.

– *Diagnostic tools*: there are tools that include a program for the calculation of doses, in addition to reference materials preloaded on the device.

– *Mobile social networking*: a South African initiative, called Love life, created a mobile social network specifically for fighting against AIDS. It focused on a more vulnerable side of people and took advantage of the intensive users of social networks and mobile devices. Obviously, the users are young people.

– *Antigen-specific diseases*: the Massachusetts Institute of Technology (USA) has come up with an idea. For example, the patient impregnates a reagent strip with urine. This reagent strip takes on a color or has another reaction. The patient can then send an SMS with the strip number and the color of the reagent anonymously and request support. Although the system is rather crude, it is effective and protects the identity of the person.

As already addressed this chapter, many applications have been created for mobile devices in the past decade. Here, some contributions are highlighted focusing on end users:

– *My Heart*: this app aims at performing an early diagnosis of CVDs, improving the patient's quality of life and reducing the costs associated with these diseases [PHI 16].

– *m-Health kit*: the Application developed by IBM uses the patient's mobile phone to collect data from devices that constantly monitor heart rate, activity and even medication. The phone keeps a data record and sends reports to physicians regularly. If the patient loses the phone, the application can destroy the medical information stored on the device using Fusion One and send a message regarding the lost/stolen device.

– *Mobile clinical assistant*: this is being developed by Intel Mobile Platform and enables medical staff to have more time for all patients. Thus, it can move from one place to another to be always connected to a database via a mobile, making simple transactions remotely, such as managing medication from a patient while serving another [INT 07].

– *Mobile Derma*: a mobile platform developed by Telefónica (a telecom operator from Spain) to track skin disease patients, allowing development at the post operative period to be followed.

For the general public, more and more mobile applications are becoming available in the healthcare field. For instance, in the Apple store there are a huge number of health-related applications (free or affordable). One-third of them are related to nutrition, diet and weight control. Other applications focus on the acquisition and maintenance of personal health records, such as the mobile platform called My Life Record which archives and stores all the user's medical data related to his/her health such as X-rays, electro cardiograms and blood tests.

8.3. A case study in cardiology

This section presents a case study with a mobile health application created at the University of Valladolid, Spain, by Borja Martínez-Pérez, Isabel de la Torre-Díez and Miguel López-Coronado.

8.3.1. *A mobile app for heart disease self-management*

The global process for the creation of Heart keeper can be divided into three phases. In the first phase, the authors discussed and obtained the design issues that the app must perform, such as the functional requirements and the general concept of the app. Once the design was concluded, the second phase, the construction could start. This phase was developed in iterative processes until the app was refined. When the final version was obtained, the third phase focused on the validation and evaluation of the solution.

8.3.1.1. *Design*

Before thinking about the design of the application to be developed, it was essential to conduct research regarding the existing applications and systems in the cardiology field. This work was finished in July 2013 [MAR 13] and the most relevant results were the following: a total of 710 relevant apps were found in the most important commercial app stores (271 in Google Play and 439 available at the Apple store). The majority of the applications found were designed for general users and healthcare professionals, the distribution being quite similar: 300 apps for general users (116 in Google Play and 184 in the Apple store) and 282 for professionals (112 in Google Play and 170 in the Apple store). The most common apps were heart rate monitors, calculators and predictors, informative guides, apps for assisting electrocardiogram (ECG) interpretation, apps with news and blood pressure trackers. One of the results that was most striking to the authors was finding only one app for heart condition management, and it was only dedicated to individuals with risk of heart failure in order to know if their risk was low or high. In line with these results, it was decided to create an app for the self-management of heart diseases broadening the scope of these diseases. These diseases are ischemic heart disease, heart valve disease, hypertension and auricular fibrillation. They included other important aspects that can influence the health of the heart, i.e. the relationships between the heart and pregnancy, the heart and physical activity, and the heart and diabetes.

The app is divided into the following main three sections:

– an informative section with medical information about the diseases that will help patients to understand their disease, its symptoms and its treatment, and a patient guide in order to inform users about best practices, prohibitions and the lifestyle they should adopt in order to improve their condition;

– a section to record the user's activities (good and bad for their conditions) and health measurements in order to act in consequence of them. Examples of these activities are rehabilitation, physical activity or excesses (in alcohol or food intake, for example), whereas typical measurements are blood pressure, glucose or cholesterol;

– a section for registering the users' medications and the hours that they should take them, offering the possibility to establish alarms to warn them. The taking of medication should be registered in order to create a daily record stored in the calendar.

8.3.1.2. *Construction*

Several operating systems were available for the implementation of the app as follows: Apple iOS, Google Android, Microsoft Windows Phone OS, BlackBerry OS and Symbian. From them, Android was selected because it is the most extended worldwide, open source and, hence, there are many tools and aid for the development of apps in this platform. Concretely, the tool used for the development of Heart keeper was the Android Software Development Kit, which includes the Eclipse Integrated Development Environment with built-in Android Development Tools.

Another important issue related to the development phase was the security and privacy the app must offer, since the data used by the app (personal health data) is very sensitive. Hence, the authors considered this issue very carefully and studied the current laws regarding security and privacy applied to mobile health apps in Europe and the United States in order to fulfil the requirements there. On first launch, Heart keeper shows a disclaimer and information about the app and its data treatment, along with an e-mail sent to the user with an address to contact the authors.

Regarding the protection of the introduced data, it was decided to implement a data storage solution in the device itself rather than in a server or in the cloud. This deployment provides significant advantages as follows: (1) the data will not circulate through Internet connections, avoiding external attacks typical of wireless links; (2) since the storage is not in the cloud, illegitimate access to the data through the Internet is also avoided; (3) the only method to access data is through the mobile device, so the only option for obtaining it is by stealing the device. In addition to these security reasons, there is another more functional reason, which is the possibility of using the app at all times, even when there is no Internet connection available, very useful for those devices with only Wi-Fi connection or for people who live in rural areas with no 3G or 4G coverage. Moreover, the most sensitive data of the user was encrypted by a password-based algorithm that uses 256-bit Secure Hash Algorithm techniques with random data input that adds more security in order to make those data inaccessible in case of losing the device or if it is stolen.

The authors were also especially careful with the implementation of the user's interface, as it has been proved that interface design and its ease of use is essential in order to attract potential users. It must be simple, intuitive even at first use but also complete, which can sometimes be very difficult to achieve.

8.3.1.3. *Validation phase*

The validation phase was divided into two phases. The first phase is the experimentation phase, based on systematic and exhaustive procedures with Heart keeper, executing all the operations offered by the app in several devices with different screen sizes. These devices are the following: Samsung Galaxy Mini GT-S6500 (3.5 inches), Samsung Galaxy S SCL GT-I9003 (4 inches), Sony Xperia Z (5 inches), Google Nexus 7 (7 inches) and Samsung Galaxy Tab 3 (9.1 inches). In this phase, the response times of the most time-consuming operations of the app were also evaluated in all the above-mentioned devices in order to check that Heart keeper is a fast enough app independently of the device used.

The second phase is the app performance evaluation performed by its users. Heart keeper was installed in the mobile devices of 16 patients with heart conditions in order to use it for 1 month. After this period of time, they answered several questions (a survey) addressing the most relevant aspects about the application. The questions are shown in Table 8.1 and the majority of them use the Likert scale, the following answers being possible: (1) strongly disagree, (2) disagree, (3) neither agree nor disagree, (4) agree and (5) strongly agree. Question 8 is the only one that uses free text.

Question	Description
1	Is the design of the app attractive?
2	Is the user's interface intuitive?
3	Is the app easy to use?
4	Do you feel that app protects your security and privacy?
5	Are the response times of the app fast enough?
6	Is the app helpful for your heart condition?
7	Are you in more control of your heart condition after using the app?
8	Would you change/improve/delete any aspect of the app?

Table 8.1. *Questions used to evaluate Heart keeper*

8.3.1.4. *Results*

Heart keeper includes a main page that shows several buttons that connects the different sections of the app. A screenshot of this window interface is shown in Figures 8.1(a) and Figure 8.1(b) shows a screenshot of the section for introducing a medication and its doses. Figures 8.1(c) and 8.1(d) show screenshots of the activities calendar and the graphs generated for the glucose registers (in this case), respectively.

8.3.1.5. *Response times*

As mentioned earlier, Heart keeper has been experimented with and evaluated in several ways. One of the experiments performed was a measure of the response times of the application when executing different actions. This measure is important since the majority of app users do not tolerate launch or waiting times of more than 2 s according to a survey from Compuware [MAR 13]. Hence, it is necessary that app may be launched in less than 2 s, and that every section can be reached almost immediately. Table 8.2 shows the measure of response times in nanoseconds (ns) when performing different actions. The indicated measures are the mean value of 10 measures for each action. The launch of the Heart keeper app takes about 2 ms in the worst case (the oldest mobile device). The operation with more time consumption is the encryption/decryption of the user's personal data, at 2.2 and 2.3 s, respectively, with the oldest device, being less than 1 s in newer devices.

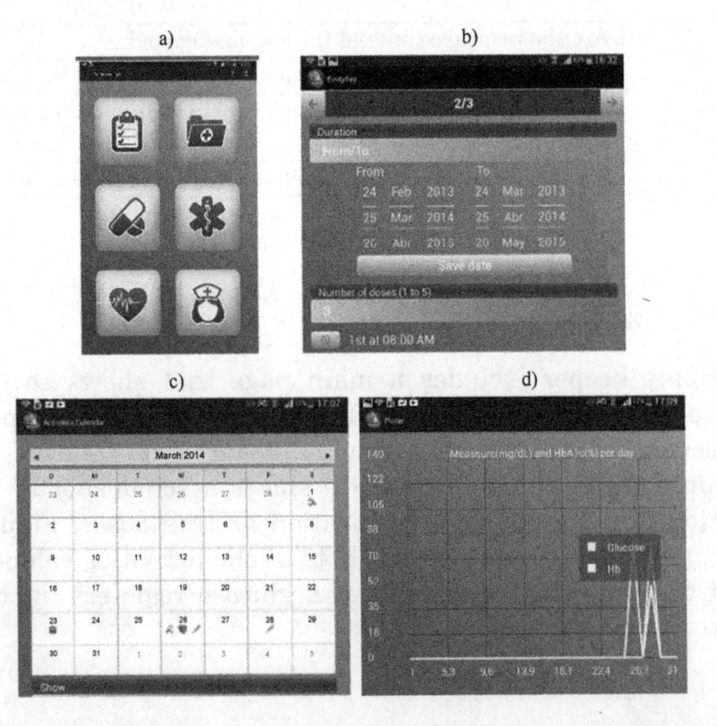

Figure 8.1. *a) Screenshot of the Heart keeper main window; b) screenshot of the creation of a medication register and its doses; c) screenshot of the activities calendar; d) screenshot of the graphs generated for the glucose registers. For a color version of this figure, see www.iste.co.uk/rodrigues/ehealth.zip*

	Samsung GT-S6500	Sony Xperia Z	Samsung Galaxy Tab 3
Launch	211.826.000,24	110.205.078,20	56.673.023,80
Encryption	2.200.953.999,60	788.012.696,50	728.293.863,35
Decryption	2.319.032.666,40	708.050.537,40	650.942.188,80
Activity DB writing	49.139.777,80	100.712.367,34	72,071391,29
Activity DB reading	25.261.667,00	44.937.134,50	6.549.713,25
Medicines DB reading with 9 registers	15.697.500,95	14.175.415,20	10.826.702,42
Blood test graph drawing with 11 registers	122.416.667,26	258.453.369,65	59.414.637,15

Table 8.2. *Mean times (ns) of some operations with Heart keeper*

8.4. Conclusions

In this chapter, the process of design, creation, implementation and performance evaluation of an app for self-management of heart conditions has been explained. The essential steps that should be followed by an app developer were considered and they are summarized as follows. The first step is based on the development of market research to know the available apps for the topic (cardiology, in this case-study) in order to find possible opportunities or deficiencies that can be covered and addressed. This is probably the most important step for the creation of a successful app. After this, the following phase is defining the type of app, its functionalities and its design. Once the app is completely designed, the next step is its creation (programming phase), choosing the operating systems where the app will be available (if not have been thought before in the design phase), since this decision is also important for the success of the app. At this phase, the authors should include the security and privacy mechanisms that the app must support according to the current laws of the countries in which it will be launched. Finally, it is very important to experiment with, demonstrate and evaluate the app in order to fix bugs and incorrect behaviors in different devices to be sure that the final version released be totally operative without errors. It is crucial that the app should be experimented with and validated by a field test (clinical trial), legally approved and the collected/measured results approved by qualified medical staff. In parallel, during the clinical trial, it is also recommended to evaluate the app in order to obtain feedback and be able to improve its usability before the app is released for regular usage.

9

Ambient Assisted Living

9.1. Introduction

In the coming years, the world will experience an important demographic shift. The elderly population is growing due to increased life expectancy and decreasing birth rates [MAG 07]. According to the United Nations, the elderly will make up around 36% of the European population by 2050 [UNI 02]. Disabilities and diseases are more prevalent with old age. Moreover, people often require more attention and healthcare with age [EUR 10]. In many cultures that stress independent living, this has led to home healthcare becoming the preferred care method for disabled and elderly people [HER 08]. In order to make independent living a possibility for these people, different companies have been investing money into researching and developing welfare technologies [SAV 09].

New devices and systems have flooded institutions and homes in many countries, mainly developed with the aim of helping people with the daily living tasks. Nowadays, ambient technologies have become a key issue in this context. These are technologies that work within a disabled person's environment. They do not necessarily require direct interaction from the user. Robotic technologies also play an important role [ENG 04].

The current demographic changes and an aging population mean that the demand for healthcare is increasing, which will lead to a shortage of healthcare professionals in a near future. Within this field the concept of Ambient Assisted Living (AAL) has emerged [GAR 15, ROD 15]. The aim of AAL is to improve the quality of life of elderly people and to increase the time they can live independently at home. One of the most important areas where AAL plays an important role in the life of the elderly is health. In recent years, many projects have been developed in order to create systems, applications and services that are easy to use both by aging people and by healthcare professionals, and which are also not intrusive when it comes to supporting the user in his or her daily life [RAS 13, FOR 05, FUC 08, SIL 15a, COS 15].

9.2. Areas of application

In Europe, a research and development program entitled the Ambient Assisted Living Joint Programme was created between 2008–2013 [AMB 12]. The main objectives of this program were the following:

– promoting the emergence of innovative ICT-based products, services and systems for aging well at home, in the community and at work, thus improving the quality of life, autonomy, participation in social life, powers and employability of older people, reducing health and social costs;

– creating in the European Union a critical mass of research, development and innovation in the area of technologies and services for aging well in the information society;

– improving conditions for industrial exploitation of research results by providing a coherent European framework to develop common approaches, including common minimum standards, and to facilitate the localization and adaptation of common solutions, which are compatible with the different social preferences and regulations at national or regional levels in Europe.

There are several projects in the area of AAL funded by the AAL Joint Programme. Major topics encompassed by this program are presented as follows:

– *Home-based empowered living*: improving the quality of life and health of the elderly in the home environment through the development of smart technologies that help in everyday activities and in household and personal care management, increasing the opportunities for part of the population to live independently for longer at their own homes. The proposed approaches are addressed to platforms for small software services embedded in immersive environments, societies based on environmentally conscious assistive tool agents, social networks assisted by the environment and smart home management.

– *Home care monitoring systems*: intelligent technologies able to "follow" the elderly inhabitants of the house in their daily activities, thus preventing health and security risks or alerting relatives or healthcare providers when abnormal situations occur. Current efforts in this context are addressed to fall detection and prevention, impotence detection and computer vision techniques for life logging [LOP 13].

– *Online ageing*: this investigates the role of the Web in the context of AAL and improving the quality of life for the elderly through social interaction, including a community social TV platform for older people, augmented by game technologies and smart furniture, a personal trainer to prevent and overcome loneliness among elderly people and a framework for the design of personalized, adaptive and ubiquitous services and applications.

– *Mobility services for independent living*: mobility, route planning, guidance and smart guiding in indoor and outdoor environments, especially in public buildings, as a pedestrian and on public transport [SIL 14].

– *AAL for rehabilitation*: natural interaction system that provides a novel solution for neurocognitive rehabilitation aimed at people with neglect syndrome.

– *AAL technologies*: the technologies in the field of ontologies for intelligent assistive solutions address modeling and recognition activity, while in home care robotics and automation ecology and adaptive robotics is proposed, consisting of mobile robotic devices, sensors and applications [CAV 13].

– *Interoperability, standards and benchmarking for AAL*: the development of standards and open platforms for AAL as well as a reliable evaluation and comparison of AAL systems.

Another project is *PERceptive Spaces prOmoting INdependent Aging* (PERSONA), whose main objective is the development of an open and scalable technology platform to support independent living that allows building over it a wide range of services for elderly people. This represents progress for creating the paradigm of ambient intelligence through the harmonization of technologies and concepts for assisted living environments.

The PERSONA project has developed an open and scalable platform that supports a wide range of AAL services quickly and easily. In this particular project, it is specified that the services required by older people can be divided into several categories as follows [VOD 16]:

– services for complementing skills and abilities of these people in the tasks of daily life guiding the user along the day;

– services for preventing injuries in the home environment, making them feel safe and giving them the feeling of being able to manage their life in their own space without needing the constant presence of a caregiver;

– services for social integration, alleviating loneliness and isolation by providing ICT-based media to support their need for companionship;

– services for mobility, supporting aging people when they leave their homes to perform activities within their neighborhood; encouraging them to do this autonomously with confidence.

9.3. Key applications

In the European Union 6th Framework Programme (FP), the strategic objective of e-Inclusion has covered assistive design for AAL technologies while other strategic objectives covered the health aspects of mobile systems, home automation, embedded technologies or micro and nano technologies, which are related to this issue. At the end of FP6, a strategic specific objective was included on AAL as a bridge toward FP7 and, in the context of its importance, as a third pillar of the i2010 initiative. AAL is part of the flagship initiative i2010 concerning Independent Living in preparation for the flagship initiative on e-Inclusion for 2008.

At this point, various projects will be addressed, some of them funded by the EU within the 6th and 7th FP of research, related to the application of AmI and AAL to e-Health.

9.3.1. *Prototype m-Health service*

The main objective of this m-Health service architecture is to enable elderly patients to self-manage their health on the move, outside any unit of special healthcare, either by controlling their illness or helping them to control the timely and correct intake of their medication. By using radiofrequency identification (RFID), passive tags become completely safe for usage for wearing or even implanting in healthcare or in health sensitive environments [SAN 14].

Due to the importance and need to preserve the privacy of patient data, security is a major concern in these systems. Therefore, both Internet of Things (IoT) devices used in healthcare systems and RFID must ensure the privacy and security of data. On the other hand, in a health environment system it is important to balance the security of the system with its availability, as this is another aspect required for the proper working of these systems.

A possible application of RFID is indoor real-time localization systems. Tag localization may be suitable for application with many objects to locate, such as tracking patients in hospitals.

9.3.1.1. *Prototype service implementation*

The entire process, from drug prescription until its intake, is controlled by an information system completely based on IoT. To sustain this AAL system based on IoT, an Object Name Service prototype was developed including new m-Health security protocols.

9.3.1.1.1. RFID for indoor location awareness and guidance

A centralized system collects tag IDs read by each RFID reader and registers the tag position in the system. Public buildings, such as hospitals and clinics, or even a patient's home facilities, are required to have a set of RFID readers preregistered in the system at known positions and with network access. Location data are stored and updated, in real time, on the server. When a RFID tag changes its position to a new zone, a stored procedure runs a check on all access control rules associated with that zone. An event is generated on each broken rule and a pre-configured associated set of actions is immediately executed. There are three types of actions, while more can be defined such as security alerts, simple notification and system updates.

Security alerts are signaled (sound or visual) and require other entities (staff, for instance) to be notified. An example is when a visitor enters a staff-only zone; at this moment a sound alert is triggered and security staff are alerted.

Notifications only require appropriate signaling. In this example, the building is also populated with information screens and this type of information is presented on the nearest screen. As an example, let us consider a visitor or a patient that has previously checked-in at the reception with a well-known destination zone. If the RFID-tag associated with this person is located out of the best path, a notification is issued as a simple signal or navigation indication (go back, go left, as examples) on the nearest screen.

The third type of action requires system state updates. If two entities are detected in the same zone, this meeting can be automatically registered. If the two entities are a patient and his medical doctor and the time frame is adequate, it can be registered as a potential medical consultation; a patient and a piece of equipment may be registered as a potential medical exam; a patient and his or her medication as a potential medication taking. This type of event can further be used on other security alerts. If a patient has not seen a physician for a long period of time, he/she may be missing, voluntarily, or not, his/her periodic consultation. In the same way, if a patient and medication were not identified in the same zone for long time, medication was not taken as expected.

Experiments conducted on hypothetical facilities show that a reduced amount of RFID readers are required for potential large security benefits.

9.3.2. *Health at Home*

The AAL Project Health at Home (H@H) was carried out included in the Ambient Assisted Living Joint Programme and lasted 3 years, from 2009 to 2011. The project aimed to develop a system for monitoring and alerting patients with chronic heart failure. By monitoring a patient's parameters and a real-time analysis, the physician receives a warning if a critical situation occurs.

H@H is a telehealth system for monitoring heart failure patients at home. The main objectives are the following:

– analyzing the effectiveness and reliability of the system;

– analyzing the quality of life related to health and patient adherence to the system;

– analyzing the satisfaction of patients and health professionals.

The H@H project aimed to provide services for aging patients with chronic heart failure, developing a system with devices that can be worn with sensors for self-monitoring pathophysiological parameters and, at the same time, allowing the medical team to monitor remote patients' situations. The project aimed to improve health services, making them more cost effective and more efficient, and improve the quality of life for the elderly.

Measuring devices and adapted mini-notebooks were used to complete this project. A representation of the complete system is shown in Figure 9.1.

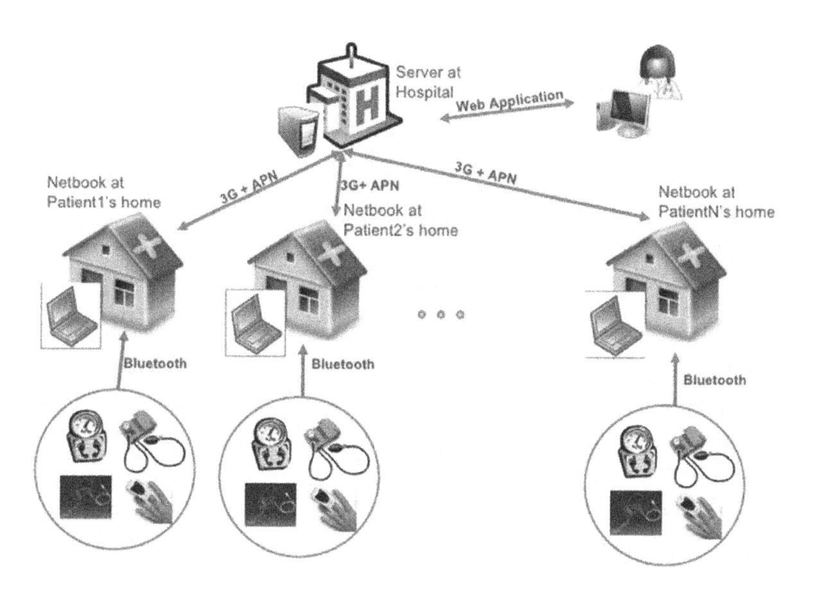

Figure 9.1. *Specification of the technology used in the H@H Project*

9.3.2. *FLORENCE project*

The FLORENCE project (multi-purpose mobile robot for ambient assisted living) aims to improve the elderly wellbeing (and their beloved ones) as well as improving the efficiency in care through AAL services, supported by a general-purpose robot platform. The Florence system with its multipurpose mobile robot platform will lay the groundwork for the use of such robots in delivering new kinds of AAL services to elderly persons and their care providers. The main objective is to make this concept acceptable for users and profitable for society and caregivers. Florence will put a robot as the connecting element between several stand-alone AAL services in a living environment, as well as between the

AAL services and the elderly person [CAV 13]. Through these care and coaching services supported by Florence, the elderly will be able to remain independent for much longer [FLO 16].

The Florence project is a small- or medium-scale focused research project in the EU FP7. It started on February 1, 2010, and lasted for 3 years, finishing by January 31, 2013 [FLO 16].

The Florence system's development has been sustained by a slow, but constant, demographic change. There are an increasing number of elderly people, while the number of younger people remains constant or even declines. Due to the advances in health treatment, a lot of previously fatal diseases have been turned into chronic diseases. This leads to an increasing demand for care, especially for the elderly. In addition to this, new family structures and more job mobility make it more and more difficult to rely on volunteer care for the elderly at home by family members. Hence, costs for both the society and the care provider are growing, which, in the end, may lead to potential undersupply of healthcare. Beyond the financial aspect, another problem is the increasing lack of social inclusion due to less stable social networks, which leads to increasing loneliness of the elderly with a negative impact on their health and safety.

The Florence system will support lifestyle and AAL services in the categories presented in Figure 9.2.

– *Keeping in touch*: the KEETOU application service implements a robotic telepresence service to provide an increased perceived level of presence in both directions. Family and friends have an increased feeling of being present by the fact they are able to control the robot and, similarly, the elderly have an increased feeling that the other person is "really" visiting them.

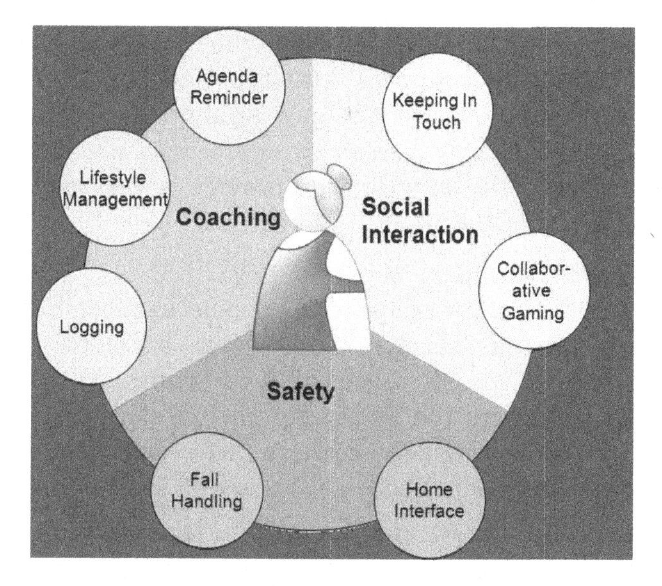

Figure 9.2. *Areas supported by FLORENCE*

– *Lifestyle improvement service*: the LIFIMP service assists the user in adopting and maintaining a healthy lifestyle. In particular, the service focuses on monitoring weight and physical activity. Building a long-term personal relationship with the user, the robot persuades the user to change his/her behavior.

– *Fall handling service*: the FALHAN service supports a service application that reacts to fall events. This reaction includes the localization of the user and communication between the robot and the user to find out what happened and if the user needs help. When the elderly needs help or does not react, an emergency call (video conference) will be provided automatically.

– *Logging service*: the LOGSYS service is based on three subservices. The first one is the data logger service, which records sensor data (for instance the laser scanner to a database). The second service is the data request service, which loads appropriate data from the database. The third service is the gait analysis service, which analyzes the laser scanner data and computes the step size and some other important parameters for the gait analysis to estimate the mobility of the elderly person. If these data are out of the expected range, the service will provide a message to the caregiver and the user.

– *Agenda reminder service*: AGEREM is a service application that allows dependent people to remain in their homes by sharing information between the elderly person and their relatives or teleassistance team. In that way, AGEREM reinforces the autonomy and safety of individuals in their own homes because it strengthens the communication channel between them and their caregivers.

– *Home interface service*: the HOMEINT service implements two use cases, the Door Guard use case and the "Energy Saving" use case. The task of the HOMEINT service in the context of Door Guard use case is to inform the user about the situation when the entrance doorbell is being activated and offer to the user a range of options to proceed. The "Energy Saving" use case aims at detecting a possible wastage of energy. The service monitors the temperature of the room and the state of the windows. In the case that a window is open and the room has a low temperature, the service concludes that energy is being wasted and informs the user about the situation, along with a set of options how to proceed.

– *Collaborative gaming*: the objective of this task is to provide a collaborative activities support platform in order to encourage people to maintain a relationship with their relatives. The provided service includes two complementary modules. The first module is based on traditional computer-based communication means (such as chats or videoconferences). The second module's extends the first module's functionalities by providing intuitive tools for sharing information about the activity taking place and for extending its interaction capabilities.

The project aims to create a low-cost solution, which is technically feasible with the current state of technology. The Florence robot is wheel-based, of 1.5-m height and screen-based with no arms. Sensor input is based on a two-dimensional laser scanner, three-dimensional structured light (Kinect) and an (optical) camera. The robot software is based on the robotic operating system – the emerging *de facto* standard in robotic software. In addition, the project focuses on a scalable platform-based approach that enables the addition/extension of third party applications.

The objective of Florence is to investigate and find out the role that can be played by robots in improving the quality of life of older people and increasing efficiency in the care of this group. More specifically, the project has focused on creating a low-cost AAL services robotic platform that supports both AAL services themselves as well as daily life, as follows [FLO 16]:

– *Coaching*: giving information about specific activities, such as physical exercises and counseling on daily activities.

– *Social inclusion*: favoring user access to social networks and allowing the user to keep in contact with his/her social environment.

– *Safety*: using Florence as a supervisor in comfort or safety situations, supervision that will be controlled by the service providers or the elderly person themselves (crisis or emergency detection, smoke detection, personalized alarms, leakage of liquid or gases, etc.).

9.3.3. *PERSONA project*

The PERSONA project has developed an open, standard and scalable technological platform for supporting independent living that allows building a wide range of AAL services quickly and easily. It demonstrates these services in implementations with real users and, in this way, assessing the social impact in order to establish an appropriate business strategy for the future development of proposed technologies and services. This project represents progress in deploying the paradigm of ambient intelligence through the harmonization of technologies and concepts for daily AAL.

PERSONA is a project included in EU FP6 that started on January 2007 with the objective of developing a platform for the ubiquitous, instant and transparent access to services for the elderly and that allow them to stay as long as possible in their usual environment.

The main challenges of the PERSONA project are the following:

– find solutions and develop AAL services for social inclusion, early detection of risks, protection of the health and personal environment, and support in movement and mobility;

– develop a technological platform that allows transparent and natural access to the offered services;

– create psychologically pleasant and user-friendly environment for older people;

– demonstrate that the solutions created are affordable and sustainable for all stakeholders: older people in situations of dependency, welfare service systems and service providers in the hypothetical market for AAL, among others.

PERSONA aims to integrate all services related to the support of independent living in a continuous way in the place of residence, covering four broad categories of the needs of an aging population:

– social integration and sense of belonging to society: the project develops a multimedia environment able to communicate quickly and intuitively with relatives and friends, while promoting the user's membership in society, enabling him/her to serve the community and allowing the provision of external services through this system, such as telerehabilitation or medical teleconsulting;

– need for activities support of daily living: PERSONA intends to implement a service able to run the workflow of the person throughout the day or during specific times of the day in order to provide guidance, for example, reminders to take medication;

– need to feel safe and secure in their own home;

– need to support a person's mobility and help them feel confident when leaving home.

The PERSONA project focuses on increasing safety services for elderly people at home. Therefore, it provides a more independent and autonomous lifestyle in their own homes.

The PERSONA project publicly presented its final results on September 15, 2010. The information obtained about developed and pilot experiments, performed products, and services were discussed.

9.3.4. *KSERA project*

Knowledgeable SErvice Robots for Ageing (KSERA) is a small- or medium-scale research project focused on the EU FP7 about service robotics for aging well. The KSERA project started on February 1, 2010 and ran for 3 years, and finished on January 31, 2013. KSERA brought together seven partners from five different countries whose main aim was the development of a socially assistive robot (SAR) that helped older people, especially those with chronic obstructive pulmonary disease (COPD), with their daily activities and care needs, and provided the means for effective self-management of their disease [KSE 16].

By 2050, 37% of the European population will be over 60 years old and it is expected that there will be fewer than two people at working age per person of 65 or older, which will lead to both an increasing demand for care and a shortage of caregivers.

Aging people need support due to their declining capabilities but also due to age-related illnesses such as COPD, which typically manifests itself at a later age (from 40 years on). According to the World Health Organization, COPD will be the third major cause of death by 2030.

The condition of those people affected by COPD depends on their own physical condition, but also on environmental pollution, such as dust in the air, excessive humidity, or low air temperature, which can cause breathing problems. Assistive technology is developed for monitoring a user's physical conditions and superintending environmental quality and housing conditions. Then, it can warn, advise and support the elderly in hazardous or dangerous situations, enabling an improved self-management and a decreased number of hospitalizations.

Intelligent home environments are one of the key facets to counterbalance the reduced number of caretakers and increase the elderly's quality of life. In the KSERA project, the aim is to seamlessly integrate smart home technology with SARs. In this project, furthermore, the main research question is addressed on how to obtain a successful and effective interaction between the human and the mobile robot to guarantee acceptance and adoption of service robotic technologies by offering an added value to the existent ubiquitous monitoring services.

During the 3 years of the project, the partners of KSERA aimed to build three houses in which the capabilities of the smart home were shown and which possessed a robot to help COPD patients in their daily lives. The robot must follow the individual through the house, giving him/her useful suggestions and tips, learn his/her habits, watch him/her closely and call a medical doctor in case of a deterioration in his/her health. Smart homes must be comfortable spaces to live, as welcoming as possible, and not cold environments controlled by robots. The ideal technology thought to be achieved is the robot that is the contact point for all domestic systems. In order to achieve these objectives, the communication between robots and humans was studied aiming to facilitate as much as possible an understanding among both parties. To make the robot useful, it should understand the patient's desires, being intelligent, and the ability to anticipate his/her needs.

Special attention was placed on the ethical issues. For example, how the robot should act in case the patient lights a cigarette or the amount of information that the robot should transmit to the central operative system. It is important in order to set clear limits because the robot would measure and would continuously have access to the patient's private information.

9.3.5. *CompanionAble project*

CompanionAble is a project whose objective was to provide the synergy of robotics and ambient intelligence technologies and their semantics. This supports the cognitive stimulation and the therapy management of the care recipient, and it is mediated by a robotic companion (mobile facilitation) working collaboratively with a smart home environment. This project started in January 2008, running for 4 years, and finished in 2012.

There are widely acknowledged imperatives for helping the elderly to live at home (semi-)independently for as long as possible. Without cognitive stimulation support, the elderly who suffer dementia and depression can deteriorate rapidly and the caregivers would face an even more demanding task. Both groups are increasingly at the risk of social exclusion.

The aims of CompanionAble are the following [COM 16]:

– mobile companion robot plus a smart home automation;

– integration of personal therapy (using screens at home and a robot with remote supervision of care staff, physicians, gerontologists, etc.);

– maintaining contacts and social life between the older person and his/her caregivers, family and friends;

– improving the social inclusion and home care (such as drug management or activities agenda) for people with chronic cognitive impairment. Figure 9.3 shows the user interface created.

Figure 9.3. *CompanionAble user interface*

The CompanionAble project focused on the social inclusion and homecare issues for an aging-dependent population suffering chronic cognitive impairment, a prevalent condition among older people. CompanionAble focused its efforts on care receptors with mild cognitive impairment (MCI), in the sense of stopping its progress, and also for those elderly and disabled people with a potential risk of suffering MCI in order to prevent it. People with very advanced deterioration that are no longer aware of what happens to them are explicitly excluded from the target population, mainly due to ethical reasons and risks that cannot be estimated reliably. In addition, generally, people with a high grade of impairment no longer live at their home for various reasons, starting with the risk of causing accidents (for example, forgetting to turn off the oven) and ending with the great need to be under direct supervision 24 hours a day. Therefore, the main objective of the project of enabling people to stay in their home for as long as possible time is not valid for this group but for the group described above.

CompanionAble provides the synergy of Robotic and Ambient Intelligence technologies and their semantic integration to provide for a caregiver's assistive environment. This supports the cognitive stimulation and therapy management of the care recipient and is mediated by a robotic companion (mobile facilitation) working collaboratively with a smart home environment (stationary facilitation).

The distinguishing advantages of the CompanionAble Framework Architecture arise from the objective of graceful, scalable and cost-effective integration. Therefore, Companion Able addresses the issues of social inclusion and homecare of persons suffering from chronic cognitive disabilities, prevalent among the increasing aging European population. A participative and inclusive co-design and scenario validation approach drove the efforts made in

CompanionAble, involving care recipients and their close caregivers as well as the wider stakeholders. This is to ensure end-to-end systemic viability, flexibility, modularity and affordability as well as a focus on overall care support governance and integration with quality of experience issues, such as dignity–privacy–security preserving responsibilities fully considered [COM 16].

A unique feature of the CompanionAble project is the synergistic combination of a robotic humanoid companion potential in home automation. It has the advantages of a fixed smart home; as in the typical care scenarios, the exclusive use of a mobile robot on the one hand or a smart home on the other hand cannot carry out all the tasks demanded. The positive effects of both individual solutions are combined to show how the synergies between the solution of a smart house and a mobile robotic humanoid companion can achieve a significant improvement in the interaction between the caregiver and the care receiver with the help system, as it is expected that the sum of both issues is greater than its parts. The combination of the robot mobility and interactions adapted to the user (for example by cognitive recognition) brings more benefits to the older person through his/her cognitive stimulation. Moreover, the flexibility to provide cognitive stimulation at any area of the house is an important benefit and an impact on the person suffering loneliness. CompanionAble complements the home automation because of its ability to perform a continuous and integrated monitoring to detect emergency situations.

They began establishing technical requirements to facilitate care through ICT and therapeutic management, determining the necessary technologies for the user multimodal observation, and the human–robot interaction that provide the foundations for the development of a fixed system, smart home and mobile robot system. This user support is given because of research activities focused on an architectural framework that allows the solving of a complex care scenario. Once the scenario of the smart house and the robot was raised, experimental studies were carried out to evaluate its effectiveness. Through the results obtained, the weaknesses and strengths of this project were evaluated. This was the starting point for developing the concept of a complete care scenario, integrating home automation and the robot for people with MCI, the main objective of the CompanionAble project.

The robot was named Hector and it holds a touch screen with menu options, eyes or an avatar that shows the emotion of the robot to achieve greater empathy with the user; a rear tray to carry small items; and a set of electronics, sensors and engines to obtain the correct performance.

CompanionAble was evaluated at a number of testbed experiments representing a diverse European user base as the proving ground for its socio–technical–ethical validation.

9.3.6. *UniversAAL project*

The UniversAAL sets as its objective to produce an open platform that provides a standardized approach making it technically feasible and economically viable to develop AAL solutions. It started in February 2010 and lasted for 4 years, ending in 2014.

As Europe's population ages, the necessary care for the increasing number of elderly people and the large workforce this will require is not affordable. For this reason, there is a huge potential market for AAL solutions. However, these solutions are not widespread because they require many resources to be deployed. To solve this problem, UniversAAL created an open platform to offer a standardized method that makes it technically feasible and economically viable to develop AAL solutions.

The potential benefits of AAL solutions are already clearly recognized, and societal trends indicate that they are attractive to a large and increasing number of people. But uptakes of such solutions has so far been limited. UniversAAL aims to reduce barriers to adoption and promote the development and widespread uptake of innovative AAL solutions. It benefits end users (for instance elderly people and people with disabilities, their caregivers and relatives) by making new solutions affordable, simple to configure, personalize and deploy, and it also benefits solution providers by making it easier and cheaper to create innovative new AAL services or adapt existing ones using a compositional approach based on existing components, services and external systems.

UniversAAL aimed to produce an open platform that provided a standardized approach, making it technically feasible and economically viable to develop AAL solutions. The platform was produced by a mixture of new developments and consolidation of the state-of-the art results from available initiatives [UNI 16].

The main objective of the project was to make it feasible and viable to conceive, design and deploy new innovative AAL services. To do this, a platform that provided the necessary technical support and acted as an open solution, common basis for both developers and end users, was produced, and support activities promoting widespread acceptance and adoption of the platform were carried out, activities that formed an integral part of the project and started at an early stage. The detailed objectives of UniversAAL are the following [UNI 16]:

– design and establish a uStore. Inspired by Apple's "App Store" concept, the uStore will provide a one-stop-shop for UniversAAL end users services;

– design and establish the universAAL developer depot;

– consolidate existing work and integrate with new developments;

– devise a technical strategy for achieving interoperability among universAAL platform elements;

– design the platform to be open, and allow interoperability with existing systems and with other domains;

– extend the range of actors involved in creating and operating AAL solutions;

– actively promote widespread adoption of the UniversAAL approach and platform;

– demonstrate the practical usefulness of the approach using a set of proof-of-concept scenarios.

UniversAAL project primary users are software developers whose business is to create AAL services and applications. This project offers them a standardized platform for the creation of such services and resources to facilitate that development [UNI 16]. The second group of users of the UniversAAL results consists of the people who will use the AAL solutions derived of this project: aging people as well as their relatives who are directly or indirectly involved in their care.

This section has described important EU projects showing examples of recent real technology deployments of AAL solutions that may impact elderly people's daily life in the near future.

9.4. Conclusion

Ambient assisted living (AAL) delivers IT solutions that aim to facilitate and improve the lives of disabled, elderly and chronically ill people, reducing the burden of their caregivers. In recent years, several projects have been created; systems, applications and services that are easy to use by aging people and healthcare professionals.

This chapter presented several projects on AAL funded by the AAL Joint Programme and the major topics encompassed by this programme. The most important EU projects were considered and described. It included examples of real technology deployments of AAL solutions. These projects and their results have had a major impact on elderly people and typical healthcare institutions.

10

Social Networks on Healthcare

10.1. Introduction

An online social network is a relatively new type of virtual community that is designed to allow members to build relationships with other adherents of their community [PRE 05, BØR 13]. Engagement in social media and online communities can enhance communication, facilitate social interaction and help to develop technical skills [ROD 11, MAR 14, XIA 14].

Social networks have already been used for the prevention, diagnosis and treatment of several diseases or conditions. Some of these social networks been used for quitting smoking [STR 12, VAN 12] or for peer support in cancer patients [SET 11, VAL 13], reducing depression, therapies for different types of cancer, etc.

Little is known about the use of social network websites for healthcare purposes. Keelan *et al.* [KEE 10] examined the use of Youtube videos and Myspace blogs as resources for finding information about immunization. Farmer *et al.* [FAR 09] showed that Facebook is providing an accessible portal for healthcare professionals and patients in order to share their experiences of diagnosis, management of the disease and research.

In the medical context, the World Health Organization (WHO) estimates that about 3% of the global population suffers from depression. This disease is probably the most common psychological disorder and that which receives most attention [WHO 07, WHO 10, WHO 12]. Other important diseases are Alzheimer's, dementia and Parkinson's. For example, Alzheimer's is a form of dementia that gradually worsens over time and affects memory. According to the WHO, about 24 million people suffer from Alzheimer's disease and these numbers are increasing due to the continuous aging of the population [GLU 04, BOU 03]. Parkinson's disease is a degenerative disorder of the central nervous system. The Parkinson's Disease Foundation estimates that 7–10 million people worldwide are living with Parkinson's disease [OUT 11, PAR 16]. Dementia is the loss of mental functions such as thinking, memory and reasoning. 35.6 million people were estimated to be living with dementia in 2011, according to the WHO, with 7.7 million new cases each year [PAR 16, PRE 05].

Colorectal cancer is an important disease given its severity and because it affects so many people. Some social groups related to colorectal cancer aim to raise awareness for people suffering from this disease, providing them links to news about the disease, diagnoses, etc. [DE 12a, DE 12b]. Breast cancer is the most common type of cancer in women and the second leading cause of death by cancer [SHA 00, GUS 01, GUS 05, ROD 12]. Diabetes is a chronic illness that consists of a group of metabolic disorders that affect different organs and tissues. It increases the blood glucose level. Diabetes and its complications are major causes of morbidity and mortality around the world [BAR 13, COW 09, BUI 11].

This chapter presents a content analysis of Facebook and Twitter groups related to different diseases and disorders such as depression, dementia, Alzheimer's and Parkinson's, diabetes, and colorrectal and breast cancer. We can note that there are already many social networks in medicine, such as Biomedexperts (http://www.biomedexperts.com), Hermes Cloud (https://twitter.com/hermescloud), Curetogether (https://twitter.com/CureTogether), Healthmap (http://www.healthmap.org), amongst others. In this case, the present analysis mainly adresses the issues of different social groups on Facebook and Twitter for the above-mentioned diseases.

10.2. Examples of social networks for different diseases

10.2.1. *Mental and neurodegenerative diseases on Facebook and Twitter*

First, a search is performed on Facebook (www.facebook.com) and Twitter (www.twitter.com) because they are the two most popular social networking websites. The search engine provided by these platforms was used. The keywords employed were as follows: "depression", "dementia", "Alzheimer" and "Parkinson". This study incorporates all types of Facebook and Twitter groups. Table 10.1 presents the main results with respect to the number of groups by disease and the number of members on Facebook and on Twitter in January 2013 [MAR 14]. Another search was completed in March 2015 and the results are similar regarding the percentages obtained.

In the following figures, the different uses of the mental and neurodegenerative groups on both Facebook and

Twitter are shown. Figures 10.1 and 10.2 display the main uses of the groups for depression on Facebook and Twitter.

	Facebook		Twitter	
Disease	No. of groups	No. of members	No. of groups	No. of followers
Depression	504	60,078	623	683,820
Parkinson	257	25,245	100	212,718
Dementia	226	12,455	99	123,968
Alzheimer	416	42,045	437	107,696
Total	1,403	139,823	1,259	1,128,202

Table 10.1. *Summary of results: number of groups and members/disease*

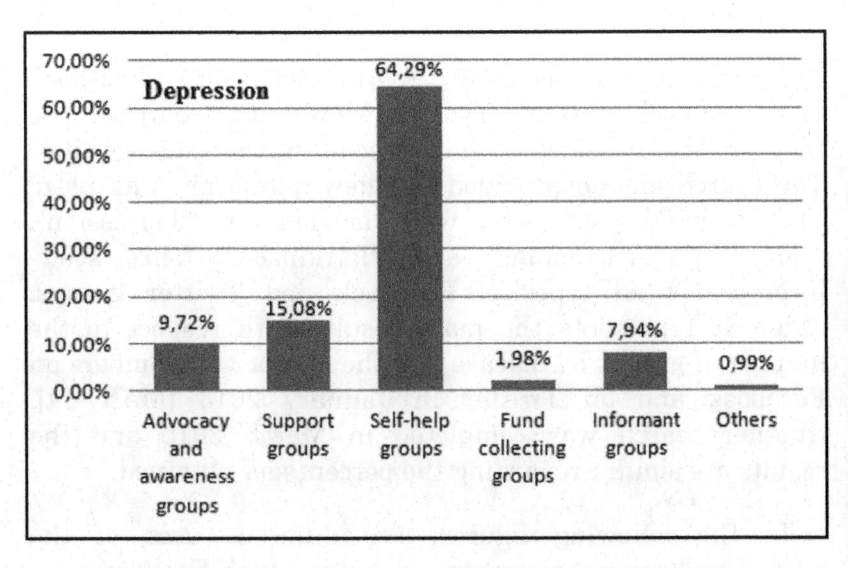

Figure 10.1. *Main issues of the Facebook groups for depression*

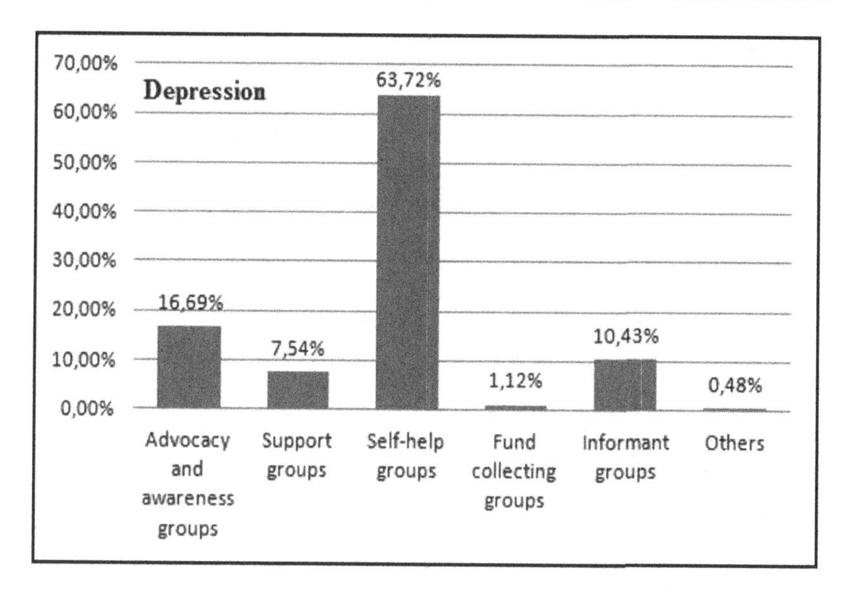

Figure 10.2. *Main issues of the Twitter groups for depression*

The majority of Facebook groups for depression are self-help groups (64.29%). With this illness, self-help groups have high relevance due to the characteristics of patients with depression. Moreover, 15.08% are groups created for supporting people affected by depression. In a similar way, on Twitter, the majority of groups are for self-help (with a percentage of 63.72%).

Regarding Parkinson's disease, Figure 10.3 shows the main objectives of the groups found on Facebook, and Figure 10.4 presents the corresponding results on Twitter.

The main group on Facebook is the "self-help" group (28.02%), a group where all members share a common problem: Parkinson's disease. On Twitter, the aim of some groups is support (around 31%). There is a diversity of organizations that offer support groups for patients, their family members and friends. Figures 10.5 and 10.6 show the main uses of the dementia groups on Facebook and Twitter, respectively.

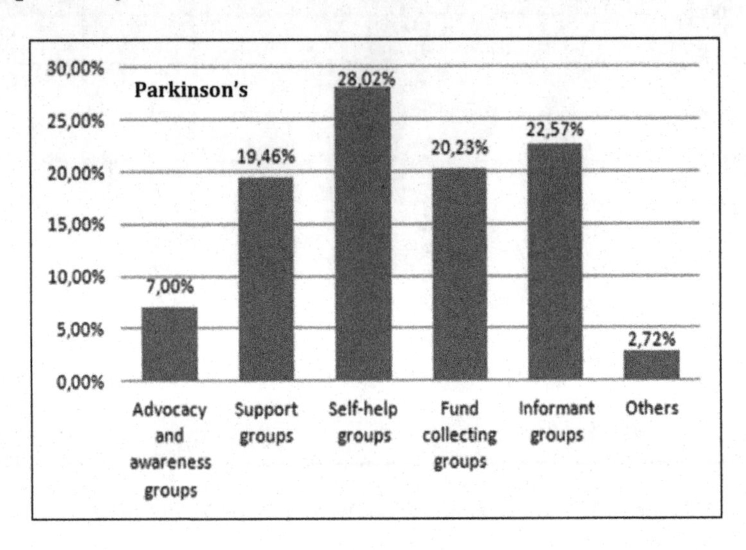

Figure 10.3. *Main issues of the Facebook groups for Parkinson's*

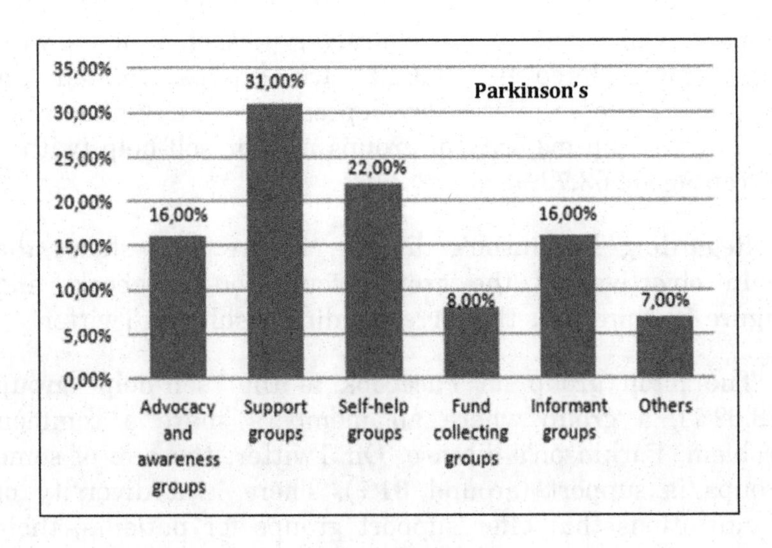

Figure 10.4. *Main issues of the Twitter for Parkinson's*

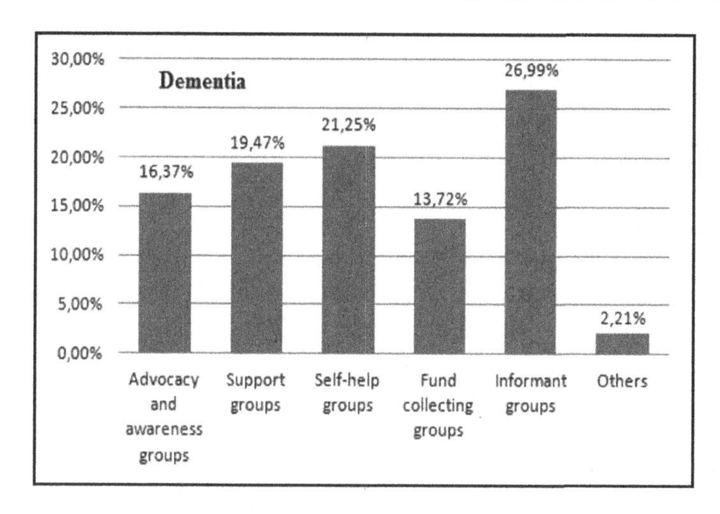

Figure 10.5. *Main issues of the Facebook groups for dementia*

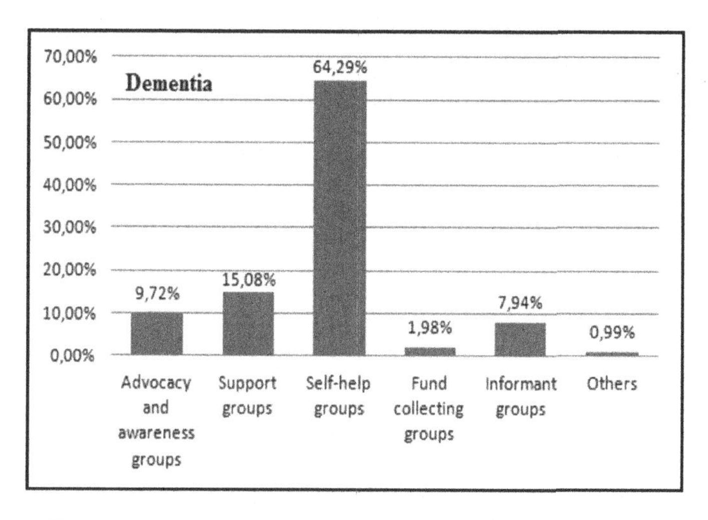

Figure 10.6. *Main issues of the Twitter groups for dementia*

The main practice of Facebook concerning dementia is to inform people about this disease (26.99%); 21.25% of groups are for self-help whereas 19.47% have the aim of supporting patients and their relatives. The objective of 64.29% of the studied groups on Twitter is self-help, while around 15% are committed to supporting patients and relatives who are fighting against the disease. Figure 10.7 shows the main uses of the Alzheimer's groups on Facebook. Figure 10.8 presents their uses on Twitter.

The main use of Facebook concerning Alzheimer's is informing people about this disease (39.90%). The goal of 20.67% of the groups is fundraising in order to continue the investigation into this illness. On Twitter, the groups mainly aim to support families, caregivers and patients (43.25%).

10.2.2. *Cancer and diabetes on Facebook and Twitter*

A search on Facebook and Twitter using the terms "colorectal cancer", "breast cancer" and "diabetes" has been performed. Figure 10.9 shows the main objectives of the groups found on Facebook and Twitter for colorectal cancer. The aim of some groups is disease awareness, i.e. to make people realize that these illnesses do not distinguish between race or social position.

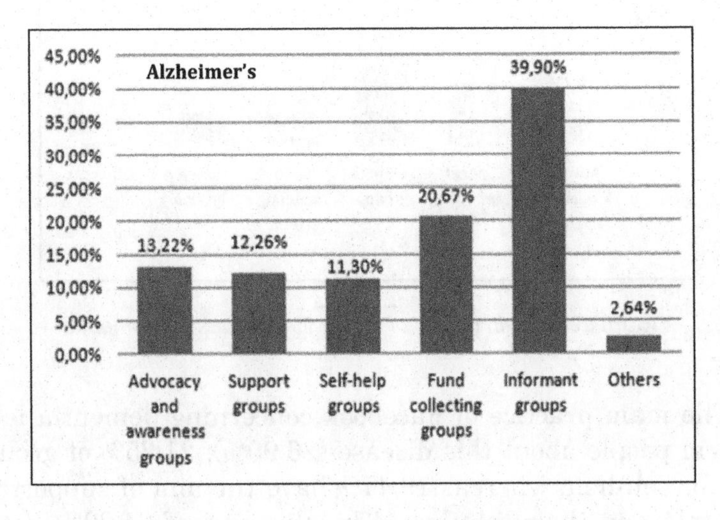

Figure 10.7. *Main issues of the Facebook groups for Alzheimer's*

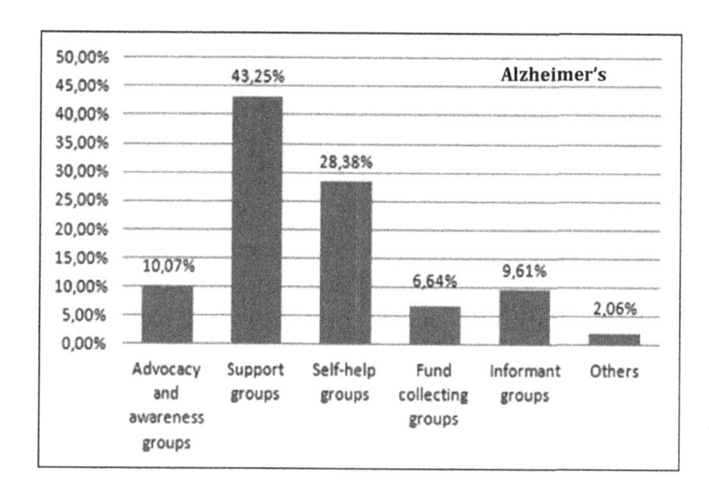

Figure 10.8. *Main issues of the Twitter groups for Alzheimer's*

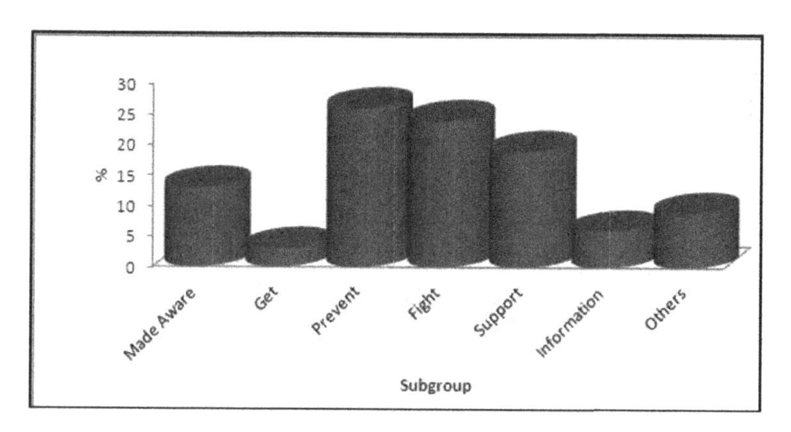

Figure 10.9. *Main issues of Facebook and Twitter groups for colorectal cancer*

The goal of 12.79% of the studied groups is disease awareness, while 3.48% of these groups aim to raise money. 25.58% of the users forming part of these groups cite disease prevention as their main objective.

Figure 10.10 shows the main purposes of breast cancer groups. The main use of social networks concerning breast cancer is disease prevention. Around 34% of the users of these groups are involved in social networks to encourage people to be periodically examined for breast cancer prevention.

Figure 10.11 shows the different purposes of the groups dedicated to diabetes. The main use of social networks for diabetes is the investigation of the illness since 25.09% of the users are involved in social networks for supporting the investigation into finding a cure for the disease.

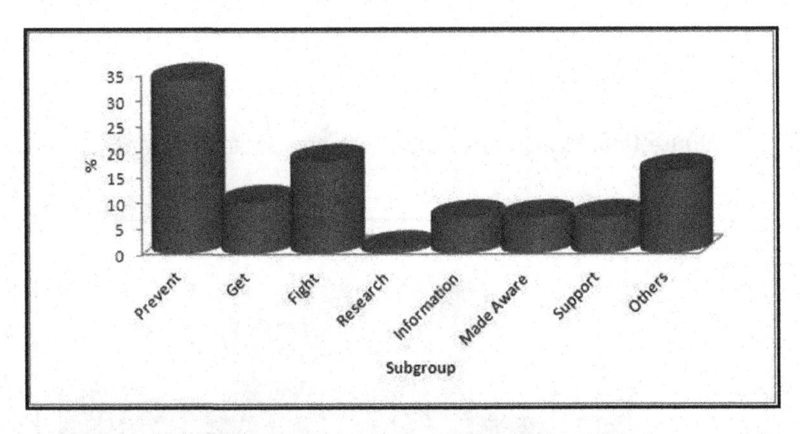

Figure 10.10. *Main issues of Facebook and Twitter groups for breast cancer*

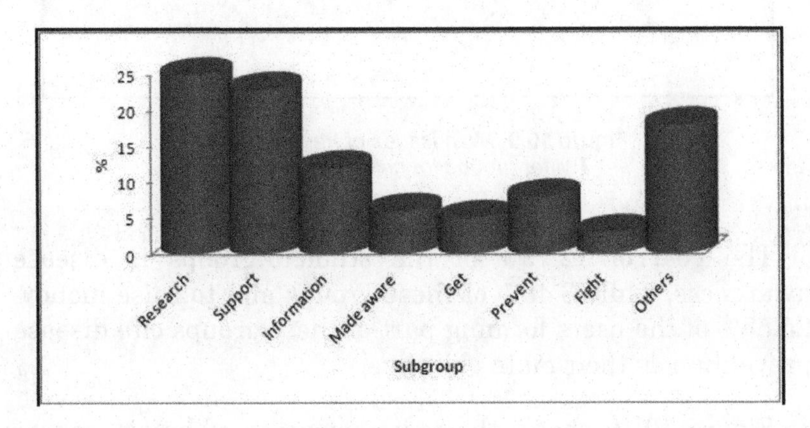

Figure 10.11. *Main issues of Facebook and Twitter groups for diabetes*

10.3. Conclusions

Social networking websites are convenient way to exchange information and support people who are in similar situations. They are also used for health reasons both by survivors and those who suffer from significant illnesses. Social networks are one of the most powerful concepts for analyzing social reality. Through social network analysis, users can know how people acquire information and resources, how information flows through social ties and also how divisions and coalitions operate.

In this chapter, the following five main types of groups have been found for mental and neurodegenerative diseases: support groups, informative groups, self-help groups, advocacy and awareness groups and fundraising groups. Taking into account the results shown, the most common groups in all the studied diseases are self-help groups and the least common are the fundraising groups. Moreover, for colorectal cancer, the greatest percentage is showed in the prevention, in the same way as breast cancer, while diabetes groups are more focused on research.

There are many groups related to diabetes. This is because diabetes is a chronic disease that affects people of all ages, while breast cancer and colorectal cancer are diseases usually only adults suffer from. Concerning colorectal and breast cancer, there is a higher number of groups for breast cancer than colorectal cancer because breast cancer is a disease that can be cured if it is detected in time.

11

Cloud Computing on e-Health

11.1. Introduction

Cloud computing is a new paradigm that is changing the way institutions, enterprises, organizations and people perceive and employ different software systems. Using cloud-based solutions, organizations have neither the need to host their software, nor maintain their own servers. Cloud computing is defined as a model that conveniently allows network access on demand to a shared set of configurable resources that can be rapidly provisioned and released with minimal management efforts or interaction with a service provider. The National Institute of Standards and Technology defines cloud computing as "... a model for enabling convenient network demand on-access to shared network resources (networks, servers, storage, applications and services), that can be rapidly provisioned and released with minimal management effort or service provider interaction".

Cloud-based solutions can be also applied to e-Health services and applications. Using a cloud solution, medical data may be hosted on the cloud and their clients (such as computers, smartphones and other devices – operating systems and Web browsers) will be able to access data with just an Internet connection. Moreover, the access to the Internet almost everywhere enables accessing all the stored medical information from any device, such as desktop computers, laptops, tablets and smartphones, since they have an Internet connection. Cloud computing is still a technology under development, which means that in the near future, the services offered will be greater. The cloud e-Health paradigm presents some barriers that must be overcome, like security and patient awareness.

Cloud computing is usually associated with computing on demand, software as a service (SaaS) and computer networks. Currently, in the fields of on-demand computing and SaaS there are two ways for providers to offer a cloud computing service while grid computing is simply a technology to deploy cloud computing. Regarding the history of the term cloud, it is attributed to the world of telecommunications, when telecom companies began offering virtual private networks with the same quality as conventional networks and lower cost solutions. The term cloud computing or, simply, cloud can be attributed to a datacenter where resources are available.

Using the cloud in order to deploy e-Health services will improve the quality of service (QoS) offered to patients. With cloud computing, a third company provides the storage and the corresponding system management and maintenance on its servers. Users can thus obtain their resources and data from the network, accessing the required information from the cloud.

In this chapter, concepts of cloud computing and its integration in e-Health are explained. Moreover, the benefits, constraints, issues and requisites of an e-Health system deployed on the cloud are analyzed. Some examples of cloud-based solutions for e-Health services will be cited in order to show that many health organizations hire these solutions to improve the services they provide to their patients and the efficiency of their workers. Several scientific publications about the deployment of cloud-based e-Health services were collected and analyzed, mainly from Med Line. Moving an e-Health system to the cloud may represent a great step forward in the digitalization of medical data. Advantages such as scalability, the economic model of pay-per-use and involving the patient as an active part of the health information management process may assume a change in the e-Health systems implementation model. Several requirements must be taken into account when medical data is uploaded to the cloud. Among those requirements, security and privacy are key issues that must be considered.

11.2. Cloud computing

Cloud computing is not exactly a new technology, but rather a combination of several technologies that, when used in a certain way, can provide different types of services that will be described below. First, in order to understand this new technology, it is interesting to know that cloud computing represents a radical change in storage and electronic resource management. With this new cloud computing approach, instead of data being stored in private servers, the customer hires a third company which provides the storage for their data [FUR 10]. This company will also provide to their clients the maintenance of the servers and access to their data. So now the resources and data will be obtained from the global network – the Internet. With this new method, the clients hire just the services they need, enabling economical savings for the management of their electronic resources. Cloud computing is based on a layered architecture depending on the services and functionalities offered by each layer [COL 11].

Cloud computing architecture is based on a front-end platform (thin client, fat client or mobile device), back-end platforms (servers, storage capacity) a cloud-based delivery and a network (Internet, Intranet, Intercloud). It follows an approach where everything is consumed or offered as a service at the different layers of the cloud architecture. Thus, Figure 11.1 illustrates the following four layers of this architecture: software as a service (SaaS), infrastructure as a service (IaaS), platform as a service (PaaS) and data storage as a service (dSaaS).

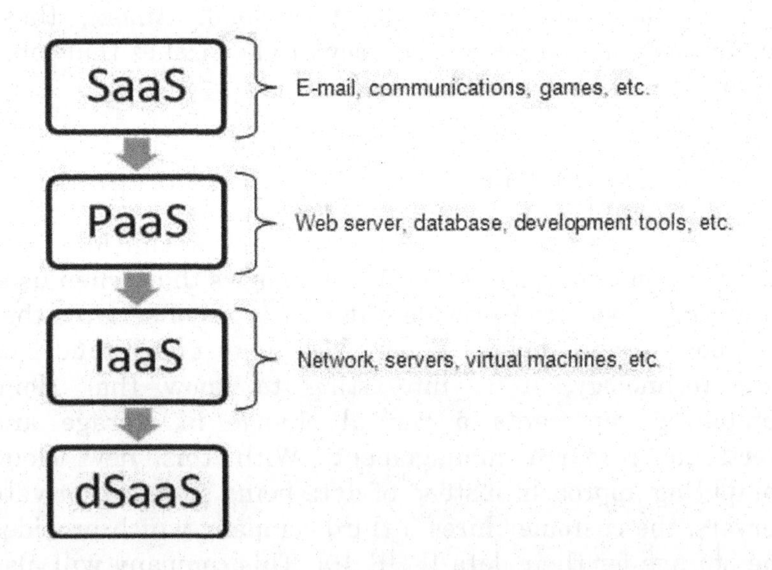

Figure 11.1. *Illustration of cloud computing architecture*

SaaS: this layer is on top of the cloud computing's architecture stack. This layer allows the user to run applications remotely from the cloud. It is a model of software distribution where the software and data handled are hosted on the servers of an information and communication technologies (ICT) company, which is accessed by clients through the Internet.

Running these applications remotely from the cloud, the necessity of having any software installed on personal computers can be avoided. With just an Internet connection, users are able to manage and handle their electronic resources. This provides a great advantage because the user can access their resources from any computer. This also provides mobility because the clients can manage their data.

IaaS: this layer provides storage and computation resources as a service. In this case, hospitals do not need to host their own private servers to store and handle data. This layer includes virtualized computers with guaranteed processing power and reserved bandwidth for storage, allowing access via Internet.

PaaS: this layer is placed immediately below the *IaaS* layer. It is based on the same concept but applied to hardware instead of an application. The *PaaS* layer adds to the *IaaS* an operating system and services for apps which are run using the cloud. In the PaaS models, cloud providers deliver a platform, including an operating system, a programming language execution environment, a database and a Web server. It also includes security and data recovery mechanisms, providing a scalable system flexible to the users' needs, so that *PaaS* is like an *IaaS* with a custom software stack for a given application.

dSaaS: the low layer of the stack is the server itself. This layer provides the hired storage services and the required bandwidth to access the resources.

For further understanding of this concept of cloud computing, the different kinds of clouds where users can host their resources will be explained below. This sorting depends on the "owner" of the cloud. There are three kinds of clouds depending on the property of the network where they are supported, as follows:

– *Private cloud*: this concept refers to cloud computing on private networks. It is a cloud infrastructure operated solely for a single organization. This type of cloud is built for the exclusive use of one client. This client will have full control over data, security and QoS. This type of cloud is also called an external cloud. In this kind of cloud, the above-mentioned problem about the security of users' resources does not exist, because the client is the only one who can access these resources. However, this sort of cloud computing is more expensive, because an enterprise is hired to develop an infrastructure which will be only used by one client, so the customer assumes the entire cost.

– *Public cloud*: in this type of cloud computing, resources are dynamically provided over the Internet via Web applications from a third-party provider. In this case, services are rendered over an open network for public use. This cloud is also called an "external cloud". This provider stores the resources of all of its clients on its servers. This type of cloud is the least secure since the resources are stored in the servers of another company (the provider). This means that if there are sensible or confidential resources being stored, the client must have total confidence in the third-party company that is storing their data. Some examples of a *public cloud* are the services provided by Amazon Web Services, Google App Engine or Microsoft Azure.

– *Hybrid cloud*: an intermediate solution for the above-mentioned approaches. The development of these hybrid clouds is based on the application of the public and private cloud. Therefore, a hybrid cloud is an alternative for a company which does not want to make an important initial inversion but has sensitive data that must be protected. In this model, sensitive and confidential data are hosted in the private cloud and the remaining resources are placed in the public one. Figure 11.2 illustrates the three types of clouds.

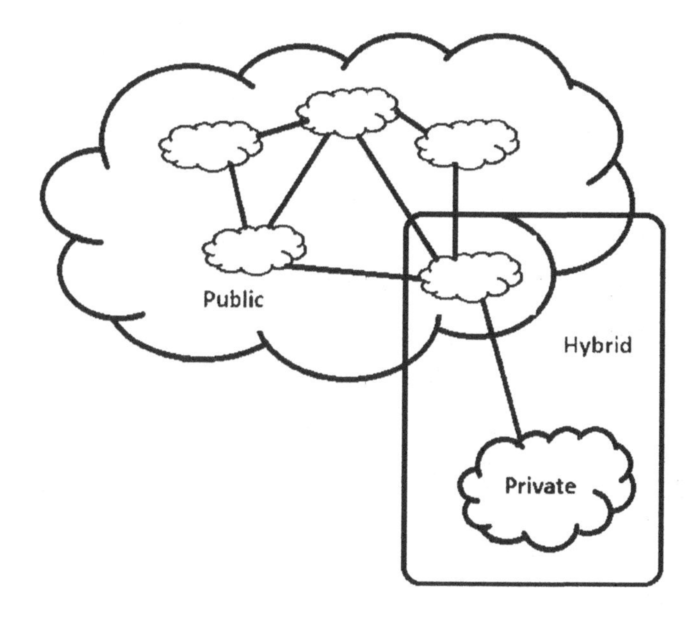

Figure 11.2. *Illustration of the three types of clouds*

A set of clouds provides a large amount of distributed computing resources, such as processors, memory, bandwidth and storage, which can be organized according to demand, growing or declining in real time.

The word cloud therefore refers to two concepts:

– *Abstract*: cloud computing removes the implementation details of the system users and developers. Applications are run on unspecified physical media, data are stored in unknown locations, management is outsourced to the service provider and access by users is extended.

– *Virtualization*: cloud computing virtualizes gathering and sharing resource systems. Storage systems are adapted to the demands made of them by users, so that resources can scale with great agility.

Cloud computing is an abstraction based on the notion of gathering physical resources and presenting them as a virtual resource. It is a new model of providing resources to improve access to applications and platforms independent of user services. The clouds may be classified as different types, and the services and applications running on clouds may or may not be provided by a cloud provider. These different types and levels of cloud services means that it is important to define the type of system being dealt with. Some available commercial examples include:

– *Google*: Google has an extensive network of data centers to serve their search engine. With this, it achieved a significant amount using advertising revenue and now offers free software to users based on that infrastructure. Google has changed the market for software to users, and is a clear example of SaaS that will be discussed later.

– *Windows Azure*: Microsoft owns the Azure platform, which allows NET Framework applications run over the Internet as an alternative to Microsoft software scheduler running on desktop platform. It is an example of PaaS.

– *Amazon Web Services*: one of the most successful businesses based on the Amazon Web Services cloud is an IaaS offering that allows users to rent virtual computers in Amazon's own infrastructure. It is an IaaS.

These new services enable cost savings and implementation at a minimum expense, as well as being scalable and always available from any geographical location.

Cloud computing requires certain protocols to communicate with other related layers of software, hardware and customers. Many of these protocols and the Internet provides a commonly used set of technologies, as follows: XML messaging is used as the format, Simple Object Access Protocol as the object model, and a set of protocols for discovery and description based on Web Services Description Language used to manage transactions.

A cloud can be created within the infrastructure of an organization or outsourced to another data center. Although resources in a cloud can be physical, more commonly they are virtualized because they are easier to modify and optimize. Virtualized cloud storage is required to support placement and data storage. From a user perspective, it is important that resources appear to be scalable to (almost) infinity, that the service can be measured and the price may be controlled by a timer.

11.3. Cloud computing and e-Health systems

This section studies the requisites, issues, benefits and constraints that a cloud solution can provide to clients in an e-Health system. Moreover, some examples of running e-Health solutions with cloud computing in several hospitals around the world are presented.

With the proliferation of cloud computing technologies, there has been a huge migration of healthcare services to the cloud. This migration of typical and centralized health solutions to the cloud model offers great efficiency in managing medical health records and reduces costs effectively [CHO 11, ABU 12, ZHO 15].

In July 2011, London's Chelsea and Westminster Hospital set a cloud computing system to manage and store their electronic health records (EHRs) system. With this system, patients have full control over who has access to their health records [HIL 08,YEL 08].

In Italy, the Hospital of Bambino Gesú (famous for being one of the largest research and treatment centers around the world in the field of pediatrics) is using cloud-based services. In Spain, the "Plan Avanza" initiated some projects like the application of cloud computing to radiotherapy treatments. Some American non-profit health organizations are using cloud computing solutions to provide patient access to medical records.

It is important to emphasize the change in mindset that this new way of using technology brings about and that those cloud-based solutions maximize all available resources to the users. It is important to consider that, depending on the agency responsible for the deployment of a cloud infrastructure, the health organization should look for the most realistic solution. Use of the cloud supposes a change in scenario and both cloud providers and health organizations must take into account the risks of this new way to host data, and try to overcome them. Consideration of the requisites, issues, benefits and constraints of this method are described in the following.

11.3.1. *Requisites*

To deploy a cloud-based e-Health system, several requirements should be fulfilled:

– *Bandwidth Internet connection*: this is an essential requirement to deploy any type of cloud-based solution. Without such a connection, medical staff would not be able to access the resources and services provided by a cloud supplier. So in order to work in a fast and a reliable way over the cloud, a broadband Internet connection is mandatory.

– *Standardized information*: for example, in an EHR system, records must be ruled by the international standards adopted in order to integrate them into the cloud [GAN 06, GUR 04]. This fact is relevant because if physicians need to share their electronic records with another healthcare center or medical staff, this is one of the main advantages provided by cloud computing [LO 07].

– *Management e-Health system or Web-based or mobile development*: it will be necessary to develop and deploy a Web application or mobile app to manage, view or update the system. There are some cloud computing providers that just allow users to work with predefined applications, such as *Google Apps*. However, there are also providers like *Amazon Web Services* that develop applications based on their cloud system to manage any type of solution regardless of the framework.

– *Server customization by the cloud provider*: many cloud computing providers offer their clients the same services regardless of their framework, offering customized options.

11.3.2. *Issues*

There are some issues that a cloud-based system can offer to the clients in order to improve an e-Health system. The most relevant issues to consider are the following:

– *Cloud computing as an evolution of e-Health systems*: The migration of e-Health systems to the cloud represents the next step after the conversion of medical records to an electronic format. With a cloud-based solution, patients and physicians can gain more advantages and better income from those digital files.

– *Improving communication with patients*: the idea of deploying a cloud solution on an e-Health system enables the patients to access their medical data. This technology allows the construction of Web platforms like forums or private messaging systems to improve communication between patients and physicians. This advance provides a faster way to contact a physician in order to solve patients' doubts, potentially avoiding unnecessary medical appointments.

– *Connecting different health care centers*: through cloud e-Health systems, data will be shared in an effective and quick way. This means that small primary care centers and hospitals deploying the same cloud solution will be able to create networks of health information exchange, giving the medical staff the chance to share their patients' medical records with other medical specialists from other centers in order to consult about their patients' treatments. So, this change will speed up many of the queries between different physicians of each healthcare center, improving the service offered to their patients. This health information network will be more important in the case of rural primary care centers in which this external support is more necessary than in a large hospital.

– *Providing medical staff a large number of services to improve the QoS*: the design of cloud computing has as its main purpose the improvement of care received by patients, by providing to medical staff a number of tools to support them in this aim. This improvement in the QoS is the result of all the benefits offered by a cloud solution [FER 12].

11.3.3. *Benefits*

Cloud computing can provide different advantages to an e-Health system, as follows:

– *Scalability and flexibility*: because of the virtualization concept (creation of virtual version), cloud computing systems can be adapted to the amount of data required by users [PIE 11]. So, due to this issue, both hospitals and primary care centers will hire a third company provider of a cloud solution to provide them with only the services they need. This third party provides resources and services for users on-demand. If, after a certain period of time, the number of patients increases, healthcare organizations simply contact their cloud computing provider to increase the hired services and adapt the system in order to manage more medical records. Without a cloud solution, before deploying the system, an estimation of the future number of patients being handled by the center would be required. If the estimation failed, the health center would have to increase the number of servers, which means a large economic cost.

With cloud computing, the greatest utilization of available resources is guaranteed, unlike if the medical center had its own servers installed, thus initially operating below peak performance. Therefore, the scalability and flexibility offered by cloud computing are considered to be an economic benefit for an e-Health system [FER 12].

– *Economic savings*: as seen in the advantages discussed earlier, the adaptive capacity offered by cloud computing results in savings, in economic terms, for the healthcare system. Moreover, it is important to mention that the use of cloud computing avoids a large initial investment in infrastructure, which is impossible to face for some healthcare organizations.

– *Increased efficiency*: with the deployment of this system, the efficiency of medical personnel will increase, since with a cloud solution medical staff will work in a quick and effective way. Health system waiting lists could thus be reduced and a better service for patients (clients) will be offered, increasing the organization productivity. This saving gives them the chance of being more ambitious in order to develop and deploy new systems, because if those systems do not work as expected, they just must contact the cloud computing provider and cancel these services [ROD 13].

– Cloud computing also enables savings in terms of management and maintenance. With all the resources stored in the cloud, hospitals do not have to hire maintenance staff to take care of the servers. The cloud provider is responsible for system management and maintenance. This maintenance includes software upgrades and database migrations performed by the cloud provider. So, with the cloud, the client only needs to maintain a sufficient bandwidth connection to the Internet in order to access the resources. This service provider is also directly responsible for any failures on the client servers, and thus for solving these problems.

– *Ease of use and wide availability*: deploying cloud computing on e-Health systems means accessing those records only with just an Internet connection and a credential. The number of mobile devices that are connected to the Internet is increasing, so the opportunities that cloud services offer, in terms of availability at any time and any place, are enormous.

Authorized medical staff can access their patients' data anywhere with an Internet connection. Web applications thus play a key role in cloud computing in order to provide straightforward access to medical records from any mobile device with an Internet connection. These Web applications must be functional, so medical staff can easily become familiar with them to access e-Health systems in a simple way, even with their smartphones. Then, a physician will be able to query and even update their patient's e-Health systems quickly and easily from any place and at any time [FER 12].

As mentioned earlier, resource storage in the cloud offers high mobility and global access. Despite these advantages, there are also several barriers and constraints to storing patients' medical records using cloud computing.

11.4.4. *Constraints*

Four barriers that may compromise the deployment of a cloud solution to an e-Health system are identified:

– *Confidence in the cloud provider*: the outsourcing of the resources to another third company requires client to have consider in the cloud provider. Medical records contain private and sensitive patient data, so it is important to guarantee the confidentiality of such data, since it is a third company that manages that information.

– *Development of a legal framework and collaboration with legal organizations*: the use of private resources must be unique to the customer (in this case, the healthcare organization) and the patient itself. Due to this fact, cloud computing providers must abide by the personal data protection laws in order to guarantee the patient's privacy. Moreover, all operations and management involving the resources must be transparent to the legal organization responsible for data protection, to avoid improper use of data by the provider.

Another problem that must be covered by legal mechanisms is the possibility of dissolving a cloud provider. In this case, these cloud providers must be forced to offer their customers a range of options and guarantees for migration of their data to another cloud service provider [SVA 10].

– *Data security*: security is essential when a health organization is looking to deploy a cloud solution for an e-Health system. A cloud company must guarantee the privacy of their customers' resources in order to avoid any unauthorized person (or organization) illegally accessing the cloud company's servers. The provider must also maintain the customer's data confidentiality, and must guarantee the security of patients' data by deploying the necessary security mechanisms in its cloud infrastructure. Transmission and network secure protocols must be deployed in order to avoid external attacks to the data. Some of the secure protocols in use are Internet Protocol Security, Secure Shell, Transport Layer Security and Secure Sockets Layer [TEJ 12].

11.4. Conclusions

It is important to emphasize the radical changes that cloud computing has initiated in e-Health. Cloud providers must present this change as a viable option for healthcare organizations interested in the migration of their e-Health systems to the cloud. These cloud providers must persuade their customers that a cloud-based solution is a cost-effective way to maximize their resources.

Another fact to take into account is that cloud computing is still under development, and in the near future will provide customized services.

An essential question for health organizations that cloud providers must answer to is how to maintain the security and privacy of health records. Cloud companies must win the trust of their clients, providing them legal guarantees in terms of property and privacy.

The fact that medical data are in the possession of a third party, different from the healthcare organization, may be a source of reluctance for patients and governments, given the sensitivity of the data. For changing the patients' and state's minds, the health organization and the cloud provider must convince and demonstrate to them the security and privacy of patients' data, even in the case of system failures. A cloud provider must secure e-Health systems against potential external attacks with security mechanisms, which prevent a non-authorized party gaining access to private data. By overcoming these problems, cloud-based solutions will offer the above advantages, and cloud customers will be able to benefit from increased accessibility and mobility.

12

Security and Privacy in e-Health Applications over the Cloud

12.1. Introduction

The main goal of cloud computing is to provide easier access to distributed resources, combining them to improve performance by avoiding the problems of large-scale computation. Therefore, cloud computing can provide virtualization, scalability, interoperability, quality of service and development models in the public, private or hybrid form of the cloud [NAT 16].

Taking into account the economic, social, technological and cultural changes contained in the term of the "information society", citizens, professionals, administrators and law makers should present their perspective on the health needs of the population. Scientific progress, improvements in diagnosis and treatments, and a healthier lifestyle have contributed to adding "years of life" and "life to years". There is also the desire to improve access to health and other services in terms of place and time, bringing them into citizens' homes and the community [ASH 03]. In this context, it is the more than timely arrival of telemedicine and telecare. In this era of knowledge, it is imperative that physicians and other health professionals offer to their customers the best possible information about the illness or disease affecting them [ANT 11]. Time, distance or physical barriers can no longer be justified as obstacles between a patients' illness and the best way to fight it. Telemedicine facilitates the use of expert advice from a specialist hospital, medical first aid, a physician or a nurse, or a global specialist in complex cases. The main advantage of telemedicine is the ability to provide support instantly when it is needed.

Needless to mention that telemedicine can play an important role in situations where urgency, geography or other conditions (such as insulation, weather and disasters) require the use of this new care model. Another scenario to promote the use of telemedicine should be in populations or regions with a critical shortage of health workers, as in the case of developing countries [LO 07]. However, as telemedicine evolves, the need for basic principles to be established prior to its deployment is becoming evident. For the successful implementation of telemedicine, it should have the same requirements as medicine: to be carried out by qualified personnel, with an unambiguous legal framework defining the rights and obligations of customers and suppliers, and with well-defined rules of quality.

E-Health can be defined as health services supported by electronic processes and applications of information and communication technology. Telecardiology, telediagnosis and electronic health records (EHRs) are examples of e-Health applications that improve the quality of patient treatment. Moreover, it aims to obtain the best available specialists and minimize movement in addition to a faster diagnosis and a second opinion from a specialist [SMI 02]. With the advent of cloud technologies typical e-Health systems are currently sustained by Web service architectures containing one or more monitoring and/or surveillance devices, such as mobile devices or wearable sensors, which should be connected to the Internet to allow information forwarding and storage (shown in Figure 12.1).

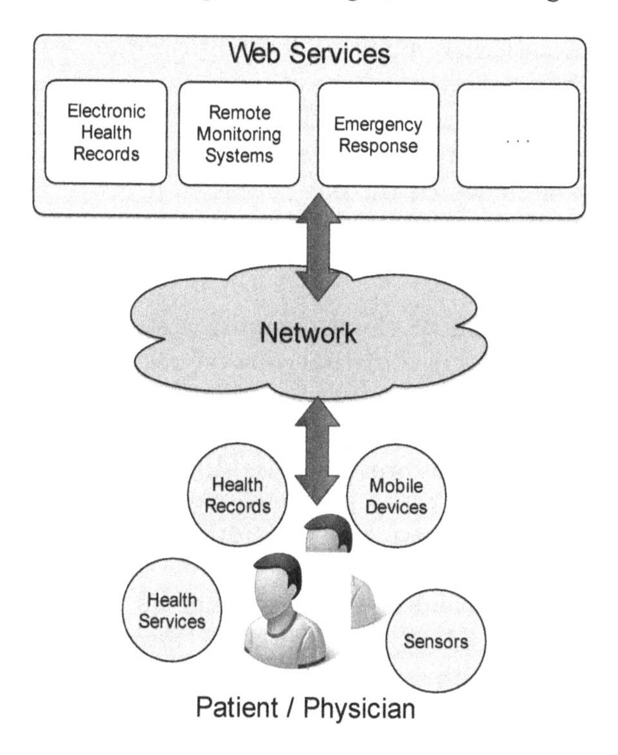

Figure 12.1. *Typical e-Health system architecture*

The protection of patient health data handled in e-Health applications must be ensured at all costs, especially when these applications include e-Health services in the cloud [MIC 13, THI 14a]. The confidentiality, integrity and security of medical data, comprising the most intimate aspects of a person, must be fully insured at the technical, institutional and legal levels. When they travel through the network, patient data must remain anonymous, and cloud providers must make use of the necessary mechanisms for this purpose, including encryption. Physicians and other professionals should observe the highest standard of ethical norms, to adapt to the information era standards.

The ability to virtualize resources in a cloud provides healthcare staff with mobility and sufficient access to query any data they need regardless of their physical location, and the ability to perform tasks with the information they need at any time. Since the data are not physically placed at the same location at which the one accessed, it must pay special attention on how to apply for these services where security and privacy are critical factors [BOT 04].

The combination of cloud computing with techniques of e-Health will provide a virtual view of resources which can be accessed regardless of geographic location or physical space. Therefore, ensuring privacy and security must be the primary objective to provide e-Health solutions based on cloud computing, it being imperative that these factors are not missed [MAR 04, SIL 13a, SIL 13b].

Problematic e-Health data exchange is currently being studied and solved by Health Level Seven International (HL7) mobile health working group [HEA 15] that creates and promotes health information technology standards and frameworks for e-Health, focusing on how data should be structured and properly secured for transmission over the network. Moreover, cryptographic algorithms are also a solid alternative and valid solution to the afore-mentioned security concerns.

Cryptographic mechanisms have proven a promising solution for several security issues in wireless networks. In this sense, cryptography may be defined as a set of techniques that aims to assure safe communication between two agents on an open channel. Moreover, it offers a solution to numerous necessities of the communication process like confidentiality, integrity and authenticity [RAW 03].

This chapter addresses the important topics related to security in e-Health. First, it provides an overview on privacy and security of e-Health systems. Some basic aspects about cloud security on e-Health will be described. After this, a secure authentication for e-Health services will be presented, and the chapter ends with the main conclusions.

12.2. Privacy and security in e-Health

E-Health data protection has been a major issue, mainly due to the sensitivity of data [JAR 15]. Since e-Health services may carry patients' sensitive and private health data (e.g. relating to HIV/AIDS or sexually transmitted diseases), it clearly becomes important to take these issues into consideration when developing such healthcare services to ensure that users' data privacy is not compromised. The main goal of an e-Health security mechanism is the same for any other system, i.e. to assure and guarantee data confidentiality, authenticity and integrity [SAH 13].

Any processing of personal health-related data must fully comply with the standards of personal data protection, while respecting the fundamental freedoms and rights of individuals to improve their wellbeing. The key right for personal data protection is based on the European Convention for the Protection of Human Rights and Fundamental Freedoms, Article 8, Charter of Fundamental Rights of the EU. More specifically, it is found in the Directive 95/46/EC on data protection and the Directive 2002/58/EC on privacy and electronic communications

(OJL 201, 31.7.2002, p. 37) and in the national laws of Member States implementing these directives.

In parallel, personal data processing is performed in EHRs that must follow the standards set by the Council of Europe Convention on the Protection of Individuals with regard to Automatic Processing of Personal Data (Council of Europe – ETS no.108), and the additional Protocol to Convention 108 regarding supervisory authorities and trans border data flows (Council of Europe – ETS No. 181); please see [COU 98].

Since patients' personal data is extremely sensitive, it requires special protection. Article 2, letter (a) of Directive 95/46/EC defines personal data as follows:

> "'Personal data' shall mean any information relating to an identified or identifiable ('data subject') individual; an identifiable person is one who can be identified, directly or indirectly, in particular by an identification number or to one or more factors specific to his physical, physiological, mental, economic, cultural or social identity."

Article 8, paragraph 1 of this Directive defines the special categories of data as follows: "Member States shall prohibit the processing of personal data revealing racial or ethnic origin, political opinions, religious or philosophical beliefs, trade-union membership, and the processing of data concerning health". This definition also applies to personal data when they have a clear and close connection with the description of the health state of a person: data about medication consumption, alcohol or drug use, generic data and all data contained in a medical record. It should also consider other sensitive data, such as administrative data (social security number, date of hospital admission, etc.), contained in medical documentation concerning a patient treatment. If some information is not relevant in the context of treatment or patient care, it should not be included in a medical record.

Medical records are also known as EHRs [LI 10]. An EHR is essentially a representation of health data in an electronic format. It enables faster and more convenient access by physicians or medical staff. A typical EHR system consists of a well-structured and organized archive containing the patient medical history in an electronic form [ISO 05]. EHR implementation improves the health provider's efficiency, reduces costs and can even increase treatments' effectiveness. Moreover, through Web service oriented architectures, it allows medical staff or patients to easily access the respective health information.

There are several limitations regarding EHR deployment among patients, including the above-mentioned security and privacy issues. Another drawback is the utilization of EHR systems with regard to interoperability [GAJ 11]. In this sense, HL7 is presented as a standard whose main goal resides in achieving interoperability among systems with different healthcare providers [HEA 16]. HL7 provides a standardized format for exchanging e-Health data among machines or devices that implement and follow its protocol. Through the usage of a protocol like HL7, different machines from different vendors can communicate through a standard interface, allowing the addition of new machines without having to modify the original source system. HL7 is currently adopted by ISO for international standardization policy, together publishing several frameworks and standards for exchange, integration, sharing and retrieval of EHRs.

To guarantee confidentiality, authentication and integrity of health data, e-Health systems have widely adopted and implemented cryptography algorithms [SOC 15, SIL 13a,

SIL 13b]. Cryptographic mechanisms are a solid and valid solution for several security issues in wireless networks. It may be defined as a set of encryption and decryption techniques that assure safe communication between two agents on an open channel [HAY 14, SHI 16].

Encryption and decryption algorithms can be defined as mechanisms for encoding messages to ensure that no one else but authorized agent should be able to read it [MAR 12]. Several algorithms were developed over recent decades to deal with the increasing need for assuring data privacy and security, in general, and they may be split into two main groups: (1) symmetric algorithms, where both encryption and decryption of a message is accomplished using the same key, and (2) asymmetric algorithms where a key is used to encrypt the message (public key) and another one is used to decrypt it (private key). Cryptography mechanisms are considered as a cost-effective response to the security requirements of e-Health applications and services in the cloud [BOO 09].

Every medical data system must also ensure that potential privacy breaches that prevent the storage and delivery of medical data in an EHR system, for example, by misuse or unauthorized use of EHR data are adequately compensated by liability for damages [FRA 01]. The analysis of potential problems from the point of view of data protection include liability issues for misuse of a system [MAR 05]. Any Member State wishing to introduce a system of this type must first perform legal and medical studies, as well as impact assessments to clarify emerging issues concerning liability that may arise in this context, for example with regard to the accuracy and completeness of data entered into the EHR, the definition of the degree of knowledge that a health professional treating a patient must have about the EHR, or the consequences provided by legislation (law) if access is not available for technical reasons, etc.

12.3. Cloud security in e-Health

While the cloud offers obvious advantages, these advantages can lead to equally large concerns. When a solution runs over a network structure, it is exposed to possible security attacks, such as denial of service (DoS). In a DoS attack, a user can gain control of a server and the attacker can stop Web services. To stop these attacks using cookies with synchronized actions, they set a limit of online users helping to neutralize DoS attacks. Another attack may occur when the cloud socket layer is incorrectly configured. Then, a client authentication will not behave as expected, triggering a security hole. Therefore, security on e-Health apps and services over cloud computing is crucial, and it is a key factor regarding their acceptance when personal data and programs are executed in an unknown physical location. Known methods such as phishing, botnets, etc., pose severe threats to data and organizational software. Then, one of the main concerns is data storage in the cloud. Data should be transferred and stored in an encrypted format, using proxies and agents to isolate clients from having direct access to the shared storage in the cloud. Records, audits and regulatory compliance are features that require accurate planning in cloud computing systems. It is also important to keep in mind the concept of presence in terms of identity (authentication). The Internet is displayed as flexible and reliable but nothing can be considered a 100% secure network. As a distributed system, cloud computing has the same vulnerabilities as Internet applications plus others that come from virtualization, shared resources and additional outsourced services. [HEI 08] on its report about security risks of cloud computing, from Gartner Group, highlight the following topics as important problems of cloud computing:

- auditing;
- data integrity;
- electronic discovery for law enforcement;
- privacy;
- recovery;
- compliance with regulations.

The risk of cloud deployment depends on the chosen cloud service model type. To evaluate the risks of an implementation over the cloud an analysis must be conducted to determine the inherent risks of cloud, used mechanisms, etc. The analysis that should be performed is the following:

1) decide and plan which resources (data, services, applications) that will be migrated to the cloud;

2) determine the sensitivity of these resources and corresponding risk. Evaluate these risks in the case of privacy loss, unauthorized access, data loss and downtime availability;

3) determine the risk associated with the particular type of cloud for each resource;

4) consider the cloud service model to be used (Infrastructure as a Service (IaaS), Software as a Service (SaaS) or Platform as a Service (PaaS)) according to clients that are responsible for security at different levels of the services stack;

5) assume that the cloud provider must know how to use the information, where it is stored and transferred in the cloud.

It is advisable to make a backup image that can prevent incidents in the case of vulnerabilities and hazards, so when there are doubts related to the system reliability, it is possible to return to that safe image easily. There is a hardware/software stack model, identified as Cloud Security Alliance, which is considered as a reference on the cloud comprising the different levels (IaaS, PaaS and SaaS). From the bottom to the top level of the stack, each service inherits the characteristics of the layer below, including advantages, weaknesses and potential risks. IaaS provides an infrastructure; PaaS adds application development frameworks, transactions and control structures; and SaaS is an operating environment with applications, management and user interface. Bottom-up IaaS has the lowest levels of functionality and integrated security, while SaaS has the highest.

For SaaS, the provider offers security as part of the service level agreement, where levels of compliance, governance and responsibility expose the entire stack. The PaaS model for the security border may be defined in order to include supplier software and a middleware layer. In this model, the client should be responsible for the security of the application and user interface on top of the stack. Finally, the model with the least integrated security is IaaS, where everything that involves any kind of software is a customer problem.

While it is true that the boundaries of cloud security are not well defined, it is not very dynamic and subject to changes. To set these boundaries, it must be known where security mechanisms are implemented, where the resources are consumed, what resources are needed, who owns them and what mechanisms are used to control these resources.

The problem that arises with storing data in the cloud comes from the fact that data may be stored in another data center, in another region or province, or even in a different country to the client location. In other network implementations there are physical network resources, such as firewalls, that act as perimeter network security, but the cloud possesses no such system. This is the reason why a solution that isolates data from direct access by clients should be deployed and used to access data layers. Then, two services are created; an agent with full access to storage without access to the client, and a proxy storage access without access to the client or the agent. Regardless of location of the proxy and the agent (they can be local or hosted in the cloud), it is important to guarantee that both are in the direct data path between the client and the data stored in the cloud. With this security solution, when a client makes a request for data, the following steps are performed:

1) the request goes to the external interface of the proxy service, which is only partially trusted;

2) the proxy, using its internal interface, forwards the request to the agent;

3) the agent requests the data storage system in the cloud;

4) the storage system returns the data to the agent;

5) the agent returns the results to the proxy;

6) to complete the response, the proxy sends the requested data to the agent.

Table 12.1 lists the responsibilities as a function of security service level. It considers the different cloud models (hybrid, private/community and public).

Many hospitals, clinics and health centers are becoming overwhelmed by the continuously growing amount of information they need to process and administer. The aim is to dedicate more attention to patients by automating recording, administering and consultation of information based on health records. The use of cloud computing technology together with e-Health applications represents a major step forward, both in terms of the quality of treatment provided to patients and the work carried out by healthcare staff.

Model	Security management infrastructure	Owner of the infrastructure	Location infrastructure	Trust condition
Hybrid	Provider and client	Provider and client	Inside and outside the facilities	With and without trust
Private/community	Client	Client	Inside and outside the facilities	With trust
Private/community	Client	Provider	Inside and outside the facilities	With trust
Private/community	Provider	Client	Inside and outside the facilities	With trust
Private/community	Provider	Provider	Inside and outside the facilities	With trust
Public	Provider	Provider	Outside the facilities	Without trust

Table 12.1. *Cloud model responsibilities as a function of security service level*

The use of the cloud-based computing technology alongside the smartcard system for authentication of physicians helps healthcare centers to electronically administer all the health data related to patients, enabling the reliable updating and modification of such data. This means that privacy, security and robustness in an extremely sensitive data system are assured. An authorized staff, physician or other health professional may access the services provided by the different e-Health applications at any time and from any location, using their smartcard to access data.

12.4. A secure authentication mechanism for e-Health cloud services

In this section, the description of key security elements associated with e-Health services on the cloud is provided. With the proliferation of Web-based services and other cloud computing technologies, there are huge migrations of services to the cloud, including health care applications. This migration of typical and centralized health solutions to the cloud brings efficiency to medical health record management and cost reduction [MIC 14, THI 14b, ZHO 15].

Regardless of which e-Health application needs to be deployed together with the cloud computing technology, all the solutions must be correctly authenticated. This is a key factor that needs to be covered, otherwise data might be accessed an used by unauthorized persons. This could result in a loss of information or fraudulent use, etc. In most cases, a private cloud has been chosen in order to increase security measures. Different encoding technologies, digital signatures, related tools and technologies have been researched in order to offer an effective and viable solution for the authentication of health professionals. To conclude, the decision has been taken to promote the use of smartcards in cloud systems as a feasible and efficient solution for maintaining identity with a suitable degree of security in this joint cloud-based system for e-Health applications or other services introduced on cloud [GUO 14, ABB 14].

Figure 12.2 details one of the consultations made by a physician, in which operation of the doctor's computer and the card acceptance device (CAD) reader is observed. The computer or computers located at the professional health staff's rooms is/are equipped with a CAD, which is a smartcard reading in charge of the customer part of the system. As described by De la Torre *et al.* [DE 15], the computer/s located in different rooms to health professionals are equipped with a CAD system. This is enough for a Java virtual machine and an open card framework (OCF) bookstore. A smartcard's OCF is simply a type of middleware, developed in Java, that enables an application to be made aware of the card's presence and to be able to interact with it in accordance with the ISO/IEC 7816-4, -8 and -9 standards. Together, these systems interact jointly with the system's healthcare software available in each terminal, where the CAD is located. The OCF is located between the CAD and the computer that hosts the application [DE 15, LUX 12].

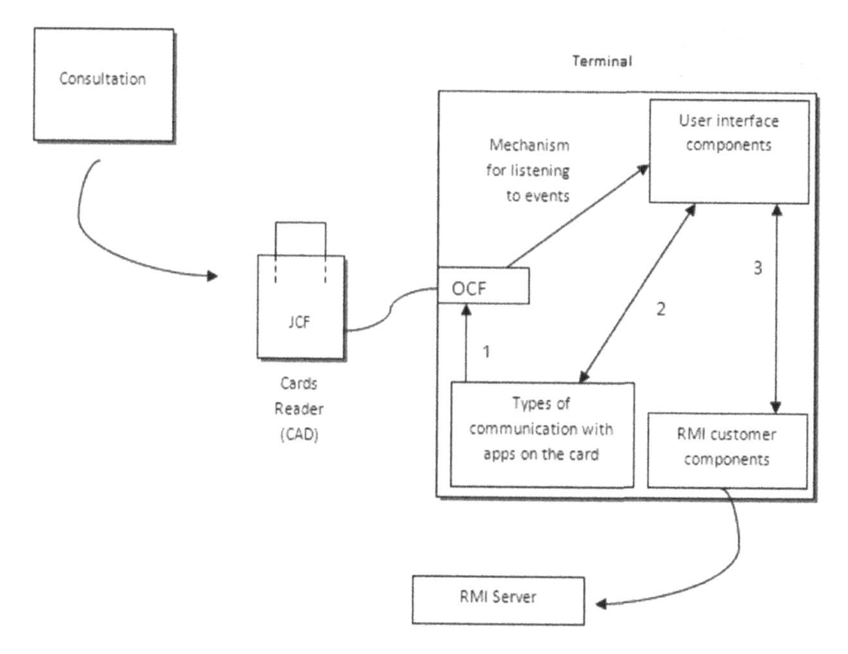

Figure 12.2. *Illustration of a physician's office consultation using smartcards*

There is also an object called a card manager, which is responsible for starting and shutting down the computer, and for establishing a secure communication channel between the smartcard and the open session at any specific time. The smartcard terminals also act as clients in the Remote Method Invocation (RMI) protocol by calling remote object methods. The remote objects have control of this, whereby the client software contain only the user's interface components (different instances of Java classes) and ways of displaying layers of architecture in the model view [COL 11].

Figure 12.3 illustrates the RMI server, which acts as the load balancer and application server when the former is deployed on cloud. Secure authentication of the data stored on the cloud is obtained and its privacy is assured, as this is extremely sensitive as it contains patients' health data. When a client wishes to update information about a patient on the clinical database, they use the suitable remote object methods with the data in an encrypted and signed format. Data are sent to the RMI server thread via the RMI channel using transmission control protocol (TCP)/internet protocol (IP) with a marshaling parameter. Then, the thread prepares the data and sends it to the remote object. The objects control the client's authentication, decode data, prepare a suitable consultation and update the information on the remote database. The result of the operation or exception is returned to the client on the same channel.

Because of the Java technology deployed (see JDBC at Figure 12.3), together with the smartcard, they are able to offer authenticated and secure access to the database hosted on the cloud. As a secure channel is established on TCP/IP, which is the network architecture used in all communications, there are no problems encountered in connecting from one point to another. Security is also assured when an authorized person uses this channel to access data.

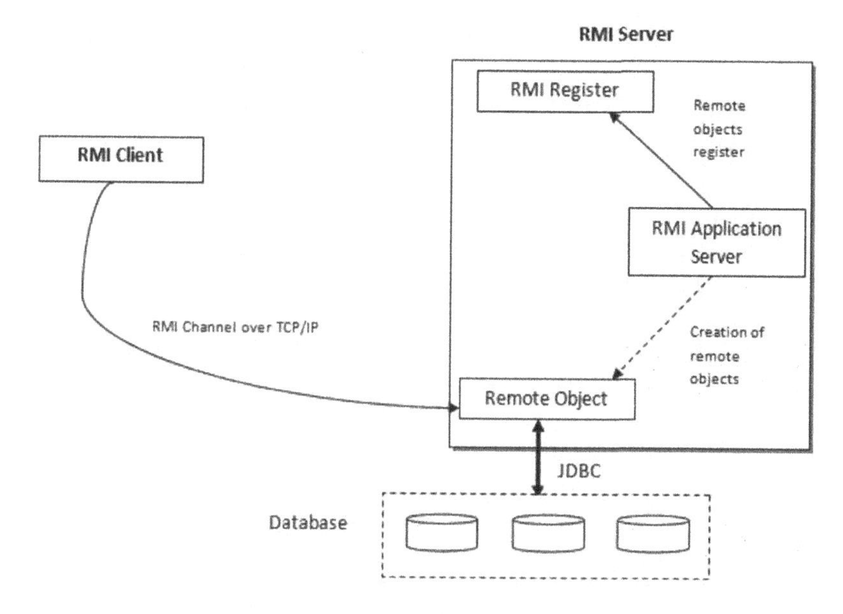

Figure 12.3. *Illustration of RMI server components operation*

12.5. Conclusions

Many clinics, hospitals and health centers are almost overwhelmed by the increasing amount of information to be processed and managed. They are able to pay more attention to patients by automating data recording, management and retrieval from medical records as much as possible. The use of cloud computing with e-Health applications is an important aid for improving both the quality of treatment given to patients and the work of socio-medical personnel. Data protection of e-Health services in the cloud is a hot topic with high importance, mainly due to the sensitivity of health data. Privacy and security mechanisms must assure health data confidentiality, integrity and authenticity.

The integration of cloud computing technology; together with the proposed smart card for physician authentication, helps socio-medical personnel to electronically manage all the data from patient health centers, and can perform updates, modifications, etc., reliably, achieving privacy, security and robustness in an extremely sensitive system data are achieved. An authorized physician or health professional can access anywhere at anytime services of different e-Health applications, taking into account the privileges given by the use of his/her smart card required to access data hosted on the cloud system.

The access control system, using firewalls configured with *IPFailover*, further improved the security solution afforded by the use of encryption keys through the proxy and agents. Moreover, the proposed storage system is able to backup elements physically separated within the cloud, increasing privacy and security over all communications and also ensuring data robustness.

In a typical scenario of cloud configuration, a client (e.g. a hospital) is not initially aware of the requirements in terms of resources needed to provide an infrastructure to host software. In these cases, the solution is to launch a battery of tests changing the required parameters, i.e. ultimately there are hired cloud resources for testing, which involve costs to customers. Using this approach where the expense is not significant, the client can perform various simulations of its future infrastructure to reach an efficient outcome in terms of cost/time. This software, displays the results itself.

For further work, it is urgent to perform a study to evaluate the impact of security attacks on the most widely known and adopted e-Health cloud services [SAH 11]. This study is crucial to identify weaknesses and open issues to reinforce privacy and security on e-Health services.

Bibliography

[ABB 14] ABBAS A., KHAN S.U., "A review on the state-of-the-art privacy-preserving approaches in the e-Health clouds", *IEEE Journal of Biomedical and Health Informatics*, vol. 18, no. 4, pp. 1431–1441, 2014.

[ABU 12] ABU KHOUSA E., MOHAMED N., AL-JAROODI J., "e-Health cloud: opportunities and challenges", *Future Internet*, vol. 4, pp. 621–645, 2012.

[AKT 10] AKTER S., RAY P., "m-Health – an ultimate platform to serve the unserved", *Yearbook of Medical Informatics*, vol. 2010, pp. 94–100, 2010.

[ALC 16] ALCATEL-LUCENT, "Delivering the benefits of remote patient monitoring to healthcare providers, patients and third-party payers", available at http://www.himssanalytics.org/uploads/product/whitepaper/4B91A32D26DE48228EEB6B3F263F0963.pdf, 28 February 2016.

[AAL 16] AAL JP, "Ambient Assisted Living Joint Programme", available at http://www.aal-europe.eu, March 10, 2016.

[ANI 07] ANSI/HL7, "The HL7 EHR system functional model", Release 1 R1-2007, 2007.

[ANT 11] ANTÓN-RODRÍGUEZ M., DE LA TORRE-DIEZ I., GUTIÉRREZ-DÍEZ P. *et al.*, "Mobile access system for the management of electronic health records of patients with mental disability", *Advances in Intelligent and Soft Computing*, vol. 91, pp. 329–336, 2011.

[APP 16] APPLE, "iTunes", available at http://www.apple.com/itunes, 2016.

[ASH 03] ASH J.S., BATES D.W., "Factors and forces affecting EHR system adoption: report of a 2004 ACMI discussion", *Journal of American Medical Information Association*, vol. 12, no. 1, pp. 8–12, 2003.

[BAI 98] BAI J., ZHANG J., DAI B., "Design and development of an interactive medical teleconsultation system over the World Wide Web", *IEEE Transactions on Information Technology in Biomedicine*, vol. 2, no. 2, pp. 74–79, 1998.

[BAR 13] BARREDA-PÉREZ M., DE LA TORRE I., LÓPEZ-CORONADO M. *et al.*, "Development and evaluation of a Web-based tool to estimate type 2 diabetes risk: Diab_Alert", *Telemedicine Journal and e-Health*, vol. 19, no. 2, pp. 81–87, 2013.

[BER 14] BERATARRECHEA A., LEE A.G., WILLNER J.M. *et al.*, "The impact of mobile health interventions on chronic disease outcomes in developing countries: a systematic review", *Telemedicine and E-Health Journal*, vol. 20, no. 1, pp. 75–82, 2014.

[BIL 12] BILGI M., GÜLALP B., EROL T. *et al.*, "Interpretation of electrocardiogram images sent through the mobile phone multimedia messaging service", *Telemedicine and E-Health Journal*, vol. 18, no. 2, pp. 126–131, 2012.

[BIS 14] BISIO I., LAVAGETTO F., MARCHESE M. *et al.*, "A smartphone-centric platform for remote health monitoring of heart failure", *International Journal of Communication Systems*, vol. 28, no. 11, pp. 1753–1771, 2014.

[BLA 16] BLACKBERRY, "BlackBerry world", available at http://appworld.blackberry.com/webstore/product/1/, 2016.

[BLU 11] BLUMROSEN G., AVISDRIS N., KUPFER R. *et al.*, "C-SMART: Efficient seamless cellular phone based patient monitoring system", *IEEE International Symposium on a World of Wireless, Mobile and Multimedia Networks*, pp. 1–6, 20–24 June 2011,

[BON 09] BOONYARATTAPHAN A., BAI Y., CHUNG S., "A security framework for e-Health service authentication and e-Health data transmission", *9th International Symposium on Communications and Information Technology*, pp. 1213–1218, Icheon, Korea, September 28–30, 2009.

[BØR 13] BØRØSUND E., CVANCAROVA M., EKSTEDT M. *et al.*, "How user characteristics affect use patterns in web-based illness management support for patients with breast and prostate cancer", *Journal of Medical Internet Research*, vol. 15, no. 3, pp. e34, 2013.

[BOT 04] BOTT O.J., "Electronic health record: standardization and implementation", *2nd Open ECG Workshop*, pp. 57–60, Berlin, Germany, January 2004.

[BOU 03] BOUCHIER H., BATH P.A., "Evaluation of websites that provide information on Alzheimer's disease", *Health Informatics Journal*, vol. 9, no. 1, pp. 17–31, 2003.

[BRO 14] BROWN-CONNOLLY N.E., CONCHA J.B., ENGLISH J., "Mobile health is worth it! Economic benefit and impact on health of a population-based mobile screening program in new Mexico", *Telemedicine and e-Health Journal*, vol. 20, no. 1, pp. 18–23, 2014.

[BUI 11] BUIJSSE B., SIMMONS R.K., GRIFFIN S.J. *et al.*, "Risk assessment tools for identifying individuals at risk of developing type 2 diabetes", *Epidemiology Review: Oxford Journals*, vol. 33, pp. 46–62, 2011.

[CAF 12] CAFAZZO A.J., CASSELMAN M., HAMMING N. *et al.*, "Design of an mhealth app for the self-management of adolescent type 1 diabetes: A pilot study", *Journal of Medical Internet Research*, vol. 14, no. 3, p. e70, 2012.

[CAL 12] CALDEIRA J.M.L.P., RODRIGUES J.J.P.C., LORENZ P., "Towards ubiquitous mobility solutions for body sensor networks on healthcare", *IEEE Communications Magazine*, vol. 50, no. 5, pp. 108–115, May 2012.

[CAL 13] CALDEIRA J.M.L.P., RODRIGUES J.J.P.C., LORENZ P., "Intra-mobility support solutions for healthcare wireless sensor networks – handover issues", *IEEE Sensors Journal*, vol. 13, no. 11, pp. 4339–4348, November 2013.

[CAL 14] CALDEIRA J.M.L.P., RODRIGUES J.J.P.C., "Body area networks for healthcare", *McGraw-Hill Yearbook of Science and Technology*, pp. 47–50, McGraw-Hill, USA, January 2014.

[CAL 15] CALDEIRA J.M.L.P., RODRIGUES J.J.P.C., LORENZ P., "MAC layer handover mechanism for continuous communication support in healthcare mobile wireless sensor networks", *Telecommunication Systems*, vol. 60, no. 1, pp. 119–132, September 2015.

[CAM 11] CAMPOS B.S., NAKAMURA E.F., FIGUEIRED C.M.S. *et al.*, "Design and implementation of a UPnP gateway for wireless sensor networks", *IEEE Symposium on Computers and Communications (ISCC)*, Kerkyra, Greece, June 28 – July 01, 2011.

[CAR 16] CAREServ, "Medical management as a service", available at http://www.cognizant.com/businesscloud/careserv-medical-management-solution, February 2 2016.

[CAV 13] CAVALLARO F.I., FACAL D., PIGINI L. *et al.*, "Multi-role shadow robotic system for independent living (SRS)", *European Commission under the 7th Framework Programme (FP7)*, 2013.

[CEN 16] CEN, "TC 251 Published Standard", available at http://standards.cen.eu/dyn/www/f?p=CENWEB:6:::NO, February 21, 2016.

[CHE 11] CHEN B., POMPILI D., "Transmission of patient vital signs using wireless body area networks", *Journal of Mobile Networks and Applications*, vol. 16, no. 6, pp. 663–682, 2011.

[CHI 13] CHIARINI G., RAY P., AKTER S. *et al.*, "m-Health technologies for chronic diseases and elders: a systematic review", *IEEE Journal of Selected Areas in Communications*, vol. 31, no. 9, pp. 6–18, 2013.

[CHO 11] CHOWDHARY S.K., YADAV A., GARG N., "Cloud computing: future prospect for e-health", *3rd International Conference on Electronics Computer Technology (ICECT)*, pp. 297–299, Kanyakumari, India, 8–10 April, 2011.

[CHR 01] CHRONAKI C.E., LELIS P., DEMOU C. *et al.*, "An HL7/CDA framework for the design and deployment of telemedicine services", *Proceedings of the 23rd Annual International Conference of the IEEE Engineering in Medicine and Biology Society*, vol. 4, pp. 3504–3507, 2001.

[COL 11] COLES-KEMP L., REDDINGTON J., WILLIAMS P.A.H., "Looking at clouds from both sides: the advantages and disadvantages of placing personal narratives in the cloud", *Information Security Technical Report*, vol. 16, nos. 3–4, pp. 115–122, 2011.

[COM 16] COMPANIONABLE, available at http://www.Companionable.net, March 21, 2016.

[COO 16] COOKING HACKS BY LIBELIUM, "e-Health Sensor Platform for Arduino and Raspberry Pi", available at http://www.cooking-hacks.com/documentation/tutorials/ehealth-v1-biometric-sensor-platform-arduino-raspberry-pi-medical, February 29 2016.

[COS 15] COSTA S.E.P., RODRIGUES J.J.P.C., SILVA B.M.C. *et al.*, "Integration of wearable solutions in AAL environments with mobility support", *Journal of Medical Systems*, vol. 39, no. 12, pp. 1–8, 2015.

[COU 98] COUNCIL OF EUROPE, "Recommendation No. R (97)5 of the Committee of Ministers to member states on the protection of medical data", *Int Dig Health Legis*, vol. 49, pp. 502–8, 1998.

[COW 09] COWIE C.C., RUST K.F., FORD E.S. *et al.*, "Full accounting of diabetes and pre-diabetes in the U.S. population in 1988-1994 and 2005-2006", *Diabetes Care*, vol. 32, pp. 287–294, 2009.

[DE 12] DE LA TORRE I., LÓPEZ-CORONADO M., RODRIGUES J.J.P.C. "How to measure the QoS of a web-based EHRs system: development of an instrument", *Journal of Medical Systems*, vol. 36, no. 6, pp. 3725–3731, 2012.

[DE 12a] DE LA TORRE I., DÍAZ F.J., ANTÓN M. *et al.*, "A telematic tool to predict the risk of colorectal cancer in white men and women: colorectal cancer alert (CRCA)", *Journal of Medical Systems*, vol. 36, no. 4, pp. 2557–2564, 2012.

[DE 12b] DE LA TORRE I., DIAZ F.J., ANTON M., "A content analysis of chronic diseases social groups on Facebook and Twitter", *Telemedicine Journal and e-Health*, vol. 18, no. 6, pp. 404–408, 2012.

[DE 15] DE LA TORRE-DÍEZ I., LOPEZ-CORONADO M., SOTO B.G.-Z. *et al.*, "Secure cloud-based solutions for different E-health services in Spanish rural health centres", *Journal of Medical Internet Research*, vol. 17, no. 7, 2015.

[DIA 12] DIALLO O., RODRIGUES J.J.P.C., SENE M., "Real-time data management on wireless sensor network: a survey", in *Journal of Network and Computer Applications*, vol. 35, no. 3, pp. 1013–1021, May 2012.

[DIA 14] DIALLO O., RODRIGUES J.J.P.C., SENE M. *et al.*, "Real-time query processing optimization for cloud-based wireless body area networks", *Information Sciences*, vol. 284, no. 14, pp. 84–94, November 2014.

[DIG 08] DICOM, "Standard parts", available at ftp://medical.nema.org/medical/dicom/2008, 2008.

[DOL 00] DOLIN R.H., ALSCHULER L., BOYER S. *et al.*, "An update on HL7's XML-based document representation standards", *AMIA Annual Symposium*, pp. 190–194, Los Angeles, CA, 2000.

[DOL 06] DOLIN R.H., ALSCHULER L., BOYER S. *et al.*, "HL7 clinical document architecture, release 2", *Journal of the American Medical Informatics Association*, vol. 13, no. 1, pp. 30–39, 2006.

[INT 16] INTEGRATING THE HEALTHCARE ENTERPRISE (IHE), available at http://www.en136 06.org/the-ceniso-en13606-standard, January 28 2016.

[ENG 04] ENGLAND C.J., "Assisted living", *The American Journal of Nursing*, vol. 104, no. 7, p. 15, 2004.

[EUR 10] EUROPEAN COMMISSION, "Overview of the European strategy in ICT for ageing well, e-inclusion", available at http://ec.europa.eu/information_society/activities/einclusion/docs/ageing/overview.pdf, 2010.

[EUR 12] EUROPEAN COMMISSION, "The 2012 ageing report: economic and budgetary projections for the 27 EU Member States (2010-2060)", available at http://ec.europa.eu/economy_finance/publications/european_economy/2012/2012-ageing-report_en.htm, 2012.

[EUR 13] EUROSTAT, "European social statistics 2013 edition", Population and social conditions. Collection: Pocketbooks, available at http://Fepp.eurostat.ec.europa.eu/cache/ITY_OFF PUB/KS-FP-13-001/EN/KS-FP-13-001-EN.PDF, 2013.

[FAH 12] FAHIM M., FATIMA I., LEE S. *et al.*, "Daily life activity tracking application for smart homes using android smartphone", *14th International Conference on Advanced Communication Technology*, pp. 241–245, Yongin, South Korea, 19–22 February 2012.

[FAL 01] FALAGAN J., "La condición de médico no supone libre acceso a la historia clínica", *Rev. Galega Actual Sanit*, vol. 1, pp. 6–9, 2001.

[FAR 09] FARMER A.D., BRUCKNER C.E., COOK M.J. *et al.*, "Social networking sites: a novel portal for communication", *Postgraduated Medicine Journal*, vol. 85, pp. 455–459, 2009.

[FAR 10] FARZANDIPOUR M., SADOUGHI F., AHMADI M., "Security requirements and solutions in electronic health records: lessons learned from a comparative study", *Journal of Medical Systems*, vol. 34, no. 4, 629–642, 2010.

[FAY 10] FAYN J., RUBEL P., "Toward a personal health society in cardiology", *IEEE Transactions on Information Technology in Biomedicine*, vol. 14, no. 2, pp. 401–409, 2010.

[FER 12] FERNÁNDEZ-CARDEÑOSA G., DE LA TORRE I., LÓPEZ-CORONADO M. *et al.*, "Analysis of cloud-based solutions on EHRs systems in different scenarios", *Journal of Medical Systems*, vol. 36, no.6, pp. 3777–3782, 2012.

[FIN 13] FINKELSTEIN J., WOOD J., "Interactive mobile system for smoking cessation", *35th Annual International Conference of Engineering in Medicine and Biology Society*, pp. 1169–1172, Osaka, Japan, July 3–7 2013.

[FIO 13] FIORDELLI M., DIVIANI N., SCHULZ P.J., "Mapping m-Health research: a decade of evolution", *Journal of Medical Internet Research*, vol. 15, no. 5, 2013.

[FLO 16] FLORENCE, "Multipurpose mobile robot for ambient assisted living", available at http://www.florence-project.eu, 2016.

[FON 13] FONTECHA J., HERVÁS R., BRAVO J. *et al.*, "A mobile and ubiquitous approach for supporting frailty assessment in elderly people", *Journal of Medical Internet Research*, vol. 15, no. 9, 2013.

[FOR 05] FORLIZZI J., "Robotic products to assist the aging population", *Interactions*, vol. 12, no. 2, pp. 16–18, 2005.

[FRA 01] FRASER H.S., MCGRATH S.J., "Information technology and telemedicine in sub-saharan Africa", *BMJ*, vol. 322, pp. 51–52, 2001.

[FRA 03] FRADEN J., *Handbook of Modern Sensors: Physics, Designs, and Applications*, 3rd ed., Springer Science, New York, 2003.

[FRE 08] FREIFELD C.C., MANDL K.D., REIS B.Y. *et al.*, "HealthMap: global injections disease monitoring through automated classification and visualization of Internet media reports", *J Am Med Infrom Assoc*, vol. 15, pp. 150–157, 2008.

[FUC 08] FUCHSBERGER V., "Ambient assisted living: elderly people's needs and how to face", *1st ACM International Workshop on Semantic Ambient Media Experiences*, pp. 21–24, 2008.

[FUT 10] FURTH B., ESCALANTE A., *Handbook of Cloud Computing*, 1st ed., Springer, Germany, 2010.

[GAG 16] GAGNON M.P., SIMONYAN D., GHANDOUR, E.K. *et al.*, "Factors influencing electronic health record adoption by physicians: a multi level analysis", *International Journal of Information Management*, vol. 36, pp. 258–270, 2016.

[GAJ 11] GAJANAYAKE R., IANNELLA R., SAHAMA T., "Sharing with care: an information accountability perspective", *IEEE Internet Computing*, vol. 15, no. 4, pp. 31–38, 2011.

[GAN 05] GANS D., KRALEWSKI J., HAMMONS T. *et al.*, "Medical groups' adoption of electronic health records and information systems", *Health Affairs Journal*, vol. 24, pp. 1323–1333, 2005.

[GAR 03] GARBAYO J.A., SANZ J., CARNICERO J. *et al.*, "La seguridad, confidencialidad y disponibilidad de la información clínica", *V Informe SEIS*, 2003.

[GAR 08] GARCIA M., BRI D., BORONAT F. *et al.*, "A new neighbor selection strategy for group-based wireless sensor networks", *4th International Conference on Networking and Services*, Gosier, Guadalupe, March 16-21, 2008.

[GAR 11] GARCIA M., SENDRA S., LLORET G. *et al.*, "Monitoring and control sensor system for fish feeding in marine fish farms", *IET Communications*, vol. 5, no. 12, pp. 1682–1690, October 2011.

[GAR 14] GARCÍA-GÓMEZ J.M., DE LA TORRE I., VICENTE J. *et al.*, "Analysis of mobile health applications for a broad spectrum of consumers: a user experience approach", *Health Informatics Journal, SAGE Publications*, vol. 20, no. 1, pp. 74–84, March 2014.

[GAR 15] GARCIA N., RODRIGUES J.J.P.C., *Ambient Assisted Living*, CRC Press/Taylor & Francis Group, 2015.

[GAR 15] GARTNER, "Gartner says emerging markets drove worldwide smartphone sales to 15.5 percent growth in third quarter of 2015", available at http://www.gartner.com/newsroom/id/3169417, November 18, 2015.

[GLU 04] GLUECKAUF R.L., KETTERSON T.U., LOOMIS J.S. *et al.*, "Online support and education for dementia caregivers: overview, utilization, and initial program evaluation", *Telemedicine and E-Health Journal*, vol. 10, no. 2, pp. 223–232, 2004.

[GOO 16] GOOGLE, "Google play", available at https://play.google.com/store, 2016.

[GRI 04] GRITZALIS D., LAMBRINOUDAKIS C., "A security architecture for interconnecting health information systems", *International Journal of Medical Informatics*, vol. 73, no. 3, pp. 305–309, 2004.

[GRI 11] GRIEVE G., "HL7 needs a fresh look because V3 has failed", 2015, available at http://www.healthintersections.com.au/? p=476, 2011.

[GRI 98] GRIMSON J., GRIMSON W., BERRY D. *et al.*, "A CORBA-based integration of distributed electronic health care records using the Synapses approach", *IEEE Transactions on Information Technology in Biomedicine*, vol. 2, no. 3, pp. 124–138, 1998.

[GUO 14] GUO L., ZHANG C., SUN J. *et al.*, "A privacy-preserving attribute-based authentication system for mobile health networks", *IEEE Transactions on Mobile Computing*, vol. 13, no. 9, pp. 1927–1941, 2014.

[GUR 04] GURLEY L., *Advantages and Disadvantages of the Electronic Medical Record*, American Academy of Medical Administrators, Cleveland, OH, 2004.

[GUS 01] GUSTAFSON D.H., HAWKINS R., PINGREE S. *et al.*, "Effect of computer support on younger women with breast cancer", *Journal of General Internal Medicine*, vol. 16, pp. 435–445, 2001.

[GUS 05] GUSTAFSON D.H., MCTAVISH F.M., STENGLE W. *et al.*, "Use and impact of eHealth system by low-income women with breast cancer", *Journal of Health Communications*, vol. 10, pp. 195–218, 2005.

[HAN 15] HAN G., ZHANG C., SHU L. *et al.*, "Impacts of deployment strategies on localization performances in underwater acoustic sensor networks", *IEEE Transactions on Industrial Electronics*, vol. 62, no. 3, pp. 1725–1733, March 2015.

[HAN 16] HAN G., LIU L., JIANG J. *et al.*, "A collaborative secure localization algorithm based on trust model in underwater wireless sensor networks", *Sensors Journal*, vol. 16, no. 2, p. 229, February 2016.

[HAU 13] HAUB C., "From population pyramids to pillars", available at http://www.prb.org/Publications/Articles/2013/population-pyramids.aspx, 2013.

[HAY 14] HAYOUNI H., HAMDI M., KIM T.H., "A survey on encryption schemes in wireless sensor networks", *7th International Conference on Advanced Software Engineering and Its Applications (ASEA)*, pp. 39–43, Haikou, December 20–23, 2014.

[HEA 08] HL7, Health Level Seven, International, available at http:// www.hl7.org, 2008.

[HEA 13] HL7, "About Health Level 7", available at http://www.hl7.org/about/index.cfm?ref=nav, 2013.

[HEA 15] HL7, "e-Health", available at http://www.hl7.org/search/index.cfm?x=0&y=0& criteria=e-health, 2015.

[HEI 08] HEISER J., NICOLETT M., "Assessing the security risks of cloud computing", available at https://www.gartner.com/doc/685308/assessing-security-risks-cloud-computing, June 3 2008.

[HEI 11] HEINISCH R., "Los efectos del envejecimiento de la población en el sistema sanitario y la protección social", available at http://www.intras.es/index.php/cendoss/temas-de-interes/mayores/cat_view/40-documentos-de-interes/45-mayores-documentos, 2011.

[HER 08] HERSH M.A., JOHNSON M.A., "Assistive technology for daily living", *Assistive Technology for Visually Impaired and Blind People*, pp. 615–657, 2008.

[HIL 05] HILLESTAD R., BIGELOW J., BOWER A. *et al.*, "Can electronic medical record systems transform health care? Potential health benefits, savings, and costs", *Health Affairs Journal*, vol. 14, no. 5, pp. 1103–1117, 2005.

[HUA 03] HUANG E.W., HSIAO S.H., LIOU D.M., "Design and implementation of a web-based HL7 message generation and validation system", *International Journal of Medical Informatics*, vol. 70, no. 1, pp. 49–58, 2003.

[IEE 05] IEEE, Standard for Information technology – Telecommunications and information exchange between systems – Local and metropolitan area networks – Specific requirements. – Part 15.1: Wireless medium access control (MAC) and physical layer (PHY) specifications for wireless personal area networks (WPANs), Institute of Electrical and Electronics Engineers Inc., New York, USA, 2005.

[IEE 06] IEEE Standard for Information technology – Telecommunications and information exchange between systems – Local and metropolitan area networks – Specific requirements Part 15.4: Wireless Medium Access Control (MAC) and Physical Layer (PHY) Specifications for Low-Rate Wireless Personal Area Networks (WPANs), pp. 0_1-305, Institute of Electrical and Electronics Engineers Inc., New York, USA, 2006.

[IEE 07] IEEE Standard for Information technology – Telecommunications and information exchange between systems – Local and metropolitan area networks – Specific requirements – Part 11: Wireless LAN Medium Access Control (MAC) and Physical Layer (PHY) Specifications, pp. 1–1184, Institute of Electrical and Electronics Engineers Inc., New York, USA, 2007.

[IMS 15] IMS, "IMS health study: patient options expand as mobile healthcare apps address wellness and chronic disease treatment needs", available at http://www.imshealth.com/en/about-us/news/ims-health-study:-patient-options-expand-as-mobile-healthcare-apps-address-wellness-and-chronic-disease-treatment-needs, 2015.

[IND 13] INDEX MUNDI, "Statistics on GDP expenditure on health", available at http://www.indexmundi.com/g/r.aspx?v=2225&l=es 2013.

[INF 16] INFINITĒ, InVentiv Medical Management, available at http://www.inventivmm.com/solutions/infinit-platform.html, February 28 2016.

[INT 07] INTEL, "mobile clinical assistant (MCA)", available at http://www.intel.com/pressroom/archive/releases/2007/20070220comp.htm(Accessed February 20, 2016).

[INT 16] INTEGRATING THE HEALTHCARE ENTERPRISE, available at http://www.ihe.net, February 21, 2016.

[INT 16] INTERNATIONAL ORGANIZATION FOR STANDARDIZATION, available at http://www.iso.org/iso/home.htm, Accessed January 28, 2016.

[ISO 05] ISO/TR 20514, *Health informatics – Electronic Health Record – Definition, Scope and Context*, American National Standards Institute (ANSI), p. 34, USA, 2005.

[IST 03] ISTEPANIAN R.S.H., LACAL J., "Emerging mobile communication technologies for health: some imperative notes on m-Health", *Engineering in Medicine and Biology Society*, vol. 2, pp. 1414–1416, 2003.

[IST 04] ISTEPANIAN R., JOVANOV E., ZHANG Y.T., "Introduction to the special section on M-Health: beyond seamless mobility and global wireless health-care connectivity", *IEEE Transactions on Information Technology in Biomedicine*, vol. 8, no. 4, pp. 405–414, 2004.

[ITU 13] ITU, "Key 2006-2013 ICT data for the world, by geographic regions and by level of development", available at http://www.itu.int/en/ITU-D/Statistics/Pages/stat/default.aspx? utm_source=twitterfeed&utm_medium=twitter, 2013.

[JAR 11] JAROWEK J., AUGUSTYNIAK P., "A cardiac telerehabilitation application for mobile devices", *Computing in Cardiology*, vol. 38, pp. 241–244, 2011.

[JAR 14] JARA H.R., SCHAFIR E., "e-Health: an introduction to the challenges of privacy and security", *Central America and Panama Convention*, pp. 1–5, Panama City, 2014.

[JIA 16] JIANG J., HAN G., GUO H. *et al.*, "Geographic multipath routing based on geospatial division in duty-cycled underwater wireless sensor networks", *Journal of Network and Computer Applications*, vol. 59, pp. 4–13, January 2016.

[KAL 02] KALRA D., Clinical foundations and information architecture for the implementation of a federated health record service, PhD Thesis, UCL, 2002.

[KAL 12] KALRA D., TAPURIA A., AUSTIN T. *et al.*, "Quality requirements for EHR archetypes", *Studies in Health Technology and Informatics*, vol. 180, pp. 48–52, 2012.

[KAL 10] KALUŽA B., MIRCHEVSKA V., DOVGAN E. *et al.*, "An agent-based approach to care in independent living", *Ambient Intelligence*, vol. 6439, pp. 177–186, 2010.

[KAN 07] KANSAL A., GORACZKO M., ZHAO F., "Building a sensor network of mobile phones", *6th International Conference on Information Processing in Sensor Networks*, pp. 547–548, Cambridge, Massachusetts, USA, April 24–27 2007.

[KEE 10] KEELAN J., PAVRI V., BALAKRISHNAN R. *et al.*, "An analysis of the human papilloma virus vaccine debate on MySpace blogs", *Vaccine*, vol. 28, no. 6, pp. 1535–1540, 2010.

[KHA 16] KHANSA L., DAVID Z., DAVIS H. *et al.*, "Health information technologies for patients with diabetes", *Technology in Society*, vol. 44, pp. 1–9, 2016.

[KIM 06] KIM E.H., "Web-based personal-centered electronic health record for elderly population", *1st Distributed Diagnosis and Home Healthcare (D2H2) Conference*, pp. 144–147, Arlington, VA, April 2–4, 2006.

[KIR 13] KIRWAN M., VANDELANOTTE C., FENNING A. *et al.*, "Diabetes self- management smartphone application for adults with type 1 diabetes: randomized controlled trial", *Journal of Medical Internet Research*, vol. 15, no. 11, p. e235, 2013.

[KOM 05] KOMIYA R., "A proposal for telemedicine reference model for future standardization", *Proceedings of 7th International Workshop on Enterprise networking and Computing in Healthcare Industry*, pp. 224–228, 2005.

[KSE 16] KSERA, available at https://www.tue.nl/en/research/research-institutes/robotics-research/projects/ksera/, 2016.

[KWA 05] KWAK Y.S., "International standards for building Electronic Health Record (EHR)", *Proceedings of 7th International Workshop on Enterprise networking and Computing in Healthcare Industry*, pp. 18–23, Healthcom, 2005.

[LAN 10] LANE N., MILUZZO E., LU H. *et al.*, "A survey ofmobile phone sensing", *IEEE Communications Magazine*, vol. 48, no. 9, pp. 140–150, 2010.

[LAN 15] LANDMAN A., CLINICAM, available at http://onlinewsj.com/news/articles/SB10001424052702303376904579137683810827104, 2015.

[LAX 00] LAXMINARAYAN S., ISTEPANIAN R.S., "UNWIRED E-MED: the next generation of wireless and Internet telemedicine systems", *IEEE Transactions Information Technology in Biomedicine*, vol. 4, no. 3, pp. 189–193, 2000.

[LI 10] LI J.H., LAND L., Ray P., "E-Health readiness framework from electronic health records perspective", *International Journal of Internet and Enterprise Management*, vol. 6, no. 4, pp. 326–348, 2010.

[LIN 10] LIN C.T., CHANG K.C., LIN C.L. *et al.*, "An intelligent telecardiology system using a wearable and wireless ECG to detect atrial fibrillation", *IEEE Transactions on Information Technology in Biomedicine*, vol. 14, no. 3, pp. 726–733, 2010.

[LLO 08] LLORET J., GARCIA M., TOMÁS J. *et al.*, "GBP-WAHSN: a group-based protocol for large wireless ad hoc and sensor networks", *Journal of Computer Science Technology*, vol. 23, pp. 461–480, 2008.

[LLO 09] LLORET J., SENDRA S., COLL H. *et al.*, "Saving energy in wireless local area sensor networks", *The Computer Journal*, vol. 53, no. 10, pp. 1658–1673, December 2009.

[LLO 11] LLORET J., BOSCH I., SENDRA S. *et al.*, "A wireless sensor network for vineyard monitoring that uses image processing", *Sensors*, vol. 11, no. 6, pp. 6165–6196, June 2011.

[LO 07] LO H.G., NEWMARK N., YOON C. *et al.*, "Electronic health records in specialty care: a time-motion study", *Journal of the American Medical Informatics Association*, vol. 14, no. 5, pp. 609–615, 2007.

[LOP 11a] LOPES I., SILVA B., RODRIGUES J.J.P.C. *et al.*, "A mobile health monitoring solution for weight control", *International Conference on Wireless Communications & Signal Processing*, Nanjing, China, 9-11 November 2011.

[LOP 13] LOPES I.C., VAIDYA B., RODRIGUES J.J.P.C., "Towards an autonomous fall detection and alerting system on a mobile and pervasive environment", *Telecommunication Systems*, vol. 52, no. 4, pp. 2299–2310, 2013.

[LUX 12] LUXTON D.D., KAYL R.A., MISHKIND M.C., "m-Health data security: the need for HIP AA compliant standardization", *Journal of Telemedicine and E- Health*, vol. 18, no. 4, pp. 284–288, 2012.

[MAA 12] MAAMAR H., BOUKERCHE A., PETRIU E., "3-d streaming supplying partner protocols for mobile collaborative exergaming for health", *IEEE Transactions on Information Technology in Biomedicine*, vol. 16, no. 6, pp. 1079–1095, 2012.

[MAC 13] MACIAS E., SUAREZ A., LLORET J., "Mobile sensing systems", *Sensors*, no. 12, pp. 17292–17321, 2013.

[MAG 07] MAGJAREVIC R., "Home care technologies for ambient assisted living", *11th Mediterranean Conference on Medical and Biomedical Engineering and Computing*, pp. 397–400, Heidelberg, Germany, 2007.

[MAR 04] MARCHESCHI P., "HL7 clinical document architecture to share cardiological images and structured data in next generation", *Computers in Cardiology*, pp. 617–620, 2004.

[MAR 05] MARGAN A., RUSTEMOVIĆ N., LONCARIĆ S., "Virtual policlinics – consultation health care system for rural areas and islands", *Acta Medica Croatica*, vol. 59, no. 3, pp. 169–178, 2005.

[MAR 12] MARTIN K.M., *Everyday Cryptography*, Oxford University Press, UK, 2012.

[MAR 13] MARTÍNEZ-PÉREZ B., DE LA TORRE-DÍEZ I., LÓPEZ-CORONADO M. *et al.*, "Mobile apps in cardiology: review", *Journal of Medical Internet Research*, vol. 15, no. 7, p. e15, 2013.

[MAR 14] MARTÍNEZ-PÉREZ B., DE LA TORRE-DÍEZ I., LÓPEZ-CORONADO M., *et al.*, "Comparison of mobile apps for the leading causes of death among different income zones: a review of the literature and app stores", *Journal of Medical Internet Research*, vol. 2, no. 1, p. e1, 2014.

[MAR 15] MARTÍNEZ-GARCÍA A., GARCÍA-GARCÍA J.A., ESCALONA M.J. *et al.*, "Working with the HL7 metamodel in a model driven engineering context", *Journal of Biomedical Informatics*, vol. 57, pp. 415–424, 2015.

[MAS 13] MASS J.F., "Apple cedes market share in smartphone operating system market as android surges and windows phone gains", available at http://www.idc.com/getdoc.jsp?containerId=prUS24257413, 2013.

[MCM 13] MCMANUS D.D., LEE J., MAITAS O. *et al.*, "A novel application for the detection of an irregular pulse using an iPhone 4S in patients with atrial fibrillation", *Heart Rhythm*, vol. 10, no. 3, pp. 315–319, 2013.

[MCN 12] MCNICKLE M., *8 Common Questions About HL7*, Healthcare IT News, HIMSS Media, 2012.

[MIC 14] MICHALAS A., PALADI N., GEHRMANN C., "Security aspects of e-Health systems migration to the cloud", *16th IEEE International Conference on e-Health Networking, Applications and Services*, pp. 212–218, Natal, Brazil, October 15–18 2014.

[MIC 15] MICHALAS A., DOWSLEY R., "Towards trusted e-Health services in the cloud", *IEEE/ACM 8th International Conference on Utility and Cloud Computing (UCC)*, pp. 618–623, Limassol, Cyprus, December 7–10 2015.

[MIC 16] MICROSOFT, "Windows phone apps+games", available at http://www.windowsphone.com/es-es/store, (accessed March 21 2016), 2016.

[MIS 14] MISRA S., ISLAM N., MAHAPATRO J. *et al.*, "Green wireless body area nano-networks: energy management and the game of survival", *IEEE Journal of Biomedical and Health Informatics (J-BHI)*, vol. 18, no. 2, pp. 467–475, March 2014.

[MON 03] MONTEAGUDO J.L., *La estandarización en Tecnologías de la Información y las Comunicaciones para Sanidad*, Instituto de Salud Carlos III, Madrid, Spain, 2003.

[MOR 11] MORIN J., *Will HL7 V3 Adoption Take Off in 2011? 5 Points and 1 Caveat*, Caristix Blog, Caristix, 2011.

[MUL 06] MULDOON C., OHARE G., OGRAD M., "Collaborative agent tuning: performance enhancement on mobile devices engineering societies in the agents world VI", *Lecture Notes in Computer Science*, vol. 3963, pp 241–258, 2006.

[MÜL13] MÜLLER A., GOETTE A., PERINGS C. *et al.*, "Potential role of telemedical service centers in managing remote monitoring data transmitted daily by cardiac implantable electronic devices: results of the early detection of cardiovascular events in device patients with heart failure (detecT-Pilot) study", *Telemedicine and E-Health Journal*, vol. 19, no. 6, pp. 460–466, 2013.

[NAI 12] NAIR M., HAN G.S., LEE H. *et al.*, "Antecedents to mobile phone diffusion in a developing economy: the case of Malaysia", *International Journal of Management*, vol. 29, no. 1, pp. 205–227, 2012.

[NAT 08a] NATIONAL ELECTRICAL MANUFACTURERS ASSOCIATION, "Digital Imaging and Communications in Medicine (DICOM). Part 1: introduction and overview", available at ftp://medical.nema.org/medical/dicom/2008/08_01pu.doc (accessed February 21, 2016), 2008.

[NAT 08b] NATIONAL ELECTRICAL MANUFACTURERS ASSOCIATION, "Digital Imaging and Communications in Medicine (DICOM). Part 2: conformance", available at ftp://medical.nema.org/medical/dicom/2008/08_02pu.doc (accessed February 21, 2016), 2008.

[NAT 08c] NATIONAL ELECTRICAL MANUFACTURERS ASSOCIATION, "Digital Imaging and Communications in Medicine (DICOM). Part 3: information object definitions", available at ftp://medical.nema.org/medical/dicom/2008/08_ 03pu.doc (accessed February 21, 2016), 2008.

[NAT 08d] NATIONAL ELECTRICAL MANUFACTURERS ASSOCIATION, "Digital Imaging and Communications in Medicine (DICOM). Part 4: Service class specifications, available at ftp://medical.nema.org/medical/dicom/2008/08_04pu.doc (accessed February 21, 2016), 2008.

[NAT 08e] NATIONAL ELECTRICAL MANUFACTURERS ASSOCIATION, "Digital Imaging and Communications in Medicine (DICOM). Part 5: data structures and encoding", available at ftp://medical.nema.org/medical/dicom/2008/08_ 05pu.doc (accessed February 21, 2016), 2008.

[NAT 08f] NATIONAL ELECTRICAL MANUFACTURERS ASSOCIATION, "Digital Imaging and Communications in Medicine (DICOM). Part 6: data dictionary", available at ftp://medical.nema.org/ medical/dicom/2008/08_06pu.doc (accessed February 21, 2016), 2008.

[NAT 08g] NATIONAL ELECTRICAL MANUFACTURERS ASSOCIATION, "Digital Imaging and Communications in Medicine (DICOM). Part 7: message exchange", available at ftp://medical. nema.org/medical/dicom/2008/08_07pu.doc (accessed February 21, 2016), 2008.

[NAT 08h] NATIONAL ELECTRICAL MANUFACTURERS ASSOCIATION, "Digital Imaging and Communications in Medicine (DICOM). Part 8: network communication support for message exchange", available at ftp://medical.nema.org/medical/dicom/2008/08_ 08pu.doc (accessed February 21, 2016), 2008.

[NAT 08i] NATIONAL ELECTRICAL MANUFACTURERS ASSOCIATION, "Digital Imaging and Communications in Medicine (DICOM). Part 10: media storage and file format for media interchange", available at ftp://medical.nema.org/medical/dicom/2008/08_ 10pu.doc (accessed February 21, 2016), 2008.

[NAT 08j] NATIONAL ELECTRICAL MANUFACTURERS ASSOCIATION, "Digital Imaging and Communications in Medicine (DICOM). Part 11: media storage application profiles", available at ftp://medical.nema.org/medical/dicom/2008/08_ 11pu.doc (accessed February 21, 2016), 2008.

[NAT 08k] NATIONAL ELECTRICAL MANUFACTURERS ASSOCIATION, "Digital Imaging and Communications in Medicine (DICOM). Part 12: media formats and physical media for media interchange", available at ftp://medical.nema.org/medical/ dicom/2008/08_ 12pu.doc (accessed February29, 2016), 2008.

[NAT 08l] NATIONAL ELECTRICAL MANUFACTURERS ASSOCIATION, "Digital Imaging and Communications in Medicine (DICOM). Part 14: grayscale standard display function", available at ftp://medical.nema.org/medical/dicom/2008/08_14 pu.doc (accessed February 21, 2016), 2008.

[NAT 08m] NATIONAL ELECTRICAL MANUFACTURERS ASSOCIATION, "Digital Imaging and Communications in Medicine (DICOM). Part 15: security and system management profiles", available at ftp://medical.nema.org/medical/dicom/2008/08_15 pu.doc (accessed February 21, 2016), 2008.

[NAT 08n] NATIONAL ELECTRICAL MANUFACTURERS ASSOCIATION, "Digital Imaging and Communications in Medicine (DICOM). Part 16: content mapping resource", available at ftp://medical.nema.org/medical/dicom/2008/08_16pu.doc (accessed February 21, 2016), 2008.

[NAT 08o] NATIONAL ELECTRICAL MANUFACTURERS ASSOCIATION, "Digital Imaging and Communications in Medicine (DICOM). Part 17: explanatory information", available at ftp://medical.nema.org/medical/dicom/2008/08_17pu.doc (accessed February 21, 2016), 2008.

[NAT 08p] NATIONAL ELECTRICAL MANUFACTURERS ASSOCIATION, "Digital Imaging and Communications in Medicine (DICOM). Part 18: web access to DICOM persistent objects (WADO)", available at ftp://medical.nema.org/medical/dicom/2008/08_18 pu.doc (accessed February 21, 2016), 2008.

[NAT 16] NATIONAL INSTITUTE OF STANDARDS AND TECHNOLOGY, Computer Security Resource Center (CSRC), available at http://www.csrc.nist.gov (accessed March 25, 2016), 2016.

[NOK 16] NOKIA, "Ovi store", available at http://store.ovi.com/ (accessed March 21, 2016), 2016.

[NUA 16] NUANCE, The Dragon Medical 360 | eScription, available at http://www.nuance.com/for-healthcare/by-benefits/medical-transcription/escription/index.htm, March 2 2016.

[NYC 04] NYCE D.S., *Linear Position Sensors: Theory and Applications*, John Wiley & Sons, New York, 2004.

[OLI 11] OLIVEIRA L.M.L., RODRIGUES J.J.P.C., "Wireless sensor networks: a survey on environmental monitoring", *Journal of Communications*, vol. 6, no. 2, pp. 143–151, April 2011.

[OPE 16] OPEN EHR, available at http://www.openehr.org/home.html (accessed March 25, 2016), 2016.

[OUT 11] OUTZEN R., "Facebook &mental health", available at http://www.inweekly.net/wordpress/?p=4212 (accessed March 16, 2016), 2011.

[PAR 16] PARKINSON'S DISEASE FOUNDATION, available at http://pdf.org (accessed March 13, 2016), 2016.

[PHI 07] PHILIPS, "My Heart project", available at http://www.research.philips.com/technologies/projects/heartcycle/myheart-gen.html (accessed March 5, 2016), 2007.

[PIE 11] PIETTE J.D., MENDOZA-AVELARES M.O., GANSER M. *et al.*, "A preliminary study of a cloud-computing model for chronic illness self-care support in an underdeveloped country", *American Journal of Preventive Medicine*, vol. 40, pp. 629–632, 2011.

[PRE 05] PREECE J., MALONEY-KRICHMAR D., "Online communities: design, theory, and practice", *Journal of Computer-Mediate Communications*, vol. 10, no. 4, 2005.

[PRE 16] PREVENTICE, "Preventice care platform", available at http://www.preventice.com/products/the-preventice-care-platform/ February 28 2016.

[QUA 16] QUALCOMM, Qualcomm Life, available at http://www.qualcomm.com/solutions/healthcare, 2016.

[QUE 13] QUEENSLAND HEALTH, "Preventive health unit: burden of disease: a snapshot in 2013", available at http://www.health.qld.gov.au/epidemiology/documents/burden-disease-study.pdf (accessed March 21, 2016), 2013.

[QUE 15] QUEST DIAGNOSTICS PATIENT SERVICE CENTER, Quest Diagnostic, available at https://www.questdiagnostics.com/hcp/psc/work%20files/hcp_psc_srch_results2.html, 2016.

[RAS 13] RASHIDI P., MIHAILIDIS A., "A survey on ambient-assisted living tools for older adults," *IEEE Journal of Biomedical and Health Informatics*, vol. 17, no. 3, pp. 579–590, 2013.

[RAW 03] RAWAT K.S., MASSIHA G.H., "Secure data transmission over wireless networks: issues and challenges", *IEEE Region 5, 2003 Annual Technical Conference*, pp. 65–68, April 2003.

[RES 13] RESEARCH2GUIDANCE, "Global mobile health market report 2013-2017", available at http://www.research2guidance.com/the-market-for-mhealth-app-services-will-reach-26-billion-by-2017/ (accessed March 13, 2016), 2013.

[RIC 11] RICHESSON R.L., NADKARNI P., "Data standards for clinical research data collection forms: current status and challenges", *Journal of the American Medical Informatics Association*, vol. 18, no. 3, pp. 341–346, 2011.

[RIV 13] RIVERA J., ROB V., "Gartner says smartphone sales grew 46.5 percent in second quarter and exceeded feature phone sales for first time", available at http://www.gartner.com/newsroom/id/2573415 (accessed March 21, 2016), 2013.

[ROD 10] RODRIGUES J.J.P.C., NEVES P.A.C.S., "A Survey on IP-based wireless sensor networks solutions", *International Journal of Communication Systems*, vol. 23, no. 8, pp. 963–981, August 2010.

[ROD 11] RODRIGUES J.J.P.C., SABINO F.M.R., ZHOU L., "Enhancing e-learning experience with online social networks", *IET Communications, Institution of Engineering and Technology (IET)*, vol. 5, no. 8, pp. 1147–1154, 2011.

[ROD 12] RODRIGUES J.J.P.C., REIS N., MOUTINHO J.A.F., DE LA TORRE I., "Breast alert: an on-line tool for predicting the lifetime risk of women breast cancer", *Journal of Medical Systems*, vol. 36, no.3, pp. 1417–1424, 2012.

[ROD 12a] RODRIGUES J.J.P.C., *Emerging Communication Technologies for E-Health and Medicine*, IGI-Global Publishers, Hershey, PA, 2012.

[ROD 12b] RODRIGUES J.J.P.C., DE LA TORRE I., SAINZ DE ABAJO B. (eds), *Telemedicine and E-Health Services, Policies and Applications: Advancements and Developments*, IGI-Global Publishers, Hershey, PA, 2012.

[ROD 13] RODRIGUES J.J.P.C., DE LA TORRE I., CARDEÑOSA G.F. *et al.*, "Analysis of the security and privacy requirements of cloud-based electronic health records systems", *Journal of Medical Internet Research*, vol. 15, no.8, 2013.

[ROD 13a] RODRIGUES J.J.P.C., PEDRO L.M.C.C., VARDASCA T. *et al.*, "Mobile health platform for pressure ulcer monitoring with EHR integration", *Health Informatics Journal*, vol. 19, no. 4, pp. 300–311, 2013.

[ROD 13b] RODRIGUES J.J.P.C., DE LA TORRE I., CARDEÑOSA G.F. *et al.*, "Security and Privacy Requisites Analysis of Cloud-based EHRs Systems", *Journal of Medical Internet Research*, vol. 15, no. 8, 2013.

[ROD 15] RODRIGUES J.J.P.C., MISRA S., WANG H. *et al.*, "Ambient assisted living communications", *IEEE Communications Magazine*, vol. 53, no. 1, pp. 24–25, 2015.

[ROM 10] ROMMAN A., "Health card (eHC)", available at http://pcrd-pal.org/newsfiles/IT%20conference%20Book%20EN.pdf#page=23, (accessed September 2), 2015.

[SÁE 13] SÁEZ C., BRESÓ A., VICENTE J. *et al.*, "An HL7-CDA wrapper for facilitating semantic interoperability to rule-based clinical decision support systems", *Computer Methods and Programs in Biomedicine*, vol. 109, no. 3, pp. 239–249, 2013.

[SAH 11] SAHADEVAIAH K., REDDY R., "Impact of security attacks on a new security protocol for mobile ad hoc networks", *Network Protocols and Algorithms*, vol. 3, no 4, pp. 122–140, 2011.

[SAH 13] SAHAMA T., SIMPSON L., LANE B., "Security and privacy in e-Health: is it possible?", *IEEE 15th International Conference on e-Health Networking, Applications & Services (HEALTHCOM)*, pp. 249–253, Lisbon, Portugal, October 9–12, 2013.

[SAN 12] SA-NGASOONGSONG A., KUNTHONG J., SARANGAN V. *et al.*, "A low-cost, portable, high-throughput wireless sensor system for phonocardiography applications", *Sensors*, vol. 12, no. 8, pp. 10851–10870, 2012.

[SAN 14] SANTOS A., MACEDO J., COSTA A.N., "Internet of things and smart objects for M-Health monitoring and control", *Procedia Technology*, vol. 16, pp. 1351–1360, 2014.

[SAV 09] SAVAGE R., YON Y., CAMPO M. *et al.*, “Market potential for ambient assisted living technology: the case of Canada”, *7th International Conference on Smart Homes and Health Telematics* pp. 57–65, Paris, France, July 1–3, 2009.

[SCH 00] SCHADOW G., HL7 Version 3 data types ballot, Draft 1, Revision 1.2, available at http://www.hl7.org/implement/standards/product_brief.cfm?product_id=186, 2000.

[SCH 13] SCHNEIDER F., “The shadow economy in Europe”, available at http://www.atkearney.com/es/paper/-/asset_publisher/dVxv4Hz2h8bS/content/the-shadow-economy-in-europe/10192 (accessed September 10, 2015), 2013.

[SEN 16] SENDRA S., Deployment of efficient wireless sensor nodes for monitoring in rural, indoor and underwater environments, PhD Thesis, Universitat Politècnica de Valencia, 2016.

[SEN 13a] SENDRA S., LLARIO F., PARRA L. *et al.*, “Smart wireless sensor network to detect and protect sheep and goats to wolf attacks, ” *Recent Advances in Communications and Networking Technology*, vol. 2, no. 2, pp. 91–101, December 2013.

[SEN 13b] SENDRA S., PARRA L., ORTUÑO V. *et al.*, “A low cost turbidity sensor development”, *7th International Conference on Sensor Technologies and Applications*, Barcelona, Spain, 25–31 August 2013.

[SEN 14a] SENDRA S., GRANELL E., LLORET J. *et al.*, “Smart collaborative mobile system for taking care of disabled and elderly people”, *Mobile Networks and Applications*, vol. 19, no. 3, pp. 287–302, 2014.

[SEN 14b] SENDRA S., LLORET A.T., LLORET J. *et al.*, “A wireless sensor network deployment to detect the degeneration of cement used in construction”, *International Journal of Ad Hoc and Ubiquitous Computing*, vol. 15, nos. 1–3, 2014.

[SEN 14c] SENDRA S., LLORET J., TURRO C. *et al.*, “IEEE 802.11a/b/g/n short scale indoor wireless sensor placement”, *International Journal of Ad Hoc and Ubiquitous Computing*, vol. 15, nos. 1–3, 2014.

[SET 11] SETOYAMA Y., YAMAZAKI Y., NAMAYAMA K., "Benefits of peer support in online Japanese breast cancer communities: differences between lurkers and posters", *Journal of Medical Internet Research*, vol. 13, no. 4, pp. e122, 2011.

[SHA 00] SHAW B.R., MCTAVISH F., HAWKINS R. *et al.*, "Experiences of women with breast cancer: exchanging social support over the CHESS computer network", *Journal of Health Communications*, vol. 5, pp. 135–159, 2000.

[SHA 09] SHAVER D., *The HL7 Evolution: Comparing HL7 Version 2 to Version 3, Including a History of Version 2*, Corepoint Health, 2009.

[SHI 16] SHIM K.A., "A survey of public-key cryptographic primitives in wireless sensor networks", *IEEE Communications Surveys & Tutorials*, vol. 18, no. 1, pp. 577–601, 2016.

[SIE 13] SIEVERDES J.C., TREIBER F., JENKINS C., "Improving diabetes management with mobile health technology", *American Journal of Medical Science*, vol. 345, no. 4, pp. 289–295, 2013.

[SIL 13] SILVA B.M.C., RODRIGUES J.J.P.C., LOPES I.M.C. *et al.*, "A novel cooperation strategy for mobile health applications", *IEEE Journal on Selected Areas in Communications*, vol. 31, no. 9, pp. 28–36, 2013.

[SIL 13a] SILVA B.M.C., RODRIGUES J.J.P.C., CANELO F. *et al.*, "Towards a Cooperative Security System for Mobile-Health Applications", *Journal of Electronic Commerce Research*, 2013.

[SIL 13b] SILVA B.M.C., RODRIGUES J.J.P.C., CANELO F. *et al.*, "A data encryption solution for mobile health apps in cooperation environments: DE4MHA", *Journal of Medical Internet Research*, vol. 13, no. 4, 2013.

[SIL 14] SILVA B.M.C., RODRIGUES J.J.P.C., SIMOES T.M.C. *et al.*, "An ambient assisted living framework for mobile environments", *IEEE-EMBS International Conference on Biomedical and Health Informatics*, Valencia, Spain, pp. 448–451, 2014.

[SIL 15a] SILVA B.M.C., RODRIGUES J.J.P.C., DE LA TORRE I. *et al.*, "Mobile-health: a review of current state", *Journal of Biomedical Informatics*, vol. 56, pp. 265–272, August 2015.

[SIL 15b] SILVA B.M.C., RODRIGUES J.J.P.C., LOPES I.M.C., "Pervasive and mobile healthcare applications", in *Ambient Assisted Living*, 1st ed., CRC Press/Taylor & Francis Group, June 2015.

[SLA 13] SLAVOV V., RAO P., PATURI S. *et al.*, "A new tool for sharing and querying of clinical documents modeled using HL7 Version 3 standard", *Computer Methods and Programs in Biomedicine*, vol. 112, pp. 529–552, 2013.

[SMA 15] SMARTPHONES AND WEB SERVICES, Ramifications and Development Challenges, Handbook of Research on Mobility and Computing, available at http://lsrg.cs.wustl.edu/~schmidt/PDF/new-ww-mobile-computing.pdf, November 2 2015.

[SMA 16] SMART INTEGRATED BIODIAGNOSTIC SYSTEMS FOR HEALTHCARE, SMARTHEALTH, available at https://www.questdiagnostics.com/hcp/psc/work%20files/hcp_psc_srch_results2.html, 2016.

[SMI 02] SMITH D., NEWELL L.M., "A physician's perspective: deploying the EMR", *Journal of Healthcare Information Management*, vol. 16, pp. 71–79, 2002.

[SOC 03] SOCIEDAD ESPAÑOLA DE INFORMÁTICA DE LA SALUD, *De la historia clínica a la historia de la salud electrónica*, Pamplona, Spain, 2003.

[SOC15] SOCEANU A., VASYLENKO M., EGNER A. *et al.*, "Managing the privacy and security of e-Health data", *20th International Conference on Control Systems and Computer Science (CSCS)*, Bucharest, Roamnia, pp. 439–446, 27–29 May 2015.

[SPA 07] SPAHNI S., LOVIS C., MERCILLE R. *et al.*, "Implementing a new ADT based on the HL7 version 3 RIM", *International Journal of Medical Informatics*, vol. 76, no.2–3, pp. 190–194, 2007.

[STR 12] STRUIK L.L., BOTTORFF J.L., JUNG M. *et al.*, "Reaching adolescent girls through social networking: a new avenue for smoking prevention messages", *The Canadian Journal of Nursing Research*, vol. 44, no. 3, pp. 84–103, 2012.

[SU 11] SU C.J., WU C.Y., "JADE implemented mobile multi-agent based, distributed information platform for pervasive health care monitoring", *Applied Soft Computing*, vol. 11, no. 1, pp. 315–325, 2011.

[SVA 10] SVANTESSON D., CLARKE R., "Privacy and consumer risks in cloud computing", *The Computer Law and Security Review*, vol. 26, no. 4, pp. 391–397, 2010.

[TAC 03] TACHAKRA S., WANG X., ISTEPANIAN R.S. *et al.*, "Mobile e-health: the un- wired evolution of telemedicine", *Telemedicine Journal and e-Health*, vol. 9, no. 3, pp. 247–257, 2003.

[TAH 16] THE AMERICAN HEALTH INFORMATION MANAGEMENT ASSOCIATION, available at http://www.ahima.org, February 26 2016.

[TEJ 12] TEJERO A., DE LA TORRE I., "Advances and current state of the security and privacy in electronic health records: survey from a social perspective", *Journal of Medical Systems*, vol. 36, no. 5, pp. 3019–3017, 2012.

[TGH 16] THE GLOBAL HEALTH INITIATIVE, available at http://www.jhumhealth.org/, March 2 2016.

[THE 14] THE HEART FOUNDATION, *Heart Disease: Scope and Impact*, available at http://www.the heartfoundation.org/heart-disease-facts/heart-disease-statistics/ (Accessed March 5, 2016), 2014.

[THI 14a] THILAKANATHAN D., ZHAO Y., CHEN S. *et al.*, "Protecting and analysing health care data on cloud", *Second International Conference on Advanced Cloud and Big Data*, pp. 143–149, Huangshan, November 20–22, 2014.

[THI 14b] THIRANANT N., SAIN N., LEE H.J., "A design of security framework for data privacy in e-health system using web service", *16th International Conference on Advanced Communication Technology*, pp. 40–43, Pyeongchang, February 16–19, 2014.

[TOM 11] TOMAS J., LLORET J., BRI D. *et al.*, "Sensors and their application for disabled and elderly people", in *Handbook of Research on Personal Autonomy Technologies and Disability Informatics*, IGI Global, 2011.

[TOP 13] TOPAZ M., ASH N., "Overview of the US policies for health information technology and lessons learned for Israel", *Harefuah*, vol. 152, no. 5, pp. 262–266, 2013.

[TOR 15] DE LA TORRE-DÍEZ I., BARGIELA-FLÓREZ B., LÓPEZ-CORONADO M. *et al.*, "Content Analysis of Neurodegenerative and Mental Diseases Social Groups", *Health Informatics Journal*, vol. 21, no. 4, pp. 267–283, December 2015.

[TRE 06] TREINS M., CURE O., SALZANO G., "On the interest of using HL7 CDA release 2 for the exchange of annotated medical documents", *19th IEEE International Symposium on Computer-Based Medical Systems*, pp. 524–532, Salt Lake City, UT, June 22–23, 2006.

[TSA 11] TSALATSANIS A., GIL-HERRERA E., YALCIN A. *et al.*, "Designing patient-centric applications for chronic disease management", *International Conference of the IEEE Engineering in Medicine and Biology Society,* Boston, MA, pp. 3146–3149, August 30–September 03, 2011.

[TUR 09] TURNER H., WHITE J., THOMPSON C. *et al.*, "Building mobile sensor networks using smartphones and web services: ramifications and development challenges", *Handbook of Research on Mobility and Computing: Evolving Technologies and Ubiquitous Impacts*, IGI Global, pp. 502–521, 2009.

[UNI 02] UNITED NATIONS, "Old population ageing, 1950 – 2050", United Nations Publications, New York, USA, 2002.

[UNI 16] UNIVERS AAL, available at http://www.universaal.org/index.php/en (Accessed March 10, 2016), 2016.

[VAL 13] VALLE C.G., TATE D.F., MAYER D.K. *et al.*, "A randomized trial of a Facebook-based physical activity intervention for young adult cancer survivors", *Journal of Cancer Survivorship*, vol. 7, no. 3, pp. 355–368, 2013.

[VAN 10] VAN DE BELT T.H., ENGELEN L.J., BERBEN S.A. *et al.* "Definition of Health 2.0 and Medicine 2.0: a systematic review", *Journal of Medical Internet Research*, vol. 12, no. 2, p. e18, 2010.

[VAN 12] VAN MIERLO T., VOCI S., LEE S. *et al.*, "Superusers in social networks for smoking cessation: analysis of demographic characteristics and posting behavior from the Canadian Cancer Society's smokers' helpline online and StopSmokingCenter.net", *Journal of Medical Internet Research*, vol. 14, no. 3, p. e66, 2012.

[VER 16] VERIZON CONVERGED HEALTH MANAGEMENT, available at http://www.verizonenterprise. com/convergedhealthmanagement/, March 2 2016.

[VOD 16] VODAFONE FOUNDATION, "Windows phone apps + games. PERSONA – PER ceptive Spaces prOmoting indepeNdent Aging", available at http://www.fundacionvodafone.es/ proyecto/proyecto-persona-perceptive-spaces-promoting-independent-aging (accessed March 21, 2016), 2016.

[WEB 16] WEBMD, LLC. WebMD for Android, available at https://play.google.com/store/search?q=medical& c=apps, February 28, 2016.

[WHI 11] WHITTAKER R., DOREY E., BRAMLEY D. *et al.*, "A theory-based video messaging mobile phone intervention for smoking cessation: randomized controlled trial", *Journal of Medical Internet Research*, vol. 13, no. 1, 2011.

[WOR 16] WORLD HEALTH ORGANIZATION, "Disease and injury regional estimates, cause-specific mortality: regional estimates for 2000-2012", available at http://gamapserver.who.int/gho/ interactive_charts/mbd/leading_cod/2012.asp (accessed March 21, 2016), 2012.

[WOR 07] WORLD HEALTH ORGANIZATION, "What are neurological disorders?", available at http://www.who.int/features/qa/55/en/ index.html, (accessed March 14, 2016), 2007.

[WOR 10] WORLD HEALTH ORGANIZATION, "Mental health: strengthening our response", available at http://www.who.int/ mediacentre/factsheets/fs220/en, (accessed March 2016), 2010.

[WHO 11] WORLD HEALTH ORGANIZATION, "mHealth: new horizons for health through mobile technologies: based on the findings of the second global survey on eHealth", available at http://www.who.int/goe/publications/goe_mhealth_web.pdf (accessed September 10, 2015), 2011.

[WHO 11a] WORLD HEALTH ORGANIZATION, "Global status report on noncommunicable diseases 2010", *World Health Organization*, available at http://whqlibdoc.who.int/publications/2011/9789240686458_eng.pdf (accessed August 15, 2014), 2011.

[WHO 11b] WORLD HEALTH ORGANIZATION, "Global atlas on cardiovascular disease prevention and control", available at http://whqlibdoc.who.int/publications/2011/9789241564373_eng.pdf (accessed March 5, 2016), 2011.

[WHO 12] WORLD HEALTH ORGANIZATION, "Depression", available at http://www.who.int/mental_health/management/depression/definition, (accessed March 14, 2016), 2012.

[WHO 14] WORLD HEALTH ORGANIZATION, "Cardiovascular Diseases (CVDs) Fact Sheet", No. 317, available at http://www.who.int/ mediacentre/factsheets/fs317/en/ (accessed March 5, 2016), 2014.

[WHO 15] WORLD HEALTH ORGANIZATION, available at http://www.who.int (accessed September 2, 2015), 2015.

[XIA 14] XIA F., AHMED A.M., YANG L.T. *et al.*, "Exploiting social relationship to enable efficient replica allocation in ad-hoc social networks", *IEEE Transactions on Parallel and Distributed Systems*, vol. 25, no.12, 2014.

[YEL 08] YELLOWLEES P.M., MARKS S.L., HOGARTH M. *et al.*, "Standards-based, open-source electronic health record systems: a desirable future for the U.S. health industry", *Telemedicine and E-Health Journal*, vol. 14, no. 3, pp. 284–288, 2008.

[YIC 08] YICK J., MUKHERJEE B., GHOSAL D., "Wireless sensor network survey", *Computer Networks*, vol. 52, pp. 2292–2330, 2008.

[YU 13] YU Y., LI J., LIU J., "M-HELP: a miniaturized total health examination system launched on a mobile phone platform", *Telemedicine and E-Health Journal*, vol. 19, no. 11, pp. 857–865, 2013.

[ZHA 16] ZHANG Y.F., TIAN Y., ZHOU T.S. *et al.*, "Integrating HL7 RIM and ontology for unified knowledge and data representation in clinical decision support systems", *Computer Methods and Programs in Biomedicine*, vol. 123, pp. 94–108, 2016.

[ZHO 15] ZHOU J., CAO Z., DONG X. *et al.*, "Security and privacy in cloud-assisted wireless wearable communications: challenges, solutions, and future directions", *IEEE Wireless Communications*, vol. 22, no. 2, pp. 136–144, 2015.

[ZHU 10] ZHU F., BOSCH M., WOO I. *et al.*, "The use of mobile devices in aiding dietary assessment and evaluation", *Journal of Selected Topics Signal Processing*, vol. 4, no. 4, pp. 756–766, 2010.

[ZUE 09] ZUEHLKE P., LI J., TALAEI-KHOEI A. *et al.*, "A functional specification for mobile e-health (m-health) systems, in: e-Health Networking", *11th International Conference on Applications and Services (Healthcom)*, pp. 74–78, 16–18 December 2009.

Index

G, H, I

L, M, O

P, Q, R

Printed in the United States
By Bookmasters